# Building the Knowledge Economy in Europe

NEW HORIZONS IN EUROPEAN POLITICS

**Series Editor:** Julie Smith, *Robinson College, Cambridge, UK*

The New Horizons in European Politics series is an invaluable forum for original research across the spectrum of European politics, promoting innovative cross-disciplinary analysis of contemporary issues and debates. Covering a diverse range of topics, the series examines issues such as: the impacts of the severe challenges brought about by the financial crisis; economic issues, including integration and monetary union; the politics of the EU and other governmental and non-governmental institutions; environmental politics and the on-going struggle to mitigate climate change; and the politics of trade, energy and security in Europe. Both international and comparative in its approach, this exciting series encompasses theoretical and empirical work from both well-established researchers and the next generation of scholars.

# Building the Knowledge Economy in Europe

New Constellations in European Research and Higher Education Governance

*Edited by*

Meng-Hsuan Chou

*NTU, Singapore*

Åse Gornitzka

*University of Oslo, Norway*

NEW HORIZONS IN EUROPEAN POLITICS

**Edward Elgar**

Cheltenham, UK • Northampton, MA, USA

Published by
Edward Elgar Publishing Limited
The Lypiatts
15 Lansdown Road
Cheltenham
Glos GL50 2JA
UK

Edward Elgar Publishing, Inc.
William Pratt House
9 Dewey Court
Northampton
Massachusetts 01060
USA

A catalogue record for this book
is available from the British Library

Library of Congress Control Number: 2013954349

This book is available electronically in the ElgarOnline.com
Social and Political Science Subject Collection, E-ISBN 978 1 78254 529 3

ISBN 978 1 78254 528 6

Typeset by Servis Filmsetting Ltd, Stockport, Cheshire
Printed and bound in Great Britain by T.J. International Ltd, Padstow

# Contents

# Contributors

**Meng-Hsuan Chou** (Nanyang Technological University, Singapore) is Nanyang Assistant Professor in Public Policy and Global Affairs. She is the Academic Coordinator of UACES's European Research Area collaborative research network.

**Mari Elken** (Nordic Institute for Studies in Innovation, Research and Education, Norway) works as a Researcher at NIFU. She is also enrolled in the Ph.D. programme at the University of Oslo and is affiliated with the research group HEIK (Higher Education: Institutional Dynamics and Knowledge Cultures), where the chapter in this volume was first conceived and written.

**Åse Gornitzka** (University of Oslo, Norway) is Professor at the Department of Political Science and is also affiliated Research Professor at Arena Centre for European Studies, University of Oslo.

**Hanne Foss Hansen** (University of Copenhagen, Denmark) is Professor at the Department of Political Science. She has published books and articles on research and higher education policy, public sector reforms and evaluations.

**Cecile Hoareau** (RAND Europe) is a Researcher at RAND Europe, a Research Associate at UC Berkeley and a Research Fellow at the University of Maastricht. Her interests lie in comparative education policies, particularly higher education.

**Julia Metz** (University of Bremen, Germany) is a Senior Researcher in the research area 'Organization and Governance Studies'. Currently she is a visiting Researcher at the WZB Social Research Centre Berlin where she works in a project on internal dynamics in the EU Commission.

**José Real-Dato** (University of Almeria, Spain) is Lecturer at the Department of Public Law. Among his research interests are the study of human resource policies in science and higher education, the theory of the policy process, and the study of political careers.

**Martina Vukasovic** (Ghent University, Belgium) has been working since December 2013 in CHEGG (Centre for Higher Education Governance

Ghent), within the Odysseus project on higher education governance. Prior to moving to Ghent, she was a member of the HEIK (Higher Education: Institutional Dynamics and Knowledge Cultures) research group at the University of Oslo, where she did her Ph.D. and where the chapter in this volume was first conceived and written.

# Foreword

The idea for this volume was conceived during the 2011 general meeting of the European Consortium for Political Research (ECPR) in Reykjavik where we convened a section for research on the Europe of Knowledge. We are grateful to all the participants that took part in the discussions and in this way contributed to the realization of this volume.

Several chapters in this volume build on research conducted in the project 'Europe of Knowledge – Between Culture and Economy', which was part of an overarching study on the transformation of European political orders (EuroTrans) at ARENA – Centre for European Studies at the University of Oslo, funded by the Research Council of Norway. This project was in turn developed on the basis of a larger research agenda presented in Peter Maassen and Johan P. Olsen's book *University Dynamics and European Integration* (Dordrecht: Springer, 2007). We are indebted to these two scholars for their inspiring ideas, and we gratefully acknowledge the support of ARENA and the Research Council of Norway.

Meng-Hsuan Chou
Åse Gornitzka

# 1. Building a European knowledge area: an introduction to the dynamics of policy domains on the rise

## Meng-Hsuan Chou and Åse Gornitzka

> The European process has very recently moved some extremely important steps ahead. Relevant as they are, they should not make one forget that Europe is not only that of the Euro, of the banks and the economy: *it must be a Europe of knowledge as well* (Sorbonne Joint Declaration 1998, emphasis added).

## INTRODUCTION[1]

A careful look at the history of European integration reveals that the knowledge domain has always been present: the founding fathers had visions of common European knowledge institutions (Corbett 2005), ideas about creating a common scientific area have been simmering for decades, and elements of science and technology cooperation were visible already at the very start (De Elera 2006). However, policies and programmes concerning education, students, teaching, learning, schools, colleges and universities, as well as research, research institutes and centres, academics and scientists have in general been at the political margins of the European integration process. Developments since the turn of the century have changed this situation dramatically and demonstrate how institutions and organizational capacity being created in this domain are ratcheting up European cooperation and intensifying the interaction between governance levels. A European 'knowledge policy area' is emerging that is radically different in key aspects from the traditional ways in which (higher) education and science policy issues were handled. How can this new 'knowledge policy area' be interpreted and how can we account for the changes underlying its emergence? In this volume, we show how European integration in these areas did not happen as a steady consensual process of functional adaptation, a consequence of irreversible lock-in effects, nor as a process of rational design and exercise of predetermined political will. No single coherent group of actors – be it the member states' governments, European institutions, interests groups or transnational actors – has been able to fully control any of the processes analysed here. Instead, these processes trigger and are the results of contestation and tensions – across governance levels, across time and between institutional actors with different interests, values, norms and ideas. In this volume these processes will be examined mainly from an institutional perspective. We show that building the Europe of Knowledge 'depends to a large extent upon the internal constitutive characteristics of existing institutions', and '[i]nstitutions that authorize, and enable, as well as constrain change' (Olsen 2007a, p. 106). Specifically, we examine: (1) how institutions and governance capacity are established at the European level; (2) the effects of institutional and sector-specific factors on policy-making; and (3) the conditions that affect how national institutions and actors respond to European governance output.

These processes of European integration concern sectors of society that are increasingly transnationally connected ('borderless knowledge') and at the same time nationally embedded and sensitive. The governance of these sectors in Europe has traditionally not been at the forefront of party-political cleavage lines mobilizing broad electorate involvement, but has engaged a narrower set of experts, stakeholders, interest groups, professional associations and scholarly communities. European integration in research and higher education are also addressing sectors where traditional governance constellations as well as the sectors' role in society at large are being questioned and redefined. These are sector-specific conditions that also affect the dynamics of European integration in these policy domains.

At a general level our analytical point of departure is that European integration in different (sub)sectors of the knowledge policy domain activates tensions along two dimensions related to how these sectors are organized and institutionalized. First, the process of task expansion at the European level in areas of core national sovereignty involves cooperation as well as conflict and tensions along the *vertical* line between national and European levels of governance (Gornitzka et al. 2007, pp. 186–190). Knowledge policies are in general more nationally embedded than most and deepening and widening European engagement is likely to trigger resistance (Börzel 2005). We argue that this *vertical* perspective must be supplemented with a *horizontal* one: integration dynamics come from tensions along the horizontal line between sectors of society and from the frictions involved when the purpose and fundamental understanding of societal institutions are challenged (Gornitzka 2010). In two knowledge sectors – higher education and research – competing visions for the Europe of Knowledge can be identified. These are linked to fundamental economic and social transformations that are in particular associated with the rise of the knowledge economy and knowledge society where knowledge is seen as the main source of wealth of nations, businesses and people (Lundvall and Rodrigues 2002).

We assume that, in the interaction between shifts in governance along the *vertical* line and tensions along the *horizontal* line, we will find the key to understanding how a Europe of Knowledge is emerging and is being institutionalized. Indeed, we argue that the construction, evolution and consolidation of the Europe of Knowledge offer crucial insights into the dynamics of contemporary European integration. The comparison between higher education and research policy will reveal *differentiated integration patterns as these two subsectors vary in level and form of institutionalization both at the national and European levels.*

To begin discussing the core issues of the Europe of Knowledge, we spell out what a *vertical* and a *horizontal* dynamic of regional integration implies in the knowledge policy domain and the general theoretical underpinnings of such a perspective. We then outline the pathways that European level involvement have followed before introducing the themes of this volume and what they tell us about the dynamics of European integration.

## INTEGRATION DYNAMICS IN THE EUROPE OF KNOWLEDGE: *VERTICAL* AND *HORIZONTAL* PERSPECTIVES

### National Sensitivity, Legitimate Diversity and the *Vertical* Perspective

A central aspect of the development of European integration is the differentiated transfer of competencies to the European level and the plurality of policy-making modes (Börzel 2005). Different shades of institutionalized interaction have taken European integration beyond the mutual adjustment among sovereign states to policy-making modes ranging from intergovernmental negotiations, joint decision-making to supranational centralization (Scharpf 2001). In European integration, the tension involved in redrawing the jurisdictional boundaries between the nation state and the European level is related to prevailing ideas about common problem-solving capacity across member states and in different societal sectors, and the legitimacy of governing modes. In some sectors of society the diversity of member states has been deemed as illegitimate and in others not, as Scharpf (2002, pp. 35–36) argues:

Given the commitment to economic integration, the defense of national diversity was tainted by the brush of illegitimate protectionism. By contrast, policy initiatives addressed to the new challenges are confronted with policy conflicts which are rooted in fundamental differences of economic and institutional conditions, policy legacies and normative orientations that have high political salience in the constituencies of member states.

This argument is relevant to address the tensions involved in European engagement in research and higher education. With around 4,000 higher education institutions, over 19 million students and 1.5 million staff, European higher education is vast and also highly diverse. The diversity includes variations of national knowledge systems historically rooted in the intricate relationship and coevolution of the nation state and higher education and research in European countries (Maassen 2009). In higher education, school and training systems, considerable national systemic diversity has developed over centuries of state involvement. An explicit research policy and innovation policies are respectively post-war and post-1980s phenomena, but still developed within the nation state frame in Europe (Georghiou 1999). This diversity is highly visible in spending on research and development (R&D) and higher education, educational attainment level, as well as the role of knowledge intensive sectors in national economies.[2] This may constitute a territorial cleavage line that can be activated in European integration between developed knowledge economies and those less developed in Europe.

Part of the diversity is rooted in national identities and legacies, which make supranational centralization highly contentious, an aspect we expect to shape the breadth and level of European integration and policy-making modes. However, national involvement in regulating and funding higher education and research has not been in a steady state. Since the 1980s, European governments have been repositioning themselves in national higher education and research systems through considerable reform efforts and experiments in changing modes of governing (Braun 2008; Gornitzka and Maassen 2000; Gornitzka et al. 2005). Hence, we cannot account for the response and involvement of national governments towards European developments without considering shifts in governance *within* national systems.

**Inter-Sectoral Tensions, Interaction and the *Horizontal* Perspective**

Nation building in Europe has been characterized by the successive build-up of territorial boundaries differentiating between distinct functional regimes (Bartolini 2005). Nation states consist of sets of institutions and institutional spheres that have their own operational logic, rules and principles legitimizing them. Science, representative democracy, and the market economy are examples of three such pillar institutions in the nation state (Olsen 2007b; 2007c). The establishment of the modern state has also been carried by a specialization of public governing arrangements for societal sectors, with individual sectoral organized capacity for policy-making and implementation. A central characteristic is the specialized policies for different areas of society developed over centuries with regularized, organized interaction between policy actors aimed at developing, deciding and implementing policies. With them, specialized subsystem actors, special interest groups and experts, have been constituted. These interact with sectorally specialized public agencies, ministries and political actors as well as sectoral industries. In its most differentiated form the modern state can be seen as a conglomerate of segments (Egeberg et al. 1978) with few institutionalized opportunities for cross-sectoral coordination.

Such sectoral segments would also share basic *ideas* about appropriate policy objectives, legitimate concerns, as well as programmes for achieving them. These constitute policy paradigms and legacies and are perpetuated in the political organization of a policy area. When public policy concerns an established area it will be informed by a relative stable set of beliefs on fundamental sectoral goals (Hall 1993). Once a policy paradigm is settled and endowed with organizational structures, rules, standard operating procedures, resources and personnel to uphold them, it has become institutionalized (see Olsen 2001; 2007c, for an in-depth analysis of what institutionalization entails).

Institutional differentiation also carries some insulation from outside influence (March and Olsen 2006, p. 17). Indeed, the differentiation of science, higher education and the university as the prime higher learning site has implications for governance structures and public policy. A differentiated policy for higher education and academic research implies recognition that policy objectives, programmes and actions are especially adjusted to the university as an institution with its own legitimate, constitutive principles (Olsen 2007b).

A similar but not identical differentiation process is notable in European integration history. Stone Sweet et al. (2001) talk, for example, about the 'Brussels complex' for the multiple arenas that have replaced the original primitive governance site. The European Commission has been especially organized according to a principle of sectoral specialization (Egeberg 2006). Interest group formation has accompanied the multiplication of access points to supranational decision-making (Mazey and Richardson 2001). For knowledge sectors the growth in the number of both European level interests groups and Europe-wide civic associations have been particularly high (Fligstein 2008). Observations have underlined the role of policy communities underpinning sectorally differentiated governance and policy-making systems. These have developed around specialized issue areas that interact on the basis of shared *ideas* (Haas 1990). The European Commission has been particularly instrumental in forging epistemic communities and disseminating legitimizing ideas within such specialized communities (Kohler-Koch 2005, p. 8).

Yet differentiation processes do not imply that such sectoral demarcation lines have reached equilibrium. Change tends to occur particularly in the interface between different institutional orders and their interactions (Holm 1995), as well as over time (Pierson 2000). Parallel to the differentiation processes into institutional spheres and policy sectors, *interaction* between sectors built on different principles is a fundamental dynamic of change. From such a perspective change should be understood in terms of 'interaction and collisions among competing institutional structures, norms, rules, identities and practices' (March and Olsen 2006, p. 16). Such interaction can result in radical change, if goals, interests, understandings and actors from one sphere *invade* another. Yet, when the logics and governing arrangements of one sector are perceived to be challenged by another, it may also trigger contestation and sectoral defence mechanisms (Gornitzka and Olsen 2006; Olsen 1997, pp. 206–207).

Less dramatic cases of intersectoral interaction are the gradual changes that can occur, for instance, when market-like solutions are imported to adjust the governance mechanisms in the academic sphere without changing the overall policy paradigm or threatening the very constitutive principles of a policy or the societal institutions it addresses (Hall 1993, p. 277). Hence the construction of governance sites is then incremental and institutional arrangements of different origins coexist. It follows that this is not a deterministic process, but one that may lead to resistance, moderation or accommodation.

From this we can expect cooperation and contestation patterns in establishing the Europe of Knowledge to reflect not only nation state (selective) resistance and sensitivity to or mobilization for European competence expansion, but also tensions concerning what kind of knowledge policy for what kind of Europe. Hence we can also expect this to be a cleavage line that *cuts across* the territorially based cleavages and the vertical tension between governance levels. Following an institutional perspective on European integration (Olsen 2007a) and research agenda (Gornitzka et al. 2007), a fundamental distinction to be made is between the understanding of schools, colleges, universities and research organizations as institutions versus instruments. Indeed, the drive towards a coherent and coordinated knowledge policy approach implicitly triggers *horizontal* tensions of integration: as the foundation for a knowledge-based economy (economic competitiveness); as an embodiment of a knowledge-based society (education for social inclusion, civic education and socializing the citizens of Europe); as an instrument of knowledge-based policy (science as a transversal problem-solver for Europe's grand challenges); and as a tool for enhancing the competitiveness of European science and higher education. These competing images indicate that research and higher education are positioned in an area of tension between culture, politics and economy, and are subject to various integration pressures within and without the European Union (EU). These visions vie for dominance in an uneasy coexistence over time triggering sequential tensions that have led to unexpected changes – as we shall show below.

## BUILDING THE EUROPE OF KNOWLEDGE IN AND OVER TIME

### Europe of Knowledge as a Term

The political and supranational origins of the phrase can be traced to the European Commission's Communication from 1997 titled 'Towards a Europe of Knowledge' (European Commission 1997b). This Communication presented the European Commission's vision for reforming the EU's internal policies within the context of Agenda 2000, setting out comprehensive overall reforms for preparing the EU for its Eastern Enlargement and amending the Common Agricultural Policy. As part of the Agenda 2000 reforms, the European Commission (1997a, p. 14) argued that the EUs 'internal policies should set the conditions for sustainable growth and employment, put knowledge at the forefront, modernize employment systems and improve living conditions'. The Europe of Knowledge Communication was a response to this call: it outlined the guidelines for future EU actions in the areas of education, training and youth.

While the Agenda 2000 Communication explicitly defined that the efforts towards consolidating the EU as a knowledge-based polity would stem from multiple policy streams (*research, innovation, education* and *training*) (European Commission 1997a, p. 19), the Communication on the Europe of Knowledge saw it as, 'an open dynamic European *educational* area' (European Commission 1997b, emphasis added, p. 2). Strikingly, only a few references were made to research and innovation. The focus on the educational side of the Europe of Knowledge points to the *horizontal* tensions between the sister sectors. Concerning what this educational area/Europe of Knowledge would substantively encompass, the

Communication gave general clues: it 'needs to be understood in the broadest possible sense, both geographically and temporally' and consists of three key dimensions – knowledge, citizenship and competence (European Commission 1997b, p. 3). We may deduce that, in its original presentation, the Europe of Knowledge would serve a socio-economic function: as a knowledge-based *society* and *economy*.

This image for the Europe of Knowledge, albeit with a stronger emphasis on the societal and cultural dimension, was upheld by four European education ministers in 1998 when they signed the Sorbonne Declaration. With the Sorbonne's signing, the *vertical* tensions of integration in creating a European Higher Education Area (EHEA) are clearly visible because this intergovernmental initiative moved the conversation outside the EU framework. The Sorbonne Declaration presented the Europe of Knowledge as an area in which the university would play a prominent role. European universities would be the 'node' through which the European citizens are connected in their lifelong pursuit of knowledge. The Sorbonne Declaration, as we have seen, referred to the Europe of Knowledge in contrast to the 'Europe of the Euro'.

The next phase in the supranational development of the Europe of Knowledge came when the European Commission issued a Communication in 2003 titled 'The Role of the Universities in the Europe of Knowledge', promoting the idea that it should also be a tool for increasing the competitiveness of European higher education on the global stage (European Commission 2003, p. 3). The European Commission's Communication 'Towards a European Research Area' (ERA) from early 2000 also referred to the Europe of Knowledge, albeit within the context of a 'Europe of innovation and knowledge' (European Commission 2000). In this core document setting out the rationale for better organization of European research through creating a common scientific area, the European Commission proposed three visions for the Europe of Knowledge: as the basis for a knowledge-based economy; as an instrument for invigorating and increasing the competitiveness of European science; and as a tool for informed policy-making and implementation. The clear emphasis on the market economy and utility of science points to the extant *horizontal* tensions in this construction process. What we may conclude from this discussion is that there is no single definition of the Europe of Knowledge. This remains the case as, in their recent review of the concept, Elken et al. (2011, p. 5) conclude: the Europe of Knowledge is 'a complex and malleable term'.

To delve deeper, we must first step back in time and identify the main elements in European integration in higher education and research: these two sectors have a history of cooperation at the supranational level before the 'Europe of Knowledge' was coined.

**European Integration and Higher Education: Coping with National Sensitivity**

Research and education have been items on the European agenda practically since the very beginning of European integration (see Corbett 2005; Guzzetti 1995). However, education (especially higher education) has been seen as an area with national prerogatives. Most historical accounts of EU's involvement in higher education frame it as a 'tug-of-war' between member states and the European Commission evolving in incremental steps due to task expansion (De Wit and Verhoeven 2001; Neave 1984). Scholarly works, especially Corbett's (2003; 2005), have identified both the historical events in the early days of European integration and elaborated a fine-grained understanding of entrepreneurs within and around the European Commission in securing the major leaps in the EU's engagement with higher education. Corbett points to how the member states' education ministers, in voicing proposals for more organized cooperation, and the European Commission, in expressing at times concern over the Community principle, contributed to supranational expansion into the educational sector.

It can be argued that the overall condition framing the tensions between the supranational and national governance levels with respect to higher education as a policy area is the issue of national sensitivity. When the university was seen as an educational institution, it was positioned in an area of legitimate national diversity especially concerning higher education's socializing role and gate-keeping functions for entrance into the national civil service. One pathway of European involvement in higher education was through its policy towards mutual recognition of professional degrees and free movement of skilled manpower. As Bartolini (2005) notes for general education, the EU's inroad into this domain was legitimized via socio-functional arguments and not as a question of the socializing role of education or for creating a common European identity.

EU history suggests that higher education has been more nationally sensitive in its cultural socializing function than in its labour market/economic role. At the same time, the university was also seen as a cultural carrier and as an independent, key societal institution transcending national borders as the Magna Charta Universitatum (1988, p. 1) proclaims: 'A university is the trustee of the European humanist tradition'. The EU did not have any legal basis for harmonization (apart from the directives for mutual recognition of professional degrees) and the member states did not show much political will to allow for the development of a supranational higher education policy. The EU continues to have a *supporting* role in education and training policies. Member states are in charge of their own education and training systems. The Treaty on the Functioning of the EU states (Article 165):

> The Community shall contribute to the development of quality education by encouraging cooperation between Member States and, if necessary, by supporting and supplementing their action, while fully respecting the responsibility of the Member States for the content of teaching and the organisation of education systems and their cultural and linguistic diversity (Official Journal of the European Union 2010, p. C 83/120).

What the EU was left with in the 1980s and 1990s was first and foremost European programmes for promoting student and staff mobility. Although the decisions to establish these programmes have been highly contentious and laborious, these programmes were institutionalized and important in establishing a European governance site for higher education. They also introduced the 'motives, means, and opportunity' to create and consolidate stakeholder associations, transnational expert communities and administrative networks (Beerkens 2008; Gornitzka 2009). In the 1990s an *informal* cooperation structure between top national officials responsible for higher education was established. Though weak, this committee was where these officials became socialized into cooperation (Corbett 2005).

The pre-Lisbon period (before 2000) is characterized by the growing momentum of the knowledge economy discourse in Europe, where one could expect higher education to be at centre stage. Yet, the European Commission had burnt its fingers on the national sensitivity towards higher education: its 1991 'Memorandum on Higher Education' received a hostile reception from member states. They opposed the economic orientation and utilitarian view of higher education supposedly permeating this document (European Commission 1991). Combined with a sense that the European Commission was trespassing on national domain (especially in the area of teacher training), the member states sent a clear message to stay off this territory. While there were tentative developments towards building up a European governance capacity for higher education in the 1990s through incentive programmes, this was about to change with the instigation of the Bologna Process.

### The Bologna Process as Voluntary Coordination for Higher Education: Stepping Outside the EU Framework

In May 1998, the German, French, Italian and British ministers in charge of higher education met on the occasion of the 800th anniversary of the Sorbonne University. The four ministers called on all European countries to join them in building an attractive EHEA based on comparable degrees and a two-cycle system for improving student mobility and employability. The Sorbonne Declaration delved straight into one of the most sensitive issues: diversity of degree structures. The central objectives exceeded what European states could have ever accepted from the European Commission (see Ravinet 2009, for details). Countries beyond the big four quickly joined and in June 1999 ministers from 29 European countries signed the Bologna Declaration, committing to coordinating their national policies based on six common objectives for establishing an EHEA by 2010 (Ravinet 2007).

Member states side-stepping the EU to pursue integrative agendas is not unprecedented. To start, following the intergovernmental logic, national ministers were in this case clearly in the driver's seat as instigators of this process. Over time, however, the actors responsible for voluntary coordination changed and became mixed. The Bologna Process saw a growing presence of national officials who connected with each other. The intergovernmental process borrowed the administrative capacity of the supranational executive and the European Commission's Directorate-General (DG) for Education became a regular participant. Consultative members were added to the Bologna Process and made it a collective forum where public and non-governmental organizations met, along with higher education experts and consultants. Measures for developing the EHEA borrowed from existing EU measures; for example, the European credit transfer system (ECTS). As Elken and Vukasovic (2014, this volume) demonstrate, the intergovernmental process has developed into a node for a *transnational* Bologna Process network.

From a *horizontal* perspective, we are able to spot the interaction between different sites of European level policy-making as a key dynamic of change. The Bologna Process is organized to reinforce the *sector internal* interaction across governance levels where actors met without any immediate demand for cross-sectoral coordination. This might be seen as a way through which member states can approach and deal with national sensitivity of a policy domain. The aspirations of the Bologna Process were ambitious, but were also restrictive in that they covered only one specific sector, paying limited attention to the overall European educational and socio-economic agendas. While it created a vision and agenda for developing national higher education systems, it made higher education vulnerable to criticisms of being a 'closed-shop' sector that did not open up for non-traditional postsecondary education developments, new providers and competence-based qualifications.

Bologna's effectiveness is contested, but even a very conservative reading suggests that it has committed signatories to a common agenda. Its effects should not automatically be equated with national policy convergence (see Witte et al. 2009). Governments have used its non-binding nature and ambiguities to bring about a variety of policy changes. The domestic impacts of these changes are conditioned by timing, national traditions and previous and on-going domestic reform trajectories. Yet changes in degree structure have taken place in a majority of higher education institutions across the Bologna signatory countries. This made them structurally more similar than they were in the 1990s; the same goes for the spread of elements that the Bologna Process 'took over' from the EU's Erasmus mobility programme (Common European Diploma Supplement and the ECTS). It has enhanced a European dimension in quality assurance, setting *European standards*, plus bolstering the *agencification* of national quality assurance systems. The national agencies are marked by domestic variations and ambitions of a common European quality policy have been co-opted by national governance traditions and nationally specific interests (see Hansen 2014, this volume). Yet they are connected through a European network of agencies with potential for European standardization of agency practices – as can also be observed in the research sector.

### European Research Policy Cooperation: from Intergovernmental to Programmed and Multi-Layered

Compared to higher education, European research cooperation has been far more developed. From the start, it was legitimized as a contribution to Europe's economic growth and industrial development (Guzzetti 1995). During the earliest period, this cooperation was about setting up the foundation for a knowledge-based *economy*. Indeed, 'science' was billed to play a starred role in European integration and a treaty basis for such cooperation was established in the Paris and Rome Treaties. While member states were keen to pursue joint collaborations, they were also cautious about retaining control over such undertakings (*vertical* tensions of integration), which took place in selected research areas such as agriculture, energy, health and environment. Meeting in various configurations of the Council of Ministers, the European research ministers decided the scope and depth of this cooperation. Hence, European research cooperation up until the 1980s can be characterized as *intergovernmental*, with the central institutions – especially the European Commission and European Parliament – playing limited advisory roles.

European research cooperation changed in the 1980s. The European Commissioner for Industry, Davignon, pushed for bundling up existing research programmes into a multi-annual research Framework Programme (FP). The idea, according to Banchoff (2002, p. 8), was to ensure that funding European research activities would directly support the Single European Market project, which goes to show a *horizontal* dynamic of integration at this stage of EU research policy development. Both the European Commission leadership and member states endorsed this approach and the Single European Act extended a treaty base for the FPs and the Community Method. Research was thus brought closer to the market and became *programmed*.

Throughout the 1990s, European research policy cooperation continued to operate along the FP-structure formalized during the previous decade. At the same time, this *programmed* approach strained the capacity of the European Commission which oversaw its preparation and implementation (Banchoff 2002). Indeed, the repeated delays in securing approval from the Council and European Parliament on the European Commission's proposal for the second FP (1987–1991) defined the tenure of the Research Commissioner Pandolfi (1989–1992). Although negotiations based on the Community Method were by no means smooth, the entry into force of the Maastricht Treaty did little to change this. This Treaty altered the decision-making procedure to co-decision, which established the Parliament as a co-legislator.

European research policy since then has gradually evolved into a very dense area of activities with a sizable share of the Community/Union budget (from €11 million to €80 billion) and a large DG for Research whose size is only surpassed by DG Translation. Indeed, DG Research established itself as the key funding agency for European research and it became the node for networks across Europe and for research collabora-tion between Europe and the rest of the world. Transnational organiza-tions mushroomed around FP preparation and implementation, which expanded in the 1990s. The fourth FP (1995–1998) was designed to solve more *technical* issues with programmes offering financial support to col-laborative projects in materials, designs and manufacturing technologies (European Court of Auditors 2008). By contrast, the fifth FP (1999–2002) was formulated to promote research that also addressed specific *social problems*. In short, the 1,200 officials in DG Research and the complex transnational constituency attached to the FPs thus became the 'FP machinery'. Its importance was consolidated when this supranational instrument became an increasingly significant funding source different from the traditional intergovernmental research cooperation structures that existed in parallel to the FPs.

The launch of the ERA in January 2000 furthered the importance of the supranational governance layer even though this new initiative strug-gled against the dominant FP organizational model (see Chou 2012). To conclude, European research cooperation became more complex and *multi-layered* with the emergence of the ERA initiative and this was largely spurred on by the adoption of the Lisbon Strategy.

**The Lisbon Strategy: the Challenge of Policy Coordination**

The EU's Lisbon Strategy was a turning point for knowledge policies with more explicit ambitions for *horizontal* policy coordination. It can be considered as a new 'governance architecture' for Europe (Borrás and Radaelli 2011) that has a substantive component (to become 'the world's most competitive and dynamic knowledge-based economy') and a procedural dimension (introduction of the 'Open Method of Coordination', OMC). As an overarching frame, the Lisbon Strategy pushed knowledge policies to the centre of the EU agenda, as transversal 'problem-solvers' (as a policy instrument) in areas such as economic growth in general, regional development, the environmental agenda and labour market policy. Among the means to the Lisbon ends was an overhaul of the European education and research systems.

The Lisbon Summit provided a diagnosis of a Europe challenged by globalization and demands of the new economy. The diagnosis concerned also European research and education systems which were argued as needing an increase in investments in human resources, improvements of education attainment levels, development of basic skills and competences in its labour force, and growth in intra-European mobility. Education and research received full attention as part of a much larger agenda and political project with the whole knowledge and skills area defined as a necessary component of an economic and social reform strategy. Hence, the link between Lisbon and the research and education sectors spurred a radical change in the cooperation mechanisms at the European level based on the OMC, especially in education (Education and Training 2010 Work Programme (E&T 2010)) (Gornitzka 2007).

For research policy the *horizontal* link between developing the ERA, the Lisbon Process and, later, the competitiveness and growth strategy was crucial (see Chou and Real-Dato 2014, this volume). Yet the introduction of the new governance mode did not have the same transformative impact as it did in the education sector (Gornitzka 2007).

For education policy the impacts of Lisbon and the OMC were considerable. The European Commission's work programme for E&T 2010 defined education cooperation and the modernization of European education systems for a decade. The Education Council agreed on the strategic objectives to guide the E&T 2010 process. Compared to the hesitant attitude towards committed cooperation in this sector only 15 to 20 years earlier, the will to agree on common goals was taken to another level. At the time, the same ministers were grappling with how to handle the policy implications of the 'shocking' results of the Organisation for Economic Co-operation and Development's (OECD) Programme for International

Student Assessment (PISA) 2000 comparative study of school children's basic skills.

DG Education championed the use of the OMC as a way to change the modus of cooperation, arguing that this was 'a method for us'. The assumed dynamics of the OMC were expected to allow the involved countries to deal with a combination of common challenges, national sensitivities and national systemic diversity. The method, however, was presented as a way of exploiting this diversity for policy learning purposes as, at the time, the education sector was involved in intersectoral rivalry – 'colliding' with the European employment strategy (EES). Reclaiming European cooperation in lifelong learning from the EES became a spur for cooperation within the education sector. Hence, the OMC's use should be read as a *sector defence* enacted by the core European institutions in the education field (Gornitzka 2007).

There was a strong awareness in DG Education that the Bologna Process occupied higher education territory (Gornitzka 2007). As a consequence, the European Commission could not easily propose a coordination process that stepped on the toes of those developing the EHEA. At the political level, most of the ministers who met in the Bologna meetings also met in the Education Council. So when they agreed to the European Commission's proposal for a 'full' E&T 2010, the Bologna Process was enlisted as an integral part of the education sector's contribution to Lisbon. Furthermore, Bologna as a governance site did become a source of inspiration, competition and support for Lisbon in other ways. In November 2002, the Education ministers of 31 countries adopted the Copenhagen Declaration on enhanced cooperation in vocational education and training, initiating a process set to mirror the Bologna Process. However, it was all along an EU process. From the moment the Bologna and Copenhagen Processes were incorporated into the E&T 2010, it was showcased as the EU's integrated policy framework for education and training.

In these contexts, the European Commission started to shape its reform agenda for higher education; more specifically, developing a vision and agenda for higher education institutions and their role within the Lisbon Strategy. It presented a vision of the university as an institution expected to play a core role in achieving the European knowledge economy ambitions. However, it would only do so if the university opened up to society and underwent drastic reforms (for an in-depth discussion of this agenda see Olsen and Maassen 2007). This reform agenda was renewed in 2011 (European Commission 2011) and can be regarded as an element in the renewed Lisbon Strategy: 'Europe 2020'.

**Europe 2020: Continuing a Competitiveness and Growth Strategy Amidst the Economic Crisis and Recession**

In June 2010, EU leaders adopted the 'Europe 2020' Strategy to replace the Lisbon Strategy. Research and education retained their place in the new strategy. New initiatives were built on existing programmes and institutions (European Commission 2010), while several Lisbon targets were recycled: for example, the 3 per cent investment for R&D; reducing school drop-out rates; increasing university degree/diploma holders.

The impact of the acute crisis is not yet well researched, but it seems that it has not resulted in the deinstitutionalization of the knowledge domain. There is no overt decentralization to the nation state level or withdrawal by the European Commission. What we can observe at this early stage of the Europe 2020 implementation is that the *vertical* and *horizontal* lines of tensions remain. For the education sector, the governance architecture seems to have been kept without major redesigns – showing signs of robustness even in face of major crisis and political upheaval.

Similarly, in the research and innovation sectors, the crisis has been used as a catalyst to 'bring ideas to the market' and the concept of the 'innovation cycle' was introduced to tightly couple EU-funded research and innovation activities. The vocal ambitions of meshing innovation policy with both research and education policy were reiterated (Maassen and Stensaker 2011). These developments were built on the Ljubljana Process for completing the ERA (Council 2008), the newly minted concept of the 'fifth freedom' (free movement of knowledge), and the new legal basis for the ERA following the entry into force of the Lisbon Treaty (not to be confused with the Lisbon Strategy) in December 2009. The European Commission has adopted a Bologna-like approach for delivering the ERA: it signed several 'ERA Pacts' with key stakeholder organizations and will 'name-and-shame' those member states and signatories failing to deliver the ERA in the coming years.

To summarize, this chapter gave an overview of the evolution of European policies towards higher education and research – two key pillars of what constitutes the Europe of Knowledge. This overview highlighted the key sector-specific conditions and multiple inherent tensions influencing the course of European integration in these domains. Below, we turn to the lessons this volume offers concerning the main dynamics in building the Europe of Knowledge specifically and regional integration more generally.

## INTEGRATION DYNAMICS IN TWO KEY KNOWLEDGE SECTORS: LESSONS FROM THIS VOLUME

Our theoretical starting point is that European cooperation in different subsectors of the knowledge domain is unleashed by institutionally embedded tensions along two dimensions: *vertical* (between governance levels) and *horizontal* (between sectors and institutional spheres). The *first lesson* the chapters in this volume provide is: *vertical* and *horizontal* tensions are not exclusive to specific sectors or policy activities. These tensions are present in everyday practices, inform key decisional moments and, indeed, may even coexist in a single policy process. Yet the specific expressions they take are influenced by sector-specific conditions within which European integration has taken place.

How have tensions between the national and the supranational governance levels been dealt with in building a European knowledge area? In Chapter 2, Chou documents the resistance from national ministers in surrendering regulatory competence to the supranational level, especially to the European executive (*vertical* tensions), in creating a 'common scientific space'. This narrative is a classic integration story with a twist: national policy-makers came to endorse the ERA concept not because the idea set out clear roadmaps for achieving their objectives. On the contrary, Chou asserts that policy actors embraced the ERA notion because the idea itself became increasingly vague and was able to accommodate multiple – sometimes even conflicting – interests. Instead of being a 'tit-for-tat' lowest common denominator outcome from rational grand bargaining, the institutionalization of the ERA concept testifies to the power of ideas and the crucial importance of institutional champions in its discursive promotion and sustainability.

Hoareau's chapter (Chapter 9) on funding higher education also highlights *vertical* tensions, but with different kinds of factors affecting the shift towards the European level. What are the conditions under which federal governments are likely to increase their redistributive functions, which are generally held by state governments? Taking the case of financial aid to students and comparing the United States and the EU, Hoareau shows that redistributive schemes are difficult to establish at the federal level given the consensus required among contributing states and the budget constraints in place preventing increases in interpersonal and interregional redistribution. Studying the United States, she argues that an economic recession alters the dynamics of this process by affecting the capacity of private lenders of loans to continue their operations. These loans, as Hoareau puts it, are 'not designed to absorb major shocks'. In her view, these findings demonstrate how negative economic shocks may become *an engine for vertical transfer of competence from the member states to the EU* on an important issue, such as student financial aid for the Europe of Knowledge. The main message from this analysis echoes core historical institutionalist argument about the conditions under which major institutional change is likely to take place.

The chapter by Gornitzka and Metz on the European Institute of Innovation and Technology (EIT) (Chapter 5) shows what happens when a combination of *vertical* and *horizontal* tensions is involved in the institution-building process. In several respects, the establishment of a higher education institution such as the EIT as an EU legal entity was unlikely. From a power-oriented perspective, one would anticipate member states vetoing the proposal from the top political leadership of the European Commission to establish such an institution in a nationally sensitive area, and in doing so blocking the attempts of the European Commission to pursuing a supranational solution and integrative agendas. From an institutional path-dependency perspective, a proposal that cuts across policy and administrative boundaries is likely to meet institutionally entrenched inertia since such an institution involves three hitherto strongly segmented policy areas: research, higher education and innovation policies. Gornitzka and Metz find that the EIT is indeed shaped by power and conflicts along the territorial cleavage line, but also by temporality and path dependency. While the will and power of key institutional actors were main factors in the institution building and in pushing this idea through to a decision, a power-oriented explanation is not a sufficient account. Several parallel events contributed to this institution's final form.

In Elken and Vukasovic, Chou and Real-Dato, and Hansen's chapters (Chapters 6, 3 and 8 respectively), *vertical* tensions of integration are the catalysts that led to the adoption of the voluntary processes they studied: the Bologna Process, Human Resource Strategy for Researchers (HRS4R) and quality assurance. These chapters zoom in on the organizational structures and query how they contribute to certain defining features of these processes – *stability* in the case of the Bologna Process, *growth* in HRS4R participation and *differentiation* in quality assurance practices in three Scandinavian countries. What these chapters highlight is that, although *vertical* tensions may have contributed to the 'design' and 'choice' of institutional structure – creating institutional set-ups for soft governance, they do not determine the outcomes of these processes. Indeed, what they tell us is that the effects of constructing the Europe of Knowledge on the evolving European political order is under certain conditions unpredictable and even situational.

Applying a network perspective to the meta-governance of the Bologna Process, in Chapter 6 Elken and Vukasovic map out the collective actor constellations from inception to the present. They find that these collective actors were able to join the Bologna Process due to the unique resources they offered: financial (the European Commission), information (expertise) or legitimacy (European University Association and the European Student Union). Elken and Vukasovic explain that the Bologna network has been relatively stable as a result of: (1) the limited numbers of entrants (collective actors); and (2) the limited range of individuals moving within this network through the collective actors. This study evidences an emerging European governance layer in higher education where it was previously absent and demonstrates how the network perspective reveals a rich dimension of an unlikely case of institutionalization – the Bologna Process.

Turning to a voluntary process in the research policy sector, in Chapter 3 Chou and Real-Dato investigate the growing participation in a European Commission-led process for HRS4R. Launched in 2008 to support national organizations and research institutes interested in translating a set of non-binding European standards for researchers, the HRS4R now consists of four cohorts, with around 50 organizations in each. The Charter for Researchers and Code of Conduct for their recruitment is a central instrument adopted for the ERA. Studying the Norwegian and Spanish organizations in the first HRS4R cohort, Chou and Real-Dato identify the factors contributing to their decisions to *voluntarily* comply, that is, endorse the Charter and Code and participate in the HRS4R. They found that both the logics of expected consequences and of appropriateness have roles in different stages of this process. While the consequential logic was most visible in the endorsement stage, appropriateness reinforces it in the formal HRS4R stages.

A key area of European level ambitions, EU and Bologna alike, is developing common European standards for quality assurance. In Hansen's chapter (Chapter 8) on developing quality assurance agencies, *vertical* tensions are visible: national governance traditions and institutional arrangements clearly influence the ways in which similar intentions and ideas about controlling and developing quality in higher education are addressed. Her analysis shows that even within the Nordic corner of the Europe of Knowledge, the differences in national governance systems in higher education in Sweden, Denmark and Norway have led to 'diverse' practices concerning how quality agencies and assurance are regulated. Using a framework informed by organizational theory and the regulatory approach, Hansen concludes that the standardizing role of European level developments is limited and 'hits' quality assurance in these countries in non-converging ways.

Similarly, examining the OMC effects on Norwegian ministries and agencies, Gornitzka in Chapter 7 finds that the OMC has had an impact on decision-making practices in some parts of national ministries and agencies – the most significant footprints of the OMC are found in research and education policy. Overall, national civil servants use the OMC in a 'learning mode' – seeking to learn from others and to share their experiences with European peers – and in a monitoring mode. Hence, the direct instrumental role of soft modes of governance in facilitating policy change is difficult to pinpoint. What the data show, however, is that the OMC has contributed to establishing regularized connections between the European administration and national ministries and agencies. The use of organized EU soft governance processes in this policy domain is clearly part of a much more general picture of going from policy-making in a national frame to organized multi-level interwoven policy-making. Domestic research and higher education policy-makers' practices are now much more oriented towards Europe than two decades ago.

The chapters by Gornitzka on the OMC (Chapter 7), Hansen on quality assurance (Chapter 8), and Chou and Real-Dato on human resource standards (Chapter 3) show that the clash of different ideas about Europe has led to different levels of Europeanization. By pointing explicitly to the domestic 'filter', these authors emphasize the importance of historical legacies on current policy and standardization efforts. This reference to the past points to the *second lesson* this volume offers on the evolution of knowledge policy cooperation and European integration: *sequential* tensions are consistently visible and should be systematically incorporated in future research in these areas. Here, *sequential* tensions of integration refer to the tensions between the past and the future in which historical legacies and path dependence become enabling/hindering factors shaping how institutions are built at the European level and how the national level responds to European governance output.

Several chapters point to the importance of the historical context, including Gornitzka and Metz's chapter on the EIT (Chapter 5). They ask: why are new European institutions established and what shapes their design? In Chapter 4 Gornitzka and Metz address this question explicitly by examining the birth of a key institutional innovation in the European research landscape – the European Research Council (ERC). The ERC was set-up in February 2007 to distribute European R&D funds based on a single assessment criterion: academic 'excellence', thereby building an institution that breaks with the established principles that have been engrained in the EU's main research policy instrument, the multi-annual FPs. With the ERC, the EU institutionalized its involvement in what was defined as *frontier* research. Starting as an idea and vision of the few, this institution became one with a governance structure, funding and an executive agency with a considerable staff and an elaborate set of rules and procedures. The case of the ERC is a testimony of how institutions *enable* change and institution building.

The *final lesson* from this volume concerns the possibility of a coherent Europe of Knowledge emerging from these contexts. Coherence, in this instance, suggests that the processes leading to the European knowledge policy area are based on calculated rational decisions in its design and expected outcomes. This has clearly not been the case. The findings from the chapters in this volume suggest that coherence would be actually rather surprising and perhaps the result of temporal 'accidents'. Yet, a European knowledge policy area *is emerging*: it is fragmented, differentiated and ordered by soft, albeit fairly robust, governance. Even though it is not far-reaching in the perspectives of current policy-makers and some stakeholders, it is certainly revolutionary from the vantage point of the founding moments. This observation speaks to the extraordinary developments that have carried European integration beyond the Single Market to one concerning knowledge policy.

## CONCLUSIONS

The European level in the 1950s has been characterized as a 'primitive site of collective governance' (Stone Sweet et al. 2001). This was most certainly the case with respect to European level governance capacity concerning research and higher education. In terms of conferring legal competencies to the EU this primitive state lingered. Yet as the European institutions developed, gradually an institutionalization of collective governance capacity for a Europe of Knowledge took place. This process partly resembles a pattern familiar from the build-up of European nation states, marked by two essential dynamics of change: institutional and sectoral differentiation on the one hand and, on the other, the transformation implied in interactions and collisions between policy sectors and institutional spheres.

These developments led to competing visions for a Europe of Knowledge, with strong and institutionally anchored promoters at multiple governance levels. Integration in the knowledge domain has occurred in the 'shadow of the past' rather than in the 'shadow of hierarchy' (Héritier and Lehmkuhl 2008). It has been carried by a progressive build-up of institutions that established capacity for and promoted certain ideas and norms about research and higher education policy cooperation. The debate concerning the Europe of Knowledge – its shape, functions and societal value – is affected by sector-specific factors embodied in the notion of policy-making under limited participation due to the 'image of policy problems' (Baumgartner and Jones 1991).

The logic(s) of integration evolved with considerable presence of transnational networks, which made the idea of a pure intergovernmental or, even supranational, logic of integration problematic. As a result, European research and higher education cooperation has witnessed processes of coevolution between intergovernmental, transnational and supranational logics. Impacts on national institutions and policies are indelible rather than legal, through European incentive programmes and the gradual socialization of national policy-makers and networks of transnational stakeholders. Indeed, the Europe of Knowledge is emerging as an experimental site of mixed modes of governance more than most other policy sectors.

## NOTES

1.  We are grateful for comments from Peter Maassen, Bjørn Stensaker, Jarle Trondal, Martina Vukasovic and Mari Elken on this chapter.
2.  See European Union (2013).

## REFERENCES

Banchoff, T. (2002), 'Institutions, inertia and European Union research policy', *Journal of Common Market Studies*, **40**(1), 1–21.

Bartolini, S. (2005), *Restructuring Europe: Centre Formation, System Building and Political Structuring Between the Nation-State and the European Union*, Oxford: Oxford University Press.

Baumgartner, F. and B. Jones (1991), 'Agenda dynamics and policy subsystems', *The Journal of Politics*, **53**(4), 1044–1074.

Beerkens, E. (2008), 'The emergence and institutionalisation of the European higher education and research area', *European Journal of Education*, **43**(4), 407–424.

Borrás, S. and C.M. Radaelli (2011), 'The politics of governance architectures: creation, change and effects of the EU Lisbon Strategy', *Journal of European Public Policy*, **18**(4), 464–484.

Börzel, T.A. (2005), 'Mind the gap! European integration between level and scope', *Journal of European Public Policy*, **12**(2), 217–236.

Braun, D. (2008), 'Lessons on the political coordination of knowledge and innovation policies', *Science and Public Policy*, **35**, 289–298.

Chou, M.-H. (2012), 'Constructing an internal market for research through sectoral and lateral strategies: layering, the European Commission and the fifth freedom', *Journal of European Public Policy*, **19**(7), 1052–1070.

Chou, M.-H. and J. Real-Dato (2014, this volume), 'Translating the "European Charter for Researchers and the Code of Conduct for the Recruitment of

Researchers" in national arenas: Norway vs Spain', in M.-H. Chou and Å. Gornitzka (eds), *Building the Knowledge Economy in Europe: New Constellations in European Research and Higher Education Governance*, Cheltenham, UK and Northampton, MA, USA: Edward Elgar, pp. 51–80.

Corbett, A. (2003), 'Ideas, institutions and policy entrepreneurs: towards a new history of higher education in the European Community', *European Journal of Education*, **38**(3), 315–330.

Corbett, A. (2005), *Universities and the Europe of Knowledge: Ideas, Institutions and Policy Entrepreneurship in European Union Higher Education Policy, 1955–2005*, Basingstoke: Palgrave Macmillan.

Council (2008), 'Council Conclusions on the Launch of the "Ljubljana Process" – Towards Full Realisation of ERA – Adoption, 9076/08', Council of the European Union, Brussels.

De Elera, Á. (2006), 'The European research area: on the way towards a European Scientific Community?', *European Law Journal*, **12**(5), 559–574.

De Wit, K. and J.C. Verhoeven (2001), 'Higher education policy of the European Union: with or against the member states?', in J. Huisman, P. Maassen and G. Neave (eds), *Higher Education and the Nation State*, Amsterdam: Pergamon Press, pp. 175–231.

Egeberg, M. (ed.) (2006), *Multilevel Union Administration. The Transformation of Executive Politics in Europe*, Houndmills: Palgrave Macmillan.

Egeberg, M., J.P. Olsen and H. Sætren (1978), 'Organisasjonssamfunnet og den segmenterte stat', in J.P. Olsen (ed.), *Politisk Organisering*, Bergen: Universitetsforlaget, pp. 115–142.

Elken, M. and M. Vukasovic (2014, this volume), 'Dynamics of voluntary coordination: actors and networks in the Bologna Process', in M.-H. Chou and Å. Gornitzka (eds), *Building the Knowledge Economy in Europe: New Constellations in European Research and Higher Education Governance*, Cheltenham, UK and Northampton, MA, USA: Edward Elgar, pp. 131–159.

Elken, M., Å. Gornitzka, P. Maassen and M. Vukasovic (2011), 'European Integration and the Transformation of Higher Education', Pre-Project: Higher Education and Professional Learning: The Effects of European Integration (The Norwegian Research Council, 197652), University of Oslo, Department of Educational Research, Oslo.

European Commission (1991), 'Memorandum on Higher Education in the European Community (349 final)', European Commission, Brussels.

European Commission (1997a), 'Agenda 2000: For a Stronger and Wider Union (2000 Final)', European Commission, Brussels.

European Commission (1997b), 'Communication on Towards a Europe of Knowledge (563 Final)', European Commission, Brussels.

European Commission (2000), 'Communication on Towards a European Research Area (6 Final)', European Commission, Brussels.

European Commission (2003), 'Communication on the Role of the Universities in the Europe of Knowledge (58 Final)', European Commission, Brussels.

European Commission (2010), 'A Strategy for Smart, Sustainable and Inclusive Growth (2020 Final)', European Commission, Brussels.

European Commission (2011), 'Supporting Growth and Jobs – an Agenda for the Modernisation of Europe's Higher Education Systems (567 Final)', European Commission, Brussels.

European Court of Auditors (2008), 'Concerning "Evaluating the EU Research and Technological Development (RTD) Framework Programmes – Could the Commission's Approach be Improved?" Together with the Commission's Replies (Special Report No. 9/2007; OJ C 26/1)', European Court of Auditors, Luxembourg.

European Union (2013), *Innovation Union Scoreboard 2013*, available at: http://ec.europa.eu/enterprise/policies/innovation/files/ius-2013_en.pdf (accessed 22 November 2013).

Fligstein, N. (2008), *Euroclash – The EU, European Identity, and the Future of Europe*, Oxford: Oxford University Press.

Georghiou, L. (1999), 'Evolving frameworks for European collaboration in research and technology', in *Conference on Civilian Technology Policy in the European Union and the United States*. Atlanta, Georgia: Elsevier Science Bv.

Gornitzka, Å. (2007), 'The Lisbon Process: a supranational policy perspective', in P. Maassen and J.P. Olsen (eds), *University Dynamics and European Integration*, Dordrecht: Springer, pp. 155–178.

Gornitzka, Å. (2009), 'Networking administration in areas of national sensitivity – the Commission and European higher education', in A. Amaral, G. Neave, C. Musselin and P. Maassen (eds), *European Integration and the Governance of Higher Education and Research*, Dordrecht: Springer, pp. 109–131.

Gornitzka, Å (2010), 'Bologna in context: a horizontal perspective on the dynamics of governance sites for a Europe of Knowledge', *European Journal of Education*, **45**(4): 535–548.

Gornitzka, Å. and P. Maassen (2000), 'Hybrid steering approaches with respect to European higher education', *Higher Education Policy*, **13**(3), 267–285.

Gornitzka, Å. and J.P. Olsen (2006), 'Europeiske endringsprosesser og høyere utdanningsinstitusjoner', *Tidsskrift for Samfunnsforskning*, **47**(2), 259–274.

Gornitzka, Å., M. Kogan and A. Amaral (eds) (2005), *Reform and Change in Higher Education: Analysing Policy Implementation*, Dordrecht: Springer.

Gornitzka, Å., P. Maassen, J.P. Olsen and B. Stensaker (2007), '"Europe of knowledge": search for a new pact', in P. Maassen and J.P. Olsen (eds), *University Dynamics and European Integration*, Dordrecht: Springer, pp. 181–214.

Guzzetti, L. (1995), *A Brief History of European Union Research Policy*, Luxembourg: Office for the Official Publications of the European Communities.

Haas, E.B. (1990), *When Knowledge is Power: Three Models of Change in International Organizations*, Berkeley: University of California Press.

Hall, P.A. (1993), 'Policy paradigms, social learning, and the state – the case of economic policy-making in Britain', *Comparative Politics*, **25**(3), 275–296.

Hansen, H.F. (2014, this volume) '"Quality agencies": the development of regulating and mediating organizations in Scandinavian higher education', in M.-H. Chou and Å. Gornitzka (eds), *Building the Knowledge Economy in Europe: New Constellations in European Research and Higher Education Governance*, Cheltenham, UK and Northampton, MA, USA: Edward Elgar, pp. 188–218.

Héritier, A. and D. Lehmkuhl (2008), 'The shadow of hierarchy and new modes of governance', *Journal of Public Policy*, **28**(1), 1–17.

Holm, P. (1995), 'The dynamics of institutionalization – transformation processes in Norwegian fisheries', *Administrative Science Quarterly*, **40**(3), 398–422.

Kohler-Koch, B. (2005), 'European goverance and system integration', *European Governance Papers (EUROGOV)*, **C-05-01**, 1–21.

Lundvall, B.-Å. and M.J. Rodrigues (2002), *The New Knowledge Economy in*

*Europe: A Strategy for International Competitiveness and Social Cohesion*, Cheltenham, UK and Northampton, MA, USA: Edward Elgar.

Maassen, P. (2009), 'The modernisation of European higher education', in A. Amaral, I. Bleiklie and C. Musselin (eds), *From Governance to Identity*, Dordrecht: Springer, pp. 95–112.

Maassen, P. and B. Stensaker (2011), 'The knowledge triangle, European higher education policy logics and policy implications', *Higher Education*, **61**(6): 757–769.

Magna Charta Universitatum (1988), available at: http://www.magna-charta.org/library/userfiles/file/mc_english.pdf (accessed 22 November 2013).

March, J.G. and J.P. Olsen (2006), 'Elaborating the "new institutionalism"', in R.A.W. Rhodes, S. Binder and B. Rockman (eds), *The Oxford Handbook of Political Institutions*, Oxford: Oxford University Press, pp. 3–20.

Mazey, S. and J. Richardson (2001) 'Institutionalizing promiscuity: Commission-Interest Group relations in the European Union', in A. Stone Sweet, W. Sandholtz and N. Fligstein (eds), *The Institutionalization of Europe*, Oxford: Oxford University Press, pp. 71–93.

Neave, G. (1984), *The EEC and Education*, Trentham: Trentham Books.

Official Journal of the European Union (2010), *Consolidated Version of the Treaty on the Functioning of the European Union*, available at: http://eur-lex.europa.eu/LexUriServ/LexUriServ.do?uri=OJ:C:2010:083:0047:0200:en:PDF (accessed 22 November 2013).

Olsen, J.P. (1997), 'Institutional design in democratic contexts', *Journal of Political Philosophy*, **5**(3), 203–229.

Olsen, J.P. (2001), 'Organizing European institutions of governance: a prelude to an institutional account to European integration', in H. Wallace (ed.), *Interlocking Dimensions of European Integration*, Houndmills: Palgrave, pp. 323–353.

Olsen, J.P. (2007a), *Europe in Search of Political Order. An Institutional Perspective on Unity/Diversity, Citizens/Their Helpers, Democratic Design/Historical Drift, and the Co-Existence of Orders*, Oxford: Oxford University Press.

Olsen, J.P. (2007b), 'The institutional dynamics of the European university', in P. Maassen and J.P. Olsen (eds), *University Dynamics and European Integration*, Dordrecht: Springer, pp. 25–55.

Olsen, J.P. (2007c), 'Mellom økonomi og kultur: Det europeiske universitetet i endring', *Norsk Statsvitenskapelig Tidsskrift*, **23**(3), 267–287.

Olsen, J.P. and P. Maassen (2007), 'European debates on the knowledge institution: the modernization of the university at the European level', in P.A.M. Maassen and J.P. Olsen (eds), *University Dynamics and European Integration*, Dordrecht: Springer, pp. 3–22.

Pierson, P. (2000), 'The limits of design: explaining institutional origins and change', *Governance: An International Journal of Policy and Administration*, **13**(4), 475–499.

Ravinet, P. (2007), 'La genèse et l'institutionnalisation du processus de Bologne: Entre chemin de traverse et sentier de dépendance', Paris: Ecole Doctorale de Sciences Po.

Ravinet, P. (2009), 'Comment le processus de Bologne a-t-il commencé? La formulation de la vision d'un Espace d'Enseignement Supérieur à la Sorbonne en 1998', *Education et Sociétés*, **24**, 29–44.

Scharpf, F.W. (2001), 'Notes toward a theory of multilevel governing in Europe', *Scandinavian Political Studies*, **24**, 1–26.

Scharpf, F.W. (2002), 'Legitimate Diversity: the New Challenge of European Integration', Les Cahiers européens de Sciences Po, Centre d'études européennes at Sciences Po, Paris.

Sorbonne Joint Declaration (1998), 'Joint Declaration on Harmonisation of the Architecture of the Europen Higher Education System by the Four Ministers in Charge for France, Germany, Italy and the United Kingdom', Sorbonne: 25 May 1998.

Stone Sweet, A., N. Fligstein and W. Sandholtz (2001), 'The institutionalization of European space', in A. Stone Sweet, W. Sandholtz and N. Fligstein (eds), *The Institutionalization of Europe*, Oxford: Oxford University Press, pp. 1–28.

Witte, J., J. Huisman and L. Purser (2009), 'European higher education reforms in the context of the Bologna Process: how did we get here, where are we and where are we going?', in OECD (ed.), *Higher Education to 2030: Volume 2, Globalisation,* Paris: OECD Publishing, pp. 205–229.

# 2. The evolution of the European Research Area as an idea in European integration

**Meng-Hsuan Chou**

## INTRODUCTION

'Research and innovation' has recently been moved closer to the top of the political and legislative agenda of the European Union (EU) – the most advanced form of existing supranational cooperation. At the heart of these developments is the completion of the European Research Area (ERA) by 2014. According to Article 179 of the Lisbon Treaty, which entered into force in December 2009, the ERA would be an area within which 'researchers, scientific knowledge and technology circulate freely' (Official Journal of the European Union 2010, p. C 83/128). Yet this notion of a common scientific space where the mobility of knowledge is unhindered is as old as the EU itself. How can we account for its emergence, evolution and survival? This chapter sets out to address this question and is structured as follows. First, I discuss briefly the idea of the ERA and the 'fifth freedom'. Next, I develop an analytical framework based on insights from studies that identify ways through which ideas affect political interactions. In this section I will also address a common methodological question faced by those proposed to use an ideational approach to study political life: is an idea epiphenomenal to interest or are its effects autonomous? I argue for adopting a dynamic approach, whereby ideas and interests are conceptualized as factors that interact to provide opportunities for actors seeking to reform sensitive policy sectors. This perspective allows us to examine how political actors confront unfamiliar (legislative) terrains, assess and select amongst solutions to what they perceive as (policy) challenges. A first-cut analysis, based mainly on documentary evidence, is then given; it points to the importance of the institutional dimension in explaining the impact of ideas in complex political interactions. The chapter concludes with a short discussion on what these developments tell us about the role of ideas in European integration.

# FROM THE FREE MOVEMENT OF *WORKERS* TO THE FREE MOVEMENT OF *KNOWLEDGE*

European integration has been animated by conflicts over how to realize the 'four freedoms'. Indeed, questions concerning how to remove barriers against the free movement of the factors of production – goods, capital, services and labour – have been central to both national and supranational debates regarding whether pan-European cooperation should be initiated in policy areas traditionally considered to be in the national *domain reservé* and, if so, to what extent the central institutions would be formally involved in these developments. While the issue of competence remains hotly contested in the fields of defence, security, migration and services, a new 'freedom' has been introduced recently that appears to embody an emerging consensus amongst EU member states, the European institutions and the constellation of public and private stakeholders: the free movement of *knowledge*.

Coined by European Commissioner Potočnik in April 2007, the 'fifth freedom' refers to the 'exchange of knowledge through the mobility of workers, researchers and students' within the ERA (European Commission 2007a, p. 1). It seeks to build on the existing EU *acquis* of the four freedoms by adding the knowledge dimension. For the European Commission, the ERA would be central to 'A Single Market for the 21st Century Europe' (European Commission 2007a). At the same time, what precisely constitutes 'knowledge' and how mobility is to be extended to *all* 'knowledge' workers (EU citizens and foreign nationals) remain an open debate and the focus of policy discussions. The March 2008 Spring European Council fully endorsed the concept and tasked the Council of Ministers and the European Commission to jointly table proposals for implementing the free movement of knowledge (European Council 2008). They responded by launching the Ljubljana Process 'Towards Full Realisation of ERA' in May 2008 (Council 2008b). In December 2008, the Competitiveness Council adopted the '2020 Vision', which stated that 'By 2020, all actors fully benefit from the "fifth freedom" across the ERA: free circulation of researchers, knowledge and technology' (Council 2008a, p. 4).

The entry into force of the Lisbon Treaty extended a treaty base for the construction of the ERA. Article 179 committed the EU and its member states to 'strengthening its scientific and technological bases by achieving a European research area in which researchers, scientific knowledge and technology circulate freely' (Official Journal of the European Union 2010, p. C 83/128). Finally, with the adoption in 2010 of the Europe 2020 Strategy (European Commission 2010b), the successor of the Lisbon Strategy for competitiveness and growth, the completion of the ERA is given a clear deadline: 2014. What is remarkable about the recent tremendous, and continuous, impetus given to the ERA is that the notion of a common scientific space is an old idea that has been proposed since the very early years of European integration.

In 1973, Ralf Dahrendorf, the then European Commissioner for Research, presented a working programme for European cooperation in the areas of science, research and education (André 2006, p. 133). At the time, Commissioner Dahrendorf had already argued that free movement of researchers was crucial for creating a common research space to underpin the European unification project, but the member states were reluctant to cede further competence claimed to be essential to bring this about (ibid., p. 134). The idea of the ERA and its core concept of researcher mobility, according to André (2006, p. 137), 'est donc apparue et disparue à plusieurs reprises (thus appeared and disappeared several times)' as both successive Commissioners for Research and several prominent national political figures tried to fully unlock the potential it seemingly promised. If the ERA is indeed an old concept, how can we account for its survival throughout these decades and for its growing prominence on the European political and policy agenda in recent years? Is it merely an idea whose time has come?

Addressing this question is important for studies of international relations, politics and public policy: analytically, it pushes us to identify the conditions under which 'old' ideas may become prominent; empirically, it provides us with insights into how actors approach collective problem-solving in sensitive policy areas. This chapter addresses this puzzle by investigating the various 'roles' that an idea plays in complex political interactions spanning multiple governance levels. The analysis will reveal the importance of the institutional dimension in these processes. In the next section I begin with a review of ideational studies to identify how ideas affect policy processes and outcomes.

## IDEAS IN COMPLEX POLITICAL INTERACTIONS

Since the 1990s, the claim that 'ideas matter' in deciding political outcomes has continued to engage scholars who seek to go beyond the explanation that politics is the 'pursuit of self-interest' (Campbell 2002, p. 21). According to Berman (2001, p. 231), what these scholars have in common is a rejection that 'non-ideational theories [. . .] account satisfactorily for a wide range of political phenomena'. The crux of their argument, Parsons (2007, p. 96) summarizes, is that the ways through which people interpret their world will affect their actions. Hence, the focus of ideational studies tends to be placed first on identifying the 'ideational' variables and then revealing how, and perhaps to what extent, they exert an effect on the outcomes in question. As the critique by Campbell (2002) reminds us, however, ideational scholars have not usually succeeded in the latter task.

This section will engage with this debate in three ways. First, it will unpack what constitutes an 'idea' and how it is used in this chapter. Second, I will review the ideational literature to identify the multiple ways that 'ideas' have been shown to determine the choices that actors make. Third, I will address the perennial question facing those who seek to delineate the ideational impact on political, policy and polity developments: are ideas epiphenomenal to interests or are their effects autonomous? This query refers explicitly to the methodological challenge of specifying the causal mechanism at work. Although the analyses are largely confined to developments in a specific policy domain, I argue for adopting a dynamic approach that conceptualizes 'ideas' and 'interests' as variables that interact to generate the outcomes under study (see also Béland 2009; Blyth 2002). In this chapter, the outcomes refer to the emergence and evolution of a common scientific area.

To operationalize this approach, I propose a set of conditions under which an idea *is more likely* to lead to its acceptance and subsequent promotion when it has been previously contested and set aside. It should be emphasized that the aim is to steer the debate towards examining how an idea becomes institutionalized rather than to offer a conclusive response to the debate on epiphenomenality; in so doing, it supports the call for adopting a pragmatic methodological approach to studying social phenomena (see Friedrichs and Kratochwil 2009). Indeed, as Campbell (2002, p. 28, emphasis added) puts it, 'the question was not whether materialist or idealistic motivations prevailed, *but how the two were blended*'.

### Defining Ideas: Macro- Versus Micro-Level Ideas

A definition of an 'idea' remains, unsurprisingly, contested. Berman (2001, p. 233) attributes the failure to explicitly differentiate and conceptualize between 'several related variables (ideas, norms, culture, identity)' as one of the main reasons behind the lack of consensus. Indeed, in Parsons's (2007, p. 96) schematic delineation of social scientific explanatory logics, an 'idea' is simply one of the several 'ideational elements' that 'carry meanings about the world'; he also cites practices, symbols, grammars, identities, norms, models and beliefs as other examples in the ideational repertoire.

In analyses of political decision- and policy-making processes, 'ideas' are often used much more concretely than simply as carriers of 'meanings about the world'. For instance, in a study of how the same 'eugenics idea' has resulted in different policies in the US and UK, Hansen and King (2001, p. 238) find that there are four categories of 'ideas': 'ideas as culture'; 'ideas as expert knowledge'; 'ideas as "programmatic beliefs"'; and 'ideas as the solution to collective action and free-rider problems'. Similarly, Campbell (2002, pp. 22–29) notes in his review of the ideational literature five types of 'ideas': cognitive paradigms and world views; frames; world culture; normative frameworks; and programmatic ideas.

Given the strong variance in how 'ideas' have been defined by scholars seeking to emphasize the ideational effect in specific processes, it is hardly surprising that ideational insights have been dismissed by those favouring both the explanatory weight of self-interests in accounting for political outcomes and the parsimonious (formal) modelling that could be carried out to 'measure' these effects. We know, however, that ambiguity is present in decision-making processes and its presence impacts the results of these processes. Ideationalists start from this assumption and go on to show how 'ideas' contribute to both information filtering and role specification and thus the actions and decisions taken. One way to reveal how 'ideas' function as 'filters' for actors is to divide them following the now familiar 'level of analysis' distinction: macro- and micro-level ideas.

*Macro-level ideas* are those 'taken-for-granted paradigms' (Campbell 2002, p. 23) such as 'world views' and 'world cultures'. These ideas 'are embedded in the symbolism of a culture and deeply affect modes of thought and discourse' (Goldstein and Keohane 1993, p. 8). The paradigmatic nature of macro-level ideas has been captured in the definition of 'policy paradigms' when Hall (1993, p. 279) stressed how they are 'embedded in the very terminology through which policy-makers communicate about their work'. Goldstein and Keohane (1993, pp. 8–9) propose 'sovereignty' and 'world religions' as instances of macro-level ideas that proffer explanations to foreign policies: 'neither human rights, nor sovereignty, nor Stalinism would have made any sense in those premodern societies in which people's lives were governed by notions of magic or fate'.

Summarising Esping-Andersen's (1999) ground-breaking study, Campbell (2002, pp. 22–23) notes that different cultural assumptions about the roles of families in the provision of welfare have led to distinct programmes in Italy and Nordic countries after the Second World War: whereas Italian policy-makers assume that families would perform childcare, those from the Scandinavian countries did not share this premise and hence the extensive publicly sponsored childcare facilities in the latter. This example allows us to incorporate into 'macro-level' ideas another category that is often distinct from 'world views', that is 'principled beliefs'. Unlike 'world views', 'principled beliefs' are 'taken-for-granted assumptions about values, attitudes, identities' (Campbell 2002, p. 23); they are normative in that they dictate what is just and unjust, or right and wrong (Goldstein and Keohane 1993, p. 9).

*Micro-level ideas* are, by contrast, those 'beliefs about cause-effect relationship which derive authority from the shared consensus of recognized elites' (Goldstein and Keohane 1993, p. 10). Often termed 'causal beliefs', on a broad level they 'provide guides for individuals on how to achieve their objectives' (ibid., p. 10), and at a specific level they include programmatic beliefs (Berman 2001) – or 'precise causal (cognitive) ideas that facilitate policy-making among elites by specifying how to solve particular policy problems' (Campbell 2002, p. 28). As Walsh (2000, p. 485) argues, 'because they have a programmatic element', 'causal beliefs' are 'policy-relevant ideas' in that they 'differ from more general ideologies and worldviews'.

McNamara (1998, pp. 4–6) demonstrates in her book, *The Currency of Ideas*, how monetarist theory trumped Keynesian policies when European governments searched for a replacement after the Oil-Crisis-induced macroeconomic policy failure. She singles out a 'causal path' that consists of policy 'failure', 'paradigm innovation' and 'emulation' as template for assessing 'why certain ideas become dominant at a given historical point, while others are put aside' (McNamara 1998, p. 5). For her, it follows that situating ideas in their historical context is the starting point to account for why some ideas are more likely to be embraced over others.

Given their association with the 'preparation' stage of the policy process, we may also add 'frames' to micro-level ideas. Stemming from studies of social movements, Campbell (2002, pp. 26–27) explains that 'frames' have been used to refer to the 'normative and sometimes cognitive ideas that are located in the foreground of policy debates' and political leaders use 'frames' strategically to persuade their constituents to endorse their policy programmes; 'reframing' could thus be seen as part of the *change*-process (Cerna and Chou 2013). As it is probably evident, the delineation between ideas at macro- and micro-levels is primarily for analytic purposes since, in practice, they are much more likely to be linked and mutually reinforcing (see Goldstein and Keohane 1993, pp. 10–11).

In this chapter, the aim is not to distinguish where macro-level ideas stop and micro-level ideas begin and vice versa. Instead, I focus mainly on the ideas at the micro-level and, to be more precise, those 'causal beliefs' that prescribe ways of understanding how best to take which course of action in policy processes. This limited focus derives primarily from the research design that confines data collection to non-psychological data that are publicly accessible (European Commission, Council and European Council documents). Before presenting the analytical framework, I first examine the ways that ideas have been empirically shown to impact policy processes.

## How Ideas Affect Policy Outcomes

Ideas affect policy outcomes in multiple ways. This review focuses on foreign policy analysis and public policy studies because these are the fields where the role of ideas in political outcomes has been traditionally taken seriously in research designs. Certainly, this review does not aim to be comprehensive; the objective is to identify a set of analytical tools for developing the framework below. To start, Goldstein and Keohane (1993, pp. 10–26), in the book *Ideas and Foreign Policy*, isolate three causal pathways: (1) ideas act as 'roadmaps' guiding actors towards particular positions within environments that are deemed to be 'uncertain' by detailing a set of 'expectations' or expected outcomes should the road be taken; (2) ideas can function as a 'focal point' or 'glue' in the presence of several equilibriums that leave all actors better off; and (3) ideas specify policies in the absence of innovation when they are embedded into an institution. The third causal path is especially powerful in that such ideas are taken for granted and no longer need to be debated nor challenged. Here, the underlying logic of action is one of 'appropriateness' rather than 'consequence' (March and Olsen 1998).

Following Kingdon (1995), Béland (2009) finds that ideas affect the policy processes in three ways. First, they are used to construct, define and articulate the problems and issues that demand a response in policy terms. In this way, ideas assist in prioritizing tasks that are most urgent vis-à-vis those that may appear to be secondary. Second, ideas provide actors with 'assumptions' concerning the contents of reforms; this is akin to the conceptualization of ideas as 'roadmaps' by Goldstein and Keohane. Third, according to Béland (2009, p. 705), ideas are used as 'discursive weapons' by actors seeking to rally others to the position that change is necessary; 'framing' is often the method through which such ideas are transformed into 'discursive weapons'. Here, the logic of action points to one of anticipated consequences.

In an account of the 'end of the Cold War', Risse-Kappen (1994, p. 186) asserts that the reform idea which had 'coalesced' at the time amongst security experts was influential because it 'satisfied [Gorbachev's] needs for coherent and consistent policy concepts'. Risse-Kappen's analysis sought to build on the then recent work of Haas (1992) on the communities of professionals and experts who were responsible for ideational transfer and dissemination. Haas (1992, p. 3) calls these networks of professionals and experts 'epistemic communities' with 'a shared set of normative and principled beliefs, which provide a value-based rationale for [. . .] a common policy enterprise'.

Other ideational studies have also stressed the crucial role that actors play in the process of policy change. For instance, Hansen and King (2001, p. 239) assert that one of three conditions for ideas to be 'translated into policy' is 'when the actors possess the requisite enthusiasm and institutional position' champion the very idea. Similarly, Béland (2009, p. 709) points to those so-called 'value amplifiers' who 'rework the meaning of a well-known value or principle in order to legitimize policy change'. This is an important insight: ideas need 'carriers', but, just as much, these 'carriers' rely on 'ideas' to convey and persuade others.

To summarize, ideas are important in political processes in more than one way: they contribute to defining the (policy) challenge; they persuade others to both the appropriateness and the utility of a particular position; they fill the ideational 'vacuum' in an institution. At the same time, they rely on actors to, first, usher them into political prominence/salience and, second, garner support for their translation into concrete policy instruments (see Lindvall 2009). Indeed, as Risse-Kappen (1994) concludes, 'Ideas do not float freely'. This insight points to the importance of actors in this process, especially to their capacity which can be determined through institutional affiliation. In the next subsection, I develop an actor-based ideational analytical framework that highlights the symbiotic relationship between ideas, actors and interests.

### An Actor-Based Ideational Analytical Framework

In the discussion in this chapter, an 'idea' refers to a set of 'causal beliefs' for proposed policy actions. What determines the 'power' of an idea is not how detailed it is in terms of its prescription. On the contrary, an actor-based ideational analytical framework postulates that an idea is more powerful when it functions as a 'focal point' on which many actors can 'hook' their materialistic and ideological interests when multiple pathways of cooperation are feasible (Garrett and Weingast 1993, p. 176). This leads to the first condition: when an idea is sufficiently vague to attract and accommodate multiple interests (especially at the supranational and national levels), the more likely that the idea will affect, and often to a greater extent, the policy outcomes. I refer to this as the *ideational scope* condition.

While this may appear to suggest that ideas play an ancillary role to the interests of actors, it in effect reveals their independent impact. As Hansen and King (2001, p. 239, emphasis added) argue, 'Through the mechanism of "cover" provision, reputation enhancement and coalition, *the impact of ideas is maximized when they serve individual interests*'; in this instance, the logic of action is one of consequentiality. To begin identifying empirically whether, and if so to what extent, this is taking place, I focus on determining if an 'ideational widening' is happening in the construction of the ERA. By 'ideational widening', I mean the 'stretching' of the ERA concept to embody multiple initiatives, conveyed through a specific discourse stressing the 'need' of a common scientific space, and realized through many or even hybrid instruments. Here, the ERA as an 'idea' has 'dual-usage': as a means to an end and as an end in itself.

To further highlight the role of actors in the change process, I turn to the methodological insights concerning 'causal mechanisms' advanced by Falleti and Lynch (2009). Challenging mainstream political scientific usage of 'causal mechanisms', Falleti and Lynch (2009, pp. 1146–1151) argue that they are 'portable' and 'abstract' concepts rather than a 'chain of intervening variables' (cf. King et al. 1994). In advancing this conceptualization of 'causal mechanisms', they emphasize the significance of clearly delineating 'contexts'. This is so because, Falleti and Lynch (2009, p. 1151) maintain, 'interaction between mechanism and context is what determines the outcome'.

Falleti and Lynch (2009, p. 1152) define context quite broadly to include 'relevant aspects of a setting (analytical, temporal, spatial, or institutional) in which a set of initial conditions leads [. . .] to an outcome of a defined scope and meaning via a specified causal mechanism or set of causal mechanisms' and propose examining developments over time (citing sequencing, timing and periodization). This acknowledgement towards process-tracing as a preferred approach is a recognition of the growing relevance of 'time' in accounts of political outcomes (see Bulmer 2009; Goetz and Meyer-Sahling 2009; Mahoney and Rueschemeyer 2003). What these research agendas have in common is an interest in identifying how institutional constraints and opportunities affected the social phenomena under examination. The empirical analysis presented in this chapter seeks to contribute to this research agenda by identifying how the actors involved in the creation of a common scientific space are institutionally anchored.

Taking their lead, I will 'contextualize' the study of the construction of the ERA by segmenting the series of developments in their particular historical and institutional settings. Specifically, I identify how European or EU institutional arrangements have either remained change-resistant or altered throughout the last six decades leading to the emergence and wide endorsement of the ERA and the fifth freedom as the way forward for European integration and cooperation in the research and innovation domains. By institutional arrangements, I refer to the rules and procedures that govern interactions between the European institutions, the member states and the representatives from the knowledge policy sectors. What is important here to account for the endurance and resilience of the ERA concept is how the institutional dynamics (that are actors, existing policies and set-ups) changed over time to support, rather than detract from, the idea. I refer to this as the condition of *institutional scope*. Put simply, the stronger the institutional dynamics supporting the ERA concept, the more likely that it will become embedded and thus increase its prominence on the political agenda. I apply this actor-based ideational analytical framework in the next section to tease out some of dynamics driving the formation of the ERA.

## THE EVOLUTION OF EUROPEAN RESEARCH COOPERATION (1950s–2014)

This section provides a first-cut analysis of how the notion of a common research space emerged, survived and thrived. These developments fall into three phases: (1) an ad hoc intergovernmental collaboration phase (1950s–early 1980s) during which the idea was initially voiced and recognized, but not yet given its own institutional framework within the supranational platform; (2) a phase of Framework Programme (FP) cooperation (mid-1980s–2000s) during which the ERA concept acquired an institutional basis, albeit structured through the distributive policy lens of the supranational funding mechanism; and (3) the phase of Lisbon and Europe 2020 cooperation (2000 onwards) during which the notion of a common scientific space consolidates its own institutional foundation. The appearance of the 'fifth freedom' as the discursive 'shorthand' for the ERA during this third phase is indicative of the European Commission's attempt to reconcile the two distinct organizational models for European research cooperation: the ERA and the FP.

The overall pattern identified is one of gradual 'ideational widening': the ERA has gradually become a 'useful' blueprint for many institutional actors over time. To bring this out, I will identify its institutional champions, the discourse used to articulate and promote the ERA concept, what happened to the idea at that point in time and why.

### Ad Hoc Intergovernmental Cooperation (1950s–1980s): ERA In Vitro

The founding fathers of the European Economic Communities (EEC), as the EU was known at the time, had envisioned that 'science' would play a key role in the unification of Europe. Consequently, they agreed quite early on that they would coordinate their respective research policies. For instance, in the 1951 Treaty of Paris that established the European Coal and Steel Community (ECSC), we find an explicit provision for 'Community-funded energy research'. Similarly, in Articles 4-11 of the European Atomic Energy Community Treaty (EURATOM), we identify provisions that would allow for closer cooperation in nuclear research. According to Elizalde (1992, p. 309, original emphasis), the EURATOM Treaty also 'included the useful concept of *multi-annual* research and training programmes' that would become the most stable feature of European cooperation. Article 41 of the Rome Treaty also signalled the interest of the signatories in pursuing joint research, but only in the agricultural field.

While the various provisions did indeed suggest strong interest, coordinated European efforts in the fields of science and research did not commence until decades later, as I shall discuss further below. The reason for this, to put it simply, is because the key decision-makers (EU member states) disagreed over the acceptable level of national control versus supranational governance. A case in point: while Jean Monnet (champion of a strong supranational body) saw EURATOM 'as the engine of a federal Europe' (Banchoff 2002, p. 7), France and Germany focused on developing and consolidating their national nuclear programmes.

The publication of *Le Défi Américain [The American Challenge]* in 1968 (Servan-Schreiber 1968) provided the discourse in favour of a common European research space. The 'American Challenge' refers to an alleged growing 'technology gap' between the US and Western European countries and it singles out three indicators. First, US public expenditure on research and development (R&D) outstripped that of the Europeans. Second, the 'best and the brightest' from Europe went to work in the US. Third, unlike European companies, private 'American firms dominated new science-based industries' (Banchoff 2002, p. 7). The message was clear: European leaders must take (immediate) actions to narrow this gap. This concern with the 'technology gap' resonated with some actors in institutional positions to introduce change.

The first call for a common European R&D policy came in 1970 from the European Commissioner for Industrial Affairs, General Research and Technology. The new European Commissioner – an Italian federalist – sought a common European R&D policy that would contribute to having 'robust' industrial policies. To this end, Commissioner Spinelli urged the Council to endorse the creation of a Community-based funding agency quite similar to the US National Science Foundation (NSF) (André 2006, p. 134). While supportive of the proposal, the Council, consisting of ministers of research, established the European Science Foundation (ESF) as an *intergovernmental* body, which continues to function on these terms to this day. Although a common European research policy does not necessarily denote the formation of a single scientific space, the push from Commissioner Spinelli to deepen supranational cooperation did trigger a move towards such an area.

Convening in Paris in 1972, the member states decided to intensify the existing joint research efforts and asked the central institutions to propose ways of doing so. The Commissioner for Research, Science and Education (a new department created in 1973) responded by tabling an 'action programme' that called for the creation of an 'European Scientific Area' (André 2006, p. 135). To implement the action lines, Commissioner Dahrendorf – a German-British academic – proposed that the Community would act as *coordinator* of national policies rather than press for wholesale *harmonization*. In proposing this approach, Commissioner Dahrendorf sought a middle way to advance cooperation at the Community level while allowing member states to retain decision-making powers over their domestic policies. This is an important observation because it shows that the earlier proposal, as envisaged by the more 'Federalist' Commissioner Spinelli, suggested a narrower or precise 'blueprint' for the common scientific space.

The Council supported this non-invasive approach and adopted four resolutions (non-binding) in January 1974 that would lead to the following: (1) creation of an advisory body – Scientific and Technical Research Committee (CREST, now the European Research Area Committee or ERAC); (2) coordination with ESF; (3) a research programme on 'forecasting, assessment and methodology'; and (4) one for 'an initial outline programme' in science and technology. De Elera (2006, p. 561) concludes, 'For almost a decade, the cooperation in the field of research was to be based on these four resolutions'.

To summarize, what we observe during this first phase of European research cooperation are: (1) the existence of legal bases for cooperation in specific scientific areas – a key 'ingredient' for any supranational undertaking; (2) an emergent discourse in favour of intensifying cooperation at the Community level that is based on the 'technology gap' between the European countries and their key competitors; and (3) the presence of actors, albeit with different visions and approaches, in institutional positions to propose change championing the idea of a common research area.

**Framework Programme Cooperation (1980s–2000s): ERA in Gestation**

The relaunch of European integration in the 1980s saw the reorganization of research policy cooperation into the FPs. This development was spurred on by a Commissioner, who, according to Banchoff (2002, p. 8), 'At a normative level [. . .] broke with his predecessors'. Banchoff argues that Davignon, as Commissioner for Industry, 'conceived of EU research policy not as a regulation of a European space for science and technology but as the distribution of research funds to flank the broader single European market project' – to this end he succeeded (ibid.).

In 1983, Commissioner Davignon secured support from the European Commission leadership and the Council to bundle up existing research programmes in the areas of energy, health and environment with new ones to form multi-annual research programmes (Gornitzka 2009, pp. 58–63). Understanding the 'context' will allow us to discern the factors contributing to the success of the Davignon initiative. At the time and in several of the key member states, according to Borrás (2003), national science policies were being reorganized to include more public participation. This reorientation was manifested in the form of large research programmes that the FPs emulated. Guzzetti (1995), in one of the few works on the history of European research policy cooperation, noted that the 'technology gap' discourse was used at the time, albeit less prominently in official documents, to deepen Community level cooperation.

The FP has functioned primarily as a funding mechanism and, according to Banchoff (2002), its very institutionalization has contributed to hindering reform efforts towards establishing a common research area (see Chou 2012 for an alternative interpretation). Using the actor-based ideational analytical framework, I could offer another account of the role of the FPs in the ERA construction. It can be argued that successive FPs have actually paved the way for the ERA to become accepted at the start of the 2000s by: (1) acting as the compromise between supranational governance and national control over research policies – a key tension that has prevented earlier and on-going efforts to construct the ERA; (2) enabling the codification of supranational competence in the research field; (3) diversifying research areas in which European level cooperation is deemed desirable; and (4) increasing the relevance of EU funding to the extent that it has become a dominant source of financial support for some national research institutes and higher education institutions.

The institutionalization effects of the FPs are especially important in gaining the acceptance of the ERA concept that was less feasible in the early 1970s because they created an audience (researchers, administrators, stakeholder groups, directorates and so on) to whom the European dimension is significant. This has come about largely due to a growth in budget size, scope of research activities funded and the development of an organizational capacity to administer the programmes. The last aspect is especially crucial because it established direct links with national administrators (Gornitzka 2009; Peterson 1991); as Elken and Vukasovic in Chapter 6 of this volume highlight, the network effect of European cooperation is significant. It is also important to acknowledge that the institutionalization of the FPs undoubtedly shaped the idea of the ERA by ensuring that funding is an indivisible and, indeed, central, component of European research policy cooperation. I will now briefly discuss the FPs to

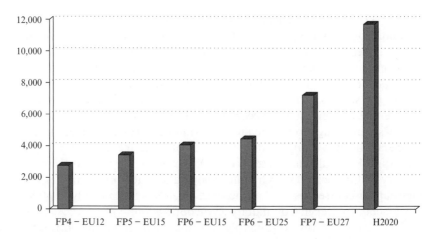

*Source:*   Chou and Gornitzka (2011, p. 18); European Parliament (2013).

*Figure 2.1     Average annual spending – FP4 to Horizon 2020 (in million
                euros)*

show how European cooperation has been a rather dynamic process and
not as static as the literature often suggests (cf. Banchoff 2002; De Elera
2006).

   Concerning FP budget sizes, we see increases from €11 million (in FP4),
to €13.7 million (FP5), to €17.8 million (FP6) and to €50.5 billion (FP7)
(European Court of Auditors 2008, p. 29); Horizon 2020, which is operational from 2014 until 2020, has a budget of €70.2 billion. In 2009 and
2010, the budget lines ('commitment appropriations') for research policy
were, respectively, €4.6 and €5.1 billion, or 3.4 per cent and 3.6 per cent
of the total annual budget (European Commission 2010a, p. 16). While it
may appear that European cooperation in the research policy field utilizes
only a comparatively small proportion of the total EU budget, it has been
historically the fifth or fourth largest budget item; it is fourth in 2010, after
agricultural, regional and employment policies (ibid.). In Figure 2.1, we
see that the average annual spending for the FPs has gradually increased
between FP4 and FP6, with the average annual spending having more than
doubled in FP7 in comparison to that of FP4. Horizon 2020 will be one of
the largest budgets – in terms of the total amount allocated – in EU history.

   After the ERA was launched in 2000, the subsequent FPs and the consolidation of the ERA became intertwined. For example, FP6 (2003–2006)
was organized explicitly to make the ERA a reality rather than an invit-
ing concept. To this end, two instruments were introduced: 'Network

of Excellence' (to develop and maintain connections between different research groups across Europe, the target audience included universities and research institutes); and 'Integrated Projects' (to generate knowledge through a 'programme approach' on 'priority themes' and universities, research organizations and industry were the target audience) (European Commission 2004, p. 1).

FP7 (2007–2013), organized as four overarching thematic programmes (Cooperation, People, Ideas and Capacities), has been path-breaking in several ways. First, its programmatic duration of seven years differs from the traditional four years of earlier FPs. Second, the formation of the European Research Council (ERC) as a FP7 thematic programme (under 'Ideas') signals a departure from the classic FP funding principles (for example, 'transnationality'). Established as an executive agency answerable to the European Commission, the ERC distributes funding to projects of basic, versus applied, research that fulfil one single criterion: excellence.[1] The Horizon 2020 continues to promote the ERA through an explicit introduction of 'ERA Chairs' to 'bridge research and innovation divide in Europe' with the pilot call launched in December 2012 and a clear reference to its urgent completion by 2014.

This short overview of the FPs aims to show the growing significance of research cooperation at the European level. This is not to say that there had been no attempts to consolidate the ERA during this period. On the contrary, André (2006) singles out Ruberti – the Italian Commissioner for Research at the time (1993–1994) – as one of the three main architects of the ERA. Indeed, as can be seen in the speeches given in Europe and abroad and the joint articles published on European research policy cooperation (see Kaiser and Prange 2004), Commissioner Ruberti was a vocal champion of the ERA concept. His short tenure and the energy devoted to other issues (that is the creation of 'Socrates' in the higher education field) did not bring the idea of the ERA to fruition. Yet, as we shall see next, the institutionalization of the FPs served as the crucial function of paving the way for formally launching the ERA concept in 2000 by having in place an organizational structure for its realization and a national audience with vested interest in its completion.

**The Lisbon and Europe 2020 Strategies (2000–2014): ERA In Vivo**

Research Commissioner Busquin formally launched the ERA in January 2000 to shore up what he argued to be a declining state of 'research in Europe' (European Commission 2000, p. 4). Citing figures comparing Europe with the US and Japan, he concluded that *inter alia* EU-wide research efforts, levels of public and private expenditure on research and the proportion of employed researchers were 'worrying'. It is important to highlight this 'gap discourse' as the preferred discursive catalyst to the flagging cooperation in this field. While the 'cast' against which the EU is now compared has changed to include countries such as China, India and Brazil, the message then and now is still clear: immediate actions are needed to close this gap.

The remedy, the European Commission proposed, was to abandon the '15+1' approach (reflecting the then number of EU member states plus the European Commission) – the source of fragmentation – that had characterized European cooperation in this sector, and establish an internal market for research (European Commission 2000). While both diagnosis and solution were not new, the March 2000 Lisbon European Council situated the concept of the ERA at the heart of its ambitious undertaking to transform the EU into the 'most competitive and dynamic knowledge-based economy in the world' (European Council 2000). In so doing, it gave the idea of a common scientific space the strongest political support, specific targets to be achieved, an approach for reaching these objectives and a deadline (by 2010) that it never had before in the evolution of European integration.

According to André (2006), what differentiated the current call for the ERA from previous ones was that Commissioner Busquin had secured support for the ERA from several key actors in the acting EU Presidency (for example, the Portuguese Prime Minister, Antonió Gutierres, and the Research Minister, José Mariano Gago) and amongst the scientific advisers and stakeholder groups. Moreover, André (2006, p. 142) notes that amongst the member states that were 'net contributors' to the Union budget, there was also concern that the FP had grown to its maximum capacity and they considered 'coordination' in areas suggested by the 2000 ERA communication as an acceptable way forward for European research cooperation. This reception, together with the ideational widening of the ERA to be discussed below, ushered the concept of a common scientific space to the top of the European agenda.

Meeting in Barcelona in March 2002, the European Council agreed that the 'overall spending on R&D and innovation in the Union should be increased with the aim of approaching 3 per cent of GDP by 2010. Two-thirds of this new investment should come from the private sector'; this became known as the '3 per cent' or the 'Barcelona' target (European Council 2002, p. 20). At Lisbon, the EU member states had endorsed the 'Open Method of Coordination' (OMC) as a modus operandi for this exercise. The OMC is considered a 'soft' approach because it is a voluntary process in which participants agreed to coordinate policy according to specific steps.

Initially, seven broad areas for action were identified for constructing the ERA; and they ranged from developing an area of 'shared values' to ensuring that there are more abundant 'human resources' (European Commission 2000, Annex I) and, in 2001, the 'international dimension of ERA' theme was added (European Commission 2002, p. 15). To establish the ERA, the European Commission called for the 'full panoply' of instruments to be activated: practical instruments (database and information systems); networks (exchange of information); financial instruments (FP); legal instruments (directives and regulations); and 'policy coordination' instruments (ibid., p. 22). The outcome of the ERA in the first half of the 2000s, given their close linkage, mirrored the result of the Lisbon Strategy in practice.

Successive reviews of the Lisbon Strategy found the Union and its member states consistently failing to reach the Barcelona target through the OMC. Indeed, shortly after FP6 was adopted, the European Commission circulated 'The European Research Area: Providing New Momentum' (2002). This Communication emphasized that the ERA 'cannot be seen solely in terms of [FP activities] and must by definition create a momentum of its own within a wider framework which draws on separate initiatives' (European Commission 2002, p. 7). After its mid-term review in 2005, the Lisbon Strategy was relaunched (Council 2009).

As part of the Lisbon relaunch, the European Commission (2007b) tabled the Green Paper on 'The European Research Area: New Perspectives' in April 2007 to initiate a public consultation on potential ways forward. Acknowledging the consultation results, the Competitiveness Council, sitting in the research configuration, formally launched in May 2008 the '"Ljubljana Process" – Towards Full Realisation of ERA' and endorsed the 'package' instrument known as the 'ERA Partnership' (Council 2008b). The ERA Partnership singled out five subjects on which there are shared interests: researchers; joint programming; research infrastructure; knowledge sharing; and international cooperation (DG Research 2009). A monitoring process, with close collaboration between the member states and the European Commission, was also initiated; but has since been integrated into the Innovation Union monitoring process.

According to the Competitiveness Council, the proposed method for creating the ERA would be 'enhanced governance based on a long-term vision on ERA developed in partnership by Member States and the Commission' (Council 2008b, para. 5). In practice, this means shared competence between the central institutions and member states, with CREST – now ERAC – acting as the governance hub. Figure 2.2 shows that five groups (that are named 'high level', 'working', 'steering' and 'forum') were created to address these topics and they report directly to

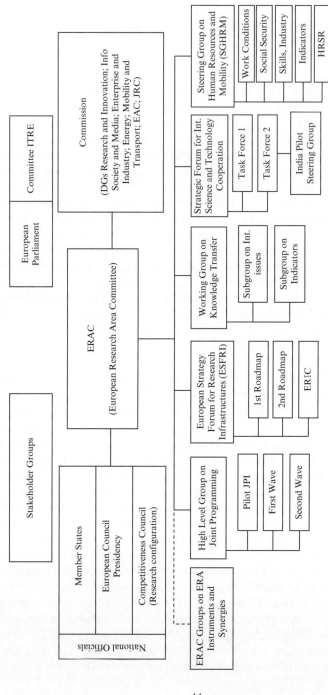

*Source:* Chou and Gornitzka (2011, p. 24).

*Figure 2.2 ERA governance*

44

the ERAC. To support their work, several sub-working groups have been organized around specific aspects (for example, working conditions), country (India), or projects ('Roadmap' and joint programming initiative). In addition, several groups are formed on an 'as-needed' basis and set time frames are assigned for their tasks. For example, the ERAC Group on ERA Instruments (and Synergies) has been created to prepare ERAC contributions to 'FP8' (as the Horizon 2020 is more commonly known).

The most important aspect concerning the ERA is that its evolution since 2000 has very much been a 'moveable feast': the ERA has come to mean different things in different contexts. For instance, in the 2002 European Commission Communication, it has been used variably to refer to a set of vaguely defined *objectives* such as 'creation of an internal market for research', 'restructuring of the European research fabric' and 'development of a European research policy [. . . taking] account of all relevant aspects of other EU and national policies' (European Commission 2002, p. 4). This earlier presentation of the ERA can be seen as, Luukkonen (2010, p. 10) argues, 'policy for science'. Yet in the more recent rendition of the ERA, as shown in the '2020 Vision' (Council 2008a), it has been depicted more as a *means* to tackle societal challenges such as climate change and poverty (that are 'Grand Challenges'); or, as Luukkonen (2010, p. 10) points out, 'science for policy'. This conceptual evolution and, indeed, interusability of the ERA is also reflected in the change of how the 'European Value-Added' is seen in the research field: from funding transnational consortia to generating competition at the European level and better integration of European research (ibid., pp. 25–26).

At the time of writing, the conclusion I could draw concerning the ERA formation is that the idea of a common scientific area has taken shape as the result of actors willing to champion the concept, a corresponding discourse urging its creation and its increased relevance over time due to the institutionalization of the FPs. More recent developments in ERA governance indicate fluidity of the concept to mean an objective (that is an 'area of knowledge') and also the 'means' to address the challenges facing European societies (for example, environment, health). The ERA landscape will most likely not assume any definitive form until after the Horizon 2020 has been implemented and the new European Commission is in place.

Speaking with Commission officials[2] in 2009 concerning the ERA concept suggests that the notion might be experiencing an 'ideational widening'. For example, when asked what the 'fifth freedom' entailed, a European Commission official responsible for promoting 'free movement of knowledge' stated that the 'ERA *is* the fifth freedom' (INTV07, 16 September 2009, original emphasis). Another European Commission official, who had been active in European research cooperation for several decades, said that the 'fifth freedom' was a 'clever manoeuvre' by Commissioner Potočnik since it encapsulated what the European Commission wanted but did not possess the tools and competence to deliver (INTV05, 28 May 2009). These comments all suggests efforts to link the ERA idea to the most successful European project to date: the Single Market. This is hardly surprising, as Borrás and Radaelli (2011, p. 474) argued in their attempt to conceptualize the Lisbon Strategy, 'Institutional ambiguity is refracted by, among other things, the fact that ideational repertoires are not stable over time and may have different meaning for different actors'. In the final section, I conclude with a discussion of what these developments tell us about the role of ideas in European integration.

## IDEAS AND EUROPEAN INTEGRATION

Speaking at the Hungarian Academy of Sciences in December 2010, Herman Van Rompuy (2010, p. 1) proclaimed that 'Europe is built on the power of ideas'. With the EU receiving the Nobel Peace Prize in 2012, this claim appears to rest on solid grounds. This chapter set out to investigate how one of these 'old' ideas – the common scientific space – emerged, survived and evolved over the last sixty years. Using an analytical framework based on insights from ideational studies, two propositions were advanced concerning the conditions under which ideas are more likely to affect policy outcomes: (1) when 'ideas' are sufficiently vague, and increasingly so, to attract and accommodate multiple interests (*ideational scope*); (2) when changes to the institutional dynamics over time support, rather than detract from, the idea (*institutional scope*).

The analysis in this chapter lends support to these propositions. It was shown that the various Commissioners for research and industry have been the champions for the common scientific space and the 'technology gap' discourse has been used since the 1970s to argue for the ERA. Over time, actors with different institutional affiliations – the Presidency and the Council – have also endorsed the ERA concept and, this in turn, contributed to its survival. The institutionalization of the FPs was significant against this context because it set the stage for the ERA concept. It did so by establishing the organizational capacity of the European Commission to coordinate with national stakeholders and, through this, a channel of communication, funding and, gradually, mutual dependence. Since the launch of the ERA concept, we could observe an 'ideational widening' to the extent that the very ambiguity of what is constitutes has become a source for its survival.

Studying the evolution of the ERA concept tells us that ideas play multiple roles in European integration: as a tool to advance this process and expand supranational competence in 'sovereign' policy domains and as an end in itself (for example, for peace in Europe). This points to the fragmentary and unfinished nature of the European polity as a key strength of its survival. If offers those searching for answers to transnational effects and national challenges a clear arena for exchange. The networks that have formed as a result of FP participation or the OMC are very likely to be channels through which these interactions are facilitated and intensified; its nexus with official interactions between elected and appointed representatives will ensure this. Given this growing complexity, an ideational perspective provides an alternative entry point to investigate the evolution of European integration and how change-resistant sectors could, one day, become transformed.

## NOTES

1. The ERC is not the only instance of organizational capacity-building: the Research Executive Agency was created in 2008 and became operational in 2009 to administer the daily operations of the 'People' thematic programme (Marie Curie Actions, MCA). This development was followed by notable European Commission organizational restructuring that included, *inter alia*, the transfer of the MCA portfolio from DG Research to DG Education in 2010. Similarly, the EU member states agreed to establish the European Institute of Innovation and Technology in 2007.
2. The interviews were carried out under the conditions of anonymity (Chatham House Rule) to ensure that speakers will freely offer their reflections, which was the point of the interview exercise. I have given the dates when the interviews have taken place.

## REFERENCES

André, M. (2006), 'L'espace européen de la recherche: histoire d'une idée', *Journal of European Integration History*, **12**(2), 131–149.
Banchoff, T. (2002), 'Institutions, inertia and European Union research policy', *Journal of Common Market Studies*, **40**(1), 1–21.
Béland, D. (2009), 'Ideas, institutions, and policy change', *Journal of European Public Policy*, **16**(5), 701–718.
Berman, S. (2001), 'Review: ideas, norms, and culture in political analysis', *Comparative Politics*, **33**(2), 231–250.
Blyth, M. (2002), *Great Transformations: Economic Ideas and Institutional Change in the Twentieth Century*, Cambridge: Cambridge University Press.
Borrás, S. (2003), *The Innovation Policy of the European Union*, Cheltenham, UK and Northampton, MA, USA: Edward Elgar.
Borrás, S. and C.M. Radaelli (2011), 'The politics of governance architectures:

creation, change and effects of the EU Lisbon Strategy', *Journal of European Public Policy*, **18**(4), 463–484.

Bulmer, S. (2009), '*Politics in Time* meets the politics of time: historical institutionalism and the EU timescape', *Journal of European Public Policy*, **16**(2), 307–324.

Campbell, J.L. (2002), 'Ideas, politics, and public policy', *Annual Review of Sociology*, **28**, 21–38.

Cerna, L. and M.-H. Chou (2013), 'The regional dimension in the global competition for talent: lessons from framing the European Scientific Visa and Blue Card', *Journal of European Public Policy*, DOI: 10.1080/13501763.2013.831114, 1–20.

Chou, M.-H. (2012), 'Constructing an internal market for research through sectoral and lateral strategies: layering, the European Commission and the fifth freedom', *Journal of European Public Policy*, **19**(7), 1052–1070.

Chou, M.-H. and Å. Gornitzka (2011), 'Den femte frihet og Kunnskapens Europa: Konsekvenser for Norge' (The Fifth Freedom and the Europe of Knowledge: Consequences for Norway), Oslo: Forskniningsoppdrag for Utvalget for utredning av Norges avtaler med EU.

Council (2008a), 'Council Conclusions on the Definition of a "2020 Vision for the European Research Area", 16767/08, 9 December 2008', Council, Brussels.

Council (2008b), 'Council Conclusions on the Launch of the "Ljubljana Process" – Towards Full Realisation of ERA – Adoption, 9076/08', Council, Brussels.

Council (2009), 'Council Resolution of 3 December 2009 on the Enhanced Governance of the European Research Area (ERA), 2009/C 323/01', Council, Brussels.

De Elera, Á. (2006), 'The European research area: on the way towards a European scientific community?', *European Law Journal*, **12**(5), 559–574.

DG Research (2009), 'The European Research Area Partnership: 2008 Initiatives', Office for Official Publications of the European Communities, Luxembourg.

Elizalde, J. (1992), 'Legal aspects of community policy on research and technology development (RTD)', *Common Market Law Review*, **29**, 309–346.

Esping-Andersen, G. (1999), *Social Foundations of Postindustrial Economies*, New York: Oxford University Press.

European Commission (2000), 'Communication from the Commission to the Council, the European Parliament, the Economic and Social Committee and the Committee of Regions – Towards a European Research Area, 6 Final', Commission, Brussels.

European Commission (2002), 'Communication from the Commission, the European Research Area: Providing New Momentum, Strengthening – Reorienting – Opening up New Perspectives, 565 Final', Commission, Brussels.

European Commission (2004), 'Classification of the FP6 Instruments: Detailed Description', Commission, Brussels.

European Commission (2007a), 'A Single Market for 21st Century Europe, 724 Final', Commission, Brussels.

European Commission (2007b), 'The European Research Area: New Perspectives, Green Paper, 161 Final', Commission, Brussels.

European Commission (2010a), 'General Budget of the European Union for the Financial Year 2010: the Figures (January 2010)', Commission, Brussels.

European Commission (2010b), 'A Strategy for Smart, Sustainable and Inclusive Growth, 2020 Final', European Commission, Brussels.

European Council (2000), 'Lisbon European Council 23 and 24 March 2000 Presidency Conclusions', European Council, Brussels.

European Council (2002), 'Barcelona European Council 15 and 16 March 2002 Presidency Conclusions', European Council, Brussels.

European Council (2008), 'Brussels European Council, 13/14 March 2008, Presidency Conclusions, 7652/1/08 Rev 1', European Council, Brussels.

European Court of Auditors (2008), 'Concerning "Evaluating the EU Research and Technological Development (RTD) Framework Programmes – Could the Commission's Approach be Improved?" Together with the Commission's Replies (Special Report No. 9/2007; OJ C 26/1)', European Court of Auditors, Luxembourg.

European Parliament (2013), 'Horizon 2020 Q&A (19-11-2013, 12:01)', available at: http://www.europarl.europa.eu/pdfs/news/expert/background/20131119BKG 25724/20131119BKG25724_en.pdf (accessed 22 November 2013).

Falleti, T.G. and J.F. Lynch (2009), 'Context and causal mechanisms in political analysis', *Comparative Political Studies*, **42**(9), 1143–1166.

Friedrichs, J. and F. Kratochwil (2009), 'On acting and knowing: how pragmatism can advance international relations research and methodology', *International Organization*, **63**(Fall 2009), 701–731.

Garrett, G. and B.R. Weingast (1993), 'Ideas, interests, and institutions: constructing the European Community's internal market', in J. Goldstein and R. Keohane (eds), *Ideas and Foreign Policy: Beliefs, Institutions and Political Change*, Ithaca: Cornell University Press, pp. 173–206.

Goetz, K. and J.H. Meyer-Sahling (2009), 'Political time in the EU: dimensions, perspectives, theories', *Journal of European Public Policy*, **16**(2), 180–201.

Goldstein, J. and R. Keohane (1993), 'Ideas and foreign policy: an analytical framework', in J. Goldstein and R. Keohane (eds), *Ideas and Foreign Policy: Beliefs, Institutions, and Political Change*, Ithaca: Cornell University Press, pp. 3–30.

Gornitzka, Å. (2009), 'Research policy and the European Union – multi-layered policy change?', in P. Clancy and D.D. Dill (eds), *The Research Mission of the University Policy Reforms and Institutional Response*, Rotterdam: Sense Publishers, pp. 53–75.

Guzzetti, L. (1995), *A Brief History of European Union Research Policy*, Luxembourg: Office for the Official Publications of the European Communities.

Haas, P.M. (1992), 'Introduction: epistemic communities and international policy coordination', *International Organization*, **46**(1), 1–35.

Hall, P.A. (1993), 'Policy paradigms, social learning, and the state: the case of economic policymaking in Britain', *Comparative Politics*, **25**(3), 275–296.

Hansen, R. and D. King (2001), 'Eugenic ideas, political interests, and policy variance: immigration and sterilization policy in Britain and the U.S.', *World Politics*, **53**(January), 237–263.

Kaiser, R. and H. Prange (2004), 'Managing diversity in a system of multi-level governance: the open method of co-ordination in innovation policy', *Journal of European Public Policy*, **11**(2), 249–266.

King, G., R.O. Keohane and S. Verba (1994), *Designing Social Inquiry: Scientific Inference in Qualitative Research*, Princeton: Princeton University Press.

Kingdon, J.W. (1995), *Agendas, Alternatives and Public Policies*, New York: HarperCollins.

Lindvall, J. (2009), 'The real but limited influence of expert ideas', *World Politics*, **61**(4), 703–730.

Luukkonen, T. (2010), 'The European Research Council in the European Research Area', The Research Institute of the Finnish Economy Helsinki.

Mahoney, J. and D. Rueschemeyer (eds) (2003), *Comparative Historical Analysis in the Social Sciences*, New York: Cambridge University Press.

March, J.G. and J.P. Olsen (1998), 'The institutional dynamics of international political orders', *International Organization*, **52**(4), 943–969.

McNamara, K. (1998), *The Currency of Ideas: Monetary Politics in the European Union*, Ithaca: Cornell University Press.

Official Journal of the European Union (2010), 'Consolidated Version of the Treaty on the Functioning of the European Union', available at: http://eur-lex.europa.eu/LexUriServ/LexUriServ.do?uri=OJ:C:2010:083:0047:0200:en:PDF (accessed 22 November 2013).

Parsons, C. (2007), *How to Map Arguments in Political Science*, Oxford: Oxford University Press.

Peterson, J. (1991), 'Technology policy in Europe: explaining the framework programme and eureka in theory and practice', *Journal of Common Market Studies*, **XXIX**(3), 269–290.

Risse-Kappen, T. (1994), 'Ideas do not float freely: transnational coalitions, domestic structures, and the end of the cold war', *International Organization*, **48**(2), 185–214.

Servan-Schreiber, J.J. (1968), *The American Challenge*, New York: Atheneum.

Van Rompuy, H. (2010), 'The Power of Ideas, Presidency of the European Council Herman Van Rompuy at the Hungarian Academy of Sciences, Budapest, 21 December 2010, PCE 318/10, SN 1080/11', European Council, the President, Brussels.

Walsh, J.I. (2000), 'When do ideas matter? Explaining the success and failures of thatcherite ideas', *Comparative Political Studies*, **33**(4), 483–516.

# 3. Translating the 'European Charter for Researchers and the Code of Conduct for the Recruitment of Researchers' in national arenas: Norway vs Spain

## Meng-Hsuan Chou and José Real-Dato

### INTRODUCTION

Researcher mobility is a central pillar of the European Research Area (ERA) and this chapter examines the main instrument formally adopted for its promotion: the 'European Charter for Researchers and the Code of Conduct for the Recruitment of Researchers' (European Commission 2005). The Charter and the Code (CC), as the name implies, is a set of 40 principles outlining the rights, duties and obligations of researchers, their employers and funders. In essence, the CC lays the foundation on which a more detailed human resource (HR) policy for researchers could be elaborated. The general idea is that, with the CC acting as a baseline for a HR policy, Europe would become a more attractive destination for research.

The CC is a non-binding instrument. The Commission of the European Union (EU) adopted it in 2005 and, while some 170 institutions representing 19 countries endorsed it by 2006, its implementation was considered 'slow' (European Commission 2007, p. 4). According to an external evaluation carried out for the European Commission, a fundamental problem concerned a general lack of awareness of the CC amongst researchers even within those institutions that formally endorsed it (European Commission 2009, p. 25). This led the European Commission to launch the 'Human Resource Strategy for Researchers' (HRS4R) in 2008 to assist institutions in the implementation of the CC at the national and institutional levels. Four cohorts (each consisting of 40–50 institutions) have joined the HRS4R as of 2014. While participation in the HRS4R is also voluntary, institutions do devote resources (organizational, financial and manpower) to meet the targets set and to prepare for multiple (internal and external) evaluations of their progress.

By studying the implementation of the CC, this chapter deals with a basic puzzle concerning voluntary policy instruments: why comply? More specifically, why do actors voluntarily implement non-binding EU measures that could contribute to changing existing (institutionalized) procedures, rules and practices? It is important to address this question in light of how increasingly complex EU governance has become in recent decades in which a panoply of binding as well as non-binding measures across different policy domains are adopted to affect similar outcomes. By explaining why research organizations would voluntarily implement measures originating from the supranational level in contested policy sectors, we consider whether integration could only move forward when legally binding measures are the modus operandi. Taking the CC as a case study and following the literature on compliance, we identify the rationales and organizational features enabling research institutions to endorse and translate non-binding instruments into their internal regulations.

To do so, this chapter is structured as follows. We begin by discussing the CC within the context of the ERA to identify the career management framework it promotes and its main supporters and opponents. For this purpose, we use official documents to which we have had access. Next, given our main research interest resides in explaining why organizations agree to adopt and, eventually, to translate non-obligatory measures into their internal working, we review the literature on compliance in the fields of EU studies and international relations – those where the subject of *compliance* has received a more exhaustive treatment – to distil a number of explanatory arguments for structuring the empirical section, where we present the research design and findings. We conclude with a systematic interpretation of our results in light of the explanations highlighted in the compliance literature.

## A PAN-EUROPEAN HUMAN RESOURCE POLICY FOR RESEARCHERS: THE CHARTER AND THE CODE

The CC proposes a career management framework that holds the researchers and their employers or funders equally responsible. The Charter, divided into two parts (see Table 3.1), is concerned with professional responsibilities of researchers and the working environment. The Code, on the other hand, sets out nine principles (plus one additional principle that we consider important) that recruiters should follow when selecting

*Table 3.1    The European Charter for Researchers*

| General principles and requirements applicable to researchers | General principles and requirements applicable to employers and funders |
|---|---|
| • Research freedom (but admitting limitations given particular research circumstances, operational constraints or intellectual property issues) | • Recognition of all researchers (including early-stage ones) as professionals |
| • Adherence to ethical principles in the discipline | • Non-discrimination on whichever basis |
| • Professional responsibility (avoiding duplications, plagiarism and so on) | • Ensuring a stimulating and safe research environment |
| • Professional attitude | • Ensuring flexible working conditions in accordance with national regulations which allow to combine family, work and career |
| • Comply with contractual and legal obligations | • Promoting contractual stability |
| • Accountability towards employers, funders and society | • Ensuring attractive funding conditions and salaries with equitable social security provisions |
| • Keeping good practices in research (safe data management and protection, workplace safety) | • Keeping gender balance at all levels |
| • Dissemination and exploitation of results | • Drawing up a specific career development strategy |
| • Public engagement (research activity and results should be made accessible to non-specialists) | • Recognition of the value of geographical, intersectoral, trans-disciplinary and virtual mobility |
| • Regular and structured relationship between research trainees and supervisors | • Ensuring researchers' access to research training and continuous development |
| • Performing supervision and managerial duties to the highest professional standards | • Ensuring access to career advice and job placement assistance |
| • Continuous professional updating and development | • Ensuring appropriate protection of intellectual property rights |
| | • Positive valuation and recognition of co-authorship |
| | • Ensuring competent supervision of early-stage researchers |
| | • Considering teaching as an option in researchers' career paths and ensuring it does not interfere with research activities |
| | • Introducing transparent and periodical evaluation/appraisal systems for all researchers |

*Table 3.1*   (continued)

| General principles and requirements applicable to researchers | General principles and requirements applicable to employers and funders |
| --- | --- |
| | • Establishing appropriate procedures to deal with complaint/appeals of researchers<br>• Ensuring clear recruitment standards, facilitating the (re)entry in the research career to disadvantaged groups and returning researchers |

*Source:*   European Commission (2005).

researchers (see Table 3.2). The CC can be seen as 'standards', a form of regulation consisting of 'pieces of general advice offered to large number of potential adopters' to be incorporated in their internal working on a voluntary basis (Brunsson and Jacobsson 2000a, p. 2). Unlike norms, standards are 'written, explicit and have an evident source and presumably not yet internalized; unlike directives [or rules, in the sense of Ostrom (2005)], they are claimed to be voluntary because those who issue standards are unable or unwilling to make others follow them' (ibid., p. 13).

The idea for the CC could be traced back to the pre-ERA years (see Chou 2012, p. 1060), but it was the formal launch of the ERA concept that pushed the issue of a 'mobile' and 'knowledgeable' workforce onto the agenda in this domain. In its 2001 Communication titled 'A Mobility Strategy for the European Research Area' (European Commission 2001), the European Commission argued for why a 'special approach' to the free movement of researchers was necessary and set out recommendations on how to achieve this goal. This was followed up by another Communication in 2003: 'Researchers in the European Research Area: One Profession, Multiple Careers' (European Commission 2003). In this Communication, the European Commission announced that it would soon launch the process to develop a '"European Researcher's Charter", a framework for the career management for human resources in R&D' and to outline the '"Code of conduct for the recruitment of researchers" based on best practice, to improve recruitment methods' (ibid., p. 23).

The CC is a 'product' of a European Commission-driven process involving both stakeholder and (ad hoc) expert groups; in this way, the preparation of the CC can be seen as both a top-down and bottom-up process. To start, the European Commission solicited inputs from various stakeholder

*Table 3.2   The European Code of Conduct for Researcher Recruitment*

| Principle | Content |
| --- | --- |
| Recruitment | Recruitment procedures should be open, efficient, transparent, supportive, internationally comparable and tailored to the type of position advertised |
| Advertisements* | They should include broad descriptions of knowledge and competencies required, working conditions and entitlements, career development prospects, and realistic time between advertisement and deadline of proposals |
| Selection | Committees should bring together expertise, adequate gender balance, and sectoral and disciplinary diversity. A variety of selection practices should be used |
| Transparency | Candidates should be informed about the recruitment process, selection criteria, number of available positions, career prospects, as well as the strengths and weaknesses of their applications after the selection |
| Judging merit | Selection should consider the whole range of experience of the candidates, their creativity and level of independence, and merits should be judged both on a quantitative and qualitative basis |
| Chronological order of CVs | Career breaks or variations in chronological order should be regarded as an evolution of a career, and thus, be evaluable as a contribution to professional development |
| Recognition of mobility experience | Geographical, sectoral, discipline or virtual should be considered as a valuable contribution to professional development |
| Recognition of qualifications | An appropriate assessment and evaluation of academic and professional, formal and non-formal, qualifications should be provided |
| Seniority | Qualifications required should be in line with the needs of the position, and recognition and evaluation should focus on judging achievements along a lifelong professional development rather than circumstances or the reputation of the institution where the qualifications were gained |
| Postdoctoral appointments | Rules and guidelines should be explicit for the recruitment and appointment of postdoctoral researchers. These should be take into account that postdoctoral status should be transitional and oriented to provide additional professional development opportunities |

*Note:*   * this is not a separate principle in the Code, but given its importance, we consider it as such.

*Source:*   European Commission (2005).

groups: the research community (for example, EuroScience and the Marie Curie Fellows Association) and trade unions (EUROCADRES and ETUCE). Young researchers also had multiple roles in drafting the CC: they gave inputs indirectly (via consultation) as well as directly through their membership in the External Advisory Group for the Marie Curie Actions (now the People's Programme) and the dedicated working group within the Steering Group on Human Resources and Mobility where the CC was finalized (Quintanilha 2004). With the exception of EU Presidencies, member states (through their national delegates sitting in the Council of Ministers configuration) played a minor role in comparison to those they have had in other policy sectors such as security and migration, yet the framing of the CC as a 'recommendation to the member states' suggested that they were the intended primary audience – the 'adopters' (Brunsson and Jacobsson 2000a) – for implementing these standards. As we shall see, however, governmental actors showed very little interest in doing so.

In 2005, several initiatives were launched to promote the CC. For instance, the European Commission, with the support of national research ministries and Rectors' Conferences (heads of higher education institutions), convened several CC seminars throughout Europe. The European Researcher's Mobility Portal, now known as Euraxess, actively promoted the CC and continues to do so to this day (European Commission 2006, p. 7). The UK Presidency hosted a conference on the CC in September 2005. Here, the participants optimistically stated that 'the Charter and Code itself is not the end of the process, but rather the beginning of a shift in perception at the European level of an understanding of research and the talented individuals that carry it out' (Kane 2005, p. 3). By the end of 2005, several national research organizations endorsed the CC or signalled their intentions to do so very shortly; yet only Lithuania had formally implemented the CC into national legislation (European Commission 2006, pp. 8–12).

The Austrian Presidency of the EU convened another conference on the CC in the first half of 2006. The theme revolved around how the CC could act as the driver for enhancing career prospects. One of its main conclusions stressed the 'voluntary' nature of the CC, noting that implementing these principles 'does not mean [applying] every single word' (Austrian Presidency of the EU 2006, p. 2). At the same time, the participants stressed that the CC implementation should be a transparent one and proposed that a 'label' be introduced to differentiate institutions implementing the CC from those who were not. Some academic participants, however, commented on how the CC principles could potentially require substantive changes to the existing practices at some national institutions (ibid., see Ramón Marimón's speech). On balance, what can be concluded from the official documents and statements is that, while reception was warm amongst the national actors (endorsement increased steadily during the first years), there was very little formal translation by governments – the intended audience (European Commission 2009, pp. 25–26).

In 2008, the European Commission renewed its efforts to promote the implementation of the CC by launching the HRS4R. This represented a shift in the European Commission's strategy, as the HRS4R is devised to stimulate voluntary compliance at the level of research funding agencies, universities and research institutes. Consisting of five steps, the participating institutions begin with Step 1 by carrying out internal analyses to identify differences between internal practice and those described in the CC (a so-called gap analysis). In these analyses, institutions should identify 'actions required' that would allow them to improve the situation. In Step 2, the institutions upload these gap analyses to their institutional webpage and also to Euraxess. The European Commission examines the gap analyses at Step 3; it either 'approves' or suggests ways to improve. If the European Commission 'approves', then a logo signifying 'HR Excellence in Research' is awarded to the institution. This logo can then be freely used in all institutional communications (virtually and in print). To retain logo usage, the institutions must carry out a self-evaluation every two years and have an external evaluation every four years (Steps 4 and 5).

Between 2009 and 2013, the European Commission has offered guidance and support to organizations belonging to one of the four successive cohorts participating in the HRS4R. Over 120 institutions are participating in the HRS4R and over 65 have achieved 'logo' status (ERA-SGHRM Working Group 2012). In light of the response from national governmental actors towards implementing the CC, this development indicates that some organizations have shown greater interest in the CC. This is particularly interesting given that participation in the HRS4R occurred during one of the most difficult economic crises Europe has faced in recent decades. Indeed, higher education institutions have been especially affected by recent cuts in public spending (see Hoareau 2014, this volume).

Given these developments, we ask: why did organizations decide to endorse and translate the CC at times of institutional resource scarcity? In asking this question, we differentiate between the 'transposition' and 'enforcement/application' stages in the process of implementing EU measures (on the different stages of implementing EU regulations, see Treib 2008, p. 6). Here, we are interested in the 'transposition' stage – that is, in the case of the CC, when national organizations adopt voluntary EU standards into internal rules. In this respect, we focus on three types of 'outputs' or 'organizational behaviour' related to the translation of the

CC into internal public policy or organizational rules: endorsement (that is, manifesting support and agreement for the CC principles through the actual signing of an endorsement letter as declaration of support); participating in the HRS4R process; and securing the HRS4R 'logo'. Each action implies an increasing level of organizational effort. We recognize that these actions may be 'symbolic' (without any immediate practical consequences) but, at the same time, we do not consider them to be merely 'cheap talk' because they entail some kind of commitment with the values implicit in the CC and, therefore, a reputational risk in case of clear contradiction. As Brunsson and Jacobsson (2000b, p.129) put it, 'Whatever strategy is chosen, the adopter of the standards will be open to criticism by others who have a different opinion on whether existing practice conforms to the standards'.

Was incorporating the CC a part of on-going national or institutional reforms (for example, the internationalization or modernization agenda)? Or was there something unique or appealing about the CC that attracted the participation of the organizations in the HRS4R process? For those organizations engaged in the HRS4R process, what accounts for the difference between those achieving 'logo' status and those that still have not? Addressing these questions will shed light on the relationship between non-binding EU recommendations and organizational decisions to comply. To do so, we turn to the literature on compliance to identify potential explanations as to why institutions comply with adopted EU instruments.

## SOFT POLICY INSTRUMENTS: WHY COMPLY?

Studies of European public administration have shown a great interest in compliance and implementation of policies adopted at the supranational level (for reviews see Angelova et al. 2012; Mastenbroek 2005; Treib 2008). The basic assumption is that for integration to 'work', adopted EU measures should be 'evenly' in place throughout its member states. Most compliance studies concentrate on the transposition of *binding* EU legislation such as directives. In their review, Angelova et al. (2012, p.1274) distinguish several explanatory arguments in the literature of which four are of particular relevance for the study of voluntary compliance. These are: 'goodness-of-fit', 'enforcement', 'culture' and 'management'. We consider how these respective explanations help us address the questions raised above concerning three specific instances of voluntary compliance with the CC: endorsement, participation in the HRS4R and obtaining the HRS4R 'logo'.

The 'goodness-of-fit' explanation is the most straightforward and, according to Angelova et al. (2012), supposedly one of the most 'robust' of all compliance theses. The basic argument is that, the greater the difference between the status quo of domestic regime or policy and the one introduced at the supranational level, the more likely that non-compliance would be observed. Here, the 'goodness-of-fit' is operationalized in different ways such as financial costs associated with transposition (Falkner et al. 2005) and national legislative legacy (Duina and Blithe 1999). However, the simple notion that national (institutional) regimes that are already a 'good fit' with the EU's may account for how and why certain institutions endorse the CC and advance more quickly than others in their implementation, is problematic. First, the 'goodness-of-fit' model has been criticized for failing to capture non-compliance even when there is a recognizable 'good fit' (Mastenbroek and Kaeding 2006). Second, the 'fit' thesis is known for its elasticity and general lack of specification: it does not isolate which mechanisms cause compliance; for example, is it because 'fit' reduces the organizational costs of compliance or is it because it refers to the 'fit' between the implementers' beliefs and the regulation's embodied values? Therefore, to some extent the 'fit' argument is implied in the other explanatory arguments discussed below.

The 'enforcement' thesis relies on the 'logic of expected consequences' (March and Olsen 1984) where compliance depends on the balance between associated costs and benefits that participating actors anticipate in return (Downs et al. 1996; Tallberg 2002). Other strands of the literature also stress the role of 'expected consequences' – for example, Brunsson and Jacobsson (2000b, pp. 133–137) underline the importance of 'situation' and 'incentives' in following standards and Börzel and Risse (2012, p. 11) point to 'domestic incentives' when discussing differential empowerment of actors – but it is conceptualized in terms of scope conditions rather than mechanisms. According to the enforcement mechanism, actors are more likely to comply if the costs of non-compliance are higher than compliance. Here, sanctioning, or the infringement procedures initiated by the European Commission, is important for ensuring compliance. While the most 'rational' of all compliance theses (Perkins and Neumayer 2007; Thomson 2010; Thomson et al. 2007), this mechanism does not allow us to account for how and why institutions decide to endorse and participate in the CC implementation since there are no visible EU sanctioning systems in place. However, it can be useful to explain continual institutional participation in the translation process (HRS4R) if there is a critical mass that allows the European Commission to leverage informal coercion. For example, it can put up a scoreboard comparing institutional performance ('logo' vs 'laggards' – the mechanisms of 'naming', 'shaming' and 'faming') or establish endorsement as a condition for accessing European funding programmes.

The 'culture' thesis stems from constructivist scholarship and socio-logical institutionalism where compliance to an adopted measure is the outcome of the 'right thing to do' (Checkel 2005). Here, compliance would result from actors behaving according to the 'logic of appropriateness' (March and Olsen 1984), grounded in previous organizational identities (Brunsson and Jacobsson 2000b, pp. 131–133) affecting substantive or procedural (that is, imitation, innovation) values; or resulting from exten-sive interactions amongst actors over a long period of time (to develop trust, learning and, ultimately, modifying identities through socialization processes) (Berglund et al. 2006). In the case of endorsing and translating the CC, we anticipate this mechanism to be working prominently at the endorsement stage and very early on in the HRS4R process because of the relatively low 'cost' associated with these steps. However, as implementa-tion progresses, it is more likely that the 'culture' thesis would only account for the participation of those institutions that perceive compliance as a 'normative commitment'.

The 'management' explanation refers to the dependence of compliance on organizational and institutional capacities more than in sanction mech-anisms. The basic assumption is that compliance would be associated with the presence of technical and bureaucratic capabilities, as well as economic resources (Chayes and Handler Chayes 1993). The idea is, as Gornitzka et al. (2007, p. 205) put it, 'If administrative capacity is built up around European standards the national take up of European standards will be easier'. There are also other structural factors affecting compliance capaci-ties, such as institutional veto players, the degree of decision-making cen-tralization, or the existence of intergovernmental or interdepartmental structures of cooperation. In their 'robustness' survey, Angelova et al. (2012, p. 1276) found that 'institutional decision-making constraints' to be the other more robust compliance findings. In this respect, the focus is often placed on accounting for non-compliance; for example, active opposition, rivalries between sectors and ministries, or misinterpretation of the adopted EU measure (Falkner et al. 2005, pp. 24–25). In our study, we assume that strong administrative capacity (either at the organizational or system level) is essential for endorsing and implementing the CC, but it is likely to be more crucial for effectively participating in the HRS4R due to the resources that need to be allocated for these activities.

In sum, following earlier compliance studies (Börzel 2010; Börzel et al. 2012; Falkner et al. 2007; Mbaye 2001; Tallberg 2002; Toshkov 2008), we investigate the complementarity between the four explanations in account-ing for how and why the institutions endorse, implement the CC and seek to achieve the HRS4R 'logo'. We expect these four theses to be invoked by participants to explain their decisions and our aim is to identify the potential links between them. In the following section we present the research design and the empirical results.

## TRANSLATING THE CHARTER AND THE CODE IN NATIONAL ARENAS: NORWAY VS SPAIN

To our knowledge, there are no existing studies about research organizations voluntarily implementing the CC. Consequently, our research design adopts the form of an exploratory comparative case study (Yin 2009, p. 29). As stated above, we focus on the initial stage of the implementation process – where the principles of the CC are 'translated' into rules at the domestic level (through changes in legal, policy or organizational regulations). More specifically, our targets (the explananda) are three specific moments of the 'translation' process – each of them involving increasing resource investment by participant organizations: formal endorsement of the CC, participation in the HRS4R and receiving the 'logo'. Therefore, we do not deal with other stages of implementation such as enforcement by policy or organizational authorities or their application on the ground.

We restricted the 'logo' analysis mainly to the first cohort of the HRS4R, as it was the only group operational at the start of this study (late 2010) and, as pioneers, they could be seen as 'innovators' amongst their peers ('imitators'). It is therefore important to identify the mechanisms that triggered their decision to endorse the CC, participate in the HRS4R and obtain the 'logo'. References to other cohorts are used to compare and contrast findings concerning the pilot group and to point out areas for future research. Cohort 1 initially comprised of 41 institutions, but a few left to join the second cohort and three interest groups were invited to participate as 'multipliers' (participant observation 2010). As of 2013, more than half are 'acknowledged': they have reached the third stage of the HRS4R and achieved 'logo' status (see Table 3.3).

Concerning the countries, we selected them according to the 'most-different' criterion, focusing on the success rate of obtaining the 'logo'. We retained the country distinction rather than the characteristics of the organizations (for example, small vs large; higher education institutions vs funding bodies) because the members of the first cohort were organized by country. Here, the countries could be divided into at least four groups according to the success criteria, ranging from very successful where all institutions were acknowledged, to those less successful where one or none had secured the logo. We were interested in the very successful and the least successful and we wanted our cases to have more than one participating

*Table 3.3   HRS4R Pilot Group*

| Country | Organization | # |
| --- | --- | --- |
| Austria | Medical University of Graz* | 1 |
| Belgium | Fonds de la Recherche Scientifique | 2 |
| | University of Hasselt | 3 |
| | Flemish Research Foundation* | 4 |
| Croatia | University of Rijeka* | 5 |
| | Agency for Mobility and EU Programmes | 6 |
| France | University of Compiègne | 7 |
| | INRA* | 8 |
| | Institut Pasteur | 9 |
| | University of Lille | 10 |
| | Université Pierre et Marie Curie | 11 |
| Germany | EMBL | 12 |
| | University of Heidelberg | 13 |
| Greece | Centre for Research and Technology Hellas | 14 |
| | National Hellenic Research Foundation | 15 |
| Hungary | Eötvös Loránd University | 16 |
| Iceland | University of Reykjavik* | 17 |
| Israel | Technion – Israel Institute of Technology | 18 |
| Italy | University of Padova | 19 |
| | University of Foggia* | 20 |
| | University of Palermo* | 21 |
| | University of Udine | 22 |
| | University of Camerino* | 23 |
| Luxembourg | CRP Santé* | 24 |
| | Fonds National de la Recherche Luxembourg | 25 |
| Norway | Research Council of Norway* | 26 |
| | Norwegian Technical University, NTNU* | 27 |
| | University of Oslo* | 28 |
| Slovenia | University of Maribor* | 29 |
| | University of Primorska* | 30 |
| Spain | Agencia de Gestió d'Ajuts Universitaris i de Recerca (AGAUR) | 31 |
| | IDIBELL | 32 |
| | IMDEA Water* | 33 |
| Switzerland | CERN | 34 |
| | University of applied sciences, Berne* | 35 |
| | ETH Zurich | 36 |
| | Swiss Rectors Conference CRUS | 37 |
| UK^ | British Council (Science) | 38 |
| | University of Bristol* | 39 |
| | VITAE | 40 |
| | University of Cambridge* | 41 |

*Notes:*   ^ UK organizations are following Concordat; * Acknowledged 'HR Excellence in Research' organizations amongst the first cohort.

*Source:*   authors' own compilation; some participants have left the pilot group and joined other cohorts.

institution with at least one acknowledged institution since this mix allowed us to compare the country cases. Based on these criteria, we had four potential countries: Norway and Slovenia (highly successful); France and Spain (less successful).

We decided to focus on Norway and Spain because they represented two extreme country cases; respectively, for example, financially well-endowed vs crisis-stricken; non-EU member vs an old member; centralized vs decentralized research systems; authorities enthusiastic vs those hesitant to embrace the CC. Moreover, these two countries represented very different compliance models, with the Norwegians following a more consensus-seeking and dialogic model (Sverdrup 2004) and the Spanish following a monitoring model where compliance relies more on follow-up enforcement. If we identified the same mechanisms to be responsible, the findings would be significant in the current context because they would signal that legally-binding measures may not be essential for further integration even at times of economic crisis.

We applied three different methods: documentary analysis of official EU texts and institutional gap analyses; semi-structured and confidential interviews with HR personnel overseeing the implementation process, officials from relevant ministries and those who were involved in promoting the CC nationally; and participant observation (one of the authors was a member of the HRS4R pilot group and participant observation is used to complement documentary and interview data). We carried out a total of 40 interviews (14 in Norway and 26 in Spain) between December 2010 and November 2012. The interviews were used to identify the following information: general awareness of the CC and the principles it promoted ('fit' with institutional and domestic policies); institutional motivation for endorsing the CC (material incentives vs values/norms embedded in organizational history, policies and practices); and organizational capacity and leadership for promoting the CC. To reference the interviews, we developed a coding system with 'NO' referring to Norwegian interviewees and 'ES' to Spanish interviewees.[1]

To start with we provide a description of the CC promotion process in the two countries prior to the launch of the HRS4R. We then identify the motivations of the respective institutions to endorse the CC and to participate in the HRS4R process.

## Promoting the Charter and the Code

### Norway

Norway has been a champion of the CC from the very beginning. Shortly after the European Commission adopted the CC in 2005, the Research

Council of Norway started to promote these principles nationally; prior to the 2005 Bologna ministerial meeting at Bergen, according to an interviewee from the University of Bergen (INTVNO9, 22 February 2012), it informed all Norwegian higher education and research institutions about the CC. Offering its support, in December 2005 the Ministry of Education and Research requested the Association of Higher Education Institutions (Universitets- og Høgskolerådet, UHR) to evaluate the impact that the CC may have on the Norwegian higher education and research system. This assessment was not carried out, however, until 2008.

We asked several interviewees to explain this delay. According to an interviewee from the UHR, when requesting further instruction from the Research Council, the instructions offered were 'quite vague'; the UHR was told that it 'should look into it' (INTVNO1, 1 February 2012). Providing another perspective, a University of Bergen interviewee said that, actually, 'The UHR problematized it a lot, [they stated that] we don't need to sign it, we have already implemented it' (INTVNO9). An interviewee from the Researchers' Union (Forskerforbundet) supported this view, 'What happened when it came and was presented in Norway, [the] reaction from many universities for example was that this is nothing new. This is how we do it in Norway' (INTVNO14, 2 March 2012). An official from the Research Council explained that the hesitance was very natural since 'This is something coming from outside. What does this really mean? Do we have to? What can we get from it?' (INTVNO2, 2 February 2012). What we may conclude is that, although there was a clear 'fit' between Norwegian regulation and the principles promoted by the CC, there was hesitance to embrace them. Interestingly, this very 'fit' was also used to argue *against* further commitment from Norwegian institutions at that time.

To signal its unambiguous support for the CC, the Research Council organized a formal endorsement ceremony at Copenhagen on 17 October 2006. In the presence of the Norwegian Minister of Education and Research and the European Commissioner for Research, the Research Council's Director General signed the CC on behalf of Norway. When asked to elaborate on what this 'formal signing' meant, an interviewee from the Research Council explained that 'it gives some sign that this is important' (INTVNO2). At the same time, this interviewee qualified the signing as a 'gimmick' because its aim was to generate 'attention nationally' (INTVNO2). It worked; on 6 February 2007, the UHR formally signed the CC and appointed a Committee to examine how the CC 'could best be implemented at Norwegian universities and university colleges' (UHR 2008). The Committee's report, completed in August 2008, became the national gap analysis and would prove to be crucial in the widespread acceptance of the CC amongst Norwegian institutions – especially those lacking resources to carry out their institutional gap analysis.

The Norwegian gap analysis found that in the main its national regulations were in line with the CC principles. The Committee, however, isolated eight principles that could be problematic when directly implemented because of its ambiguous formulation (for example, the 'research environment' principle), existing schemes (the 'professional recognition' principle would be challenging for maintaining the Norwegian 'quota scheme' for Ph.D.'s since they have student status), or a general lack of a viable pan-European solution (pension portability) (UHR 2008). Two principles stood out for being very difficult to enforce: introducing an evaluation/appraisal system at the level of individual researchers ('career counselling') and providing unsuccessful applicants with feedback on their weaknesses and strengths. The Committee argued that implementing these principles would be time-consuming and costly; some of the processes may be too sensitive and 'must be handled with discretion' (ibid.).

The UHR and the Research Council jointly launched the national gap analysis in January 2009 at a seminar on the topic of 'Global Competition for Talented Researchers' according to our interviewee in the Research Council (INTVNO2). The CC was presented as a tool to 'clarify and simplify recruitment and funding processes' so that Norway can 'successfully compete for the best international researchers' (Euraxess 2009). At that meeting, the Minister of Education and Research also politically supported the CC translation and the Norwegian internal HRS4R group met for the first time. This 'national group', according to its designer in the Research Council, 'was something we thought of even before the HR Strategy group on the EU level' (INTVNO2). The idea was to enable informal dialogue amongst Norwegian universities on 'Recruitment [and] how to build that good research environment'; the group has now expanded to include university colleges and industrial partners (INTVNO2). What we may conclude is that complying with the CC – voluntarily, but visibly – was important to Norwegian political actors who actively promoted these principles and steered the process from top-down. As we shall now discuss, it was an entirely different process in Spain.

### Spain

An EU member since 1986, decentralization is a basic feature of the Spanish research system. The state and the autonomous regions are both constitutionally entitled to develop their own policies and institutional structures, but they share authority on regulating universities. The regions are responsible for funding universities while the federal government is tasked with coordinating the entire system through the National Plan of

Research, Development and Innovation – a tool criticized for being ineffective (Sanz 1997; Tortosa 2006). HR policy in research is regulated in two ways: by the civil service code or through employer administrative or labour contracts, which include pre- and postdoctoral grants. During the 2000s, research grant holders launched a campaign to improve the precarious working conditions of contract researchers. Organized as the Young Researchers Federation (FJI), these stakeholders were involved in drafting the CC through the institutional framework of the European Council of Doctoral Candidates (Eurodoc); the European Commission invited Eurodoc to participate and a FJI member was its delegate. In this way, the FJI can be considered as the main CC champion in Spain.

When the CC was adopted in 2005, the Ministry of Education and Science was studying how to change postdoctoral grants into labour contracts and replace doctoral grants with a '2+2' system. The resulting regulation adopted in January 2006 – *Estatuto del personal investigador en formación* – allegedly implemented the CC principles. The subsequent calls issued under the National Plan did indeed mention the CC, but we have observed that the programmes funded or managed by the research centres dependent on these funding schemes did not reference the CC in their calls.

In 2008, the Ministry of Science and Innovation and the Council of Universities jointly committed to promote the CC implementation. In a report issued in September 2008, the Council of Universities declared that 'in view of the importance of the decision' it will 'study [the CC], promote its application and identify those problems and obstacles that could hinder its implementation, undertaking initiatives to solve them' (Consejo de Universidades 2008). To that end, the report confirmed that the Council would create an 'organizational node' within its secretariat (dependent on the Ministry of Science and Innovation). According to the then General Secretary of the Council, however, such a node was never created (INTVES9, 25 February 2011). The promotion of the CC in Spain occurred primarily through the Euraxess network and indirectly via the promotion of Marie Curie Co-Fund programmes (Ministry of Science and Innovation 2011).

The Spanish Law on Science, Technology and Innovation adopted in May 2011 cited the CC as inspiring the new regulatory framework concerning research personnel. Speaking with the General Director of Research in office when the bill was sent to Parliament, we were told that the law is fully compliant with the CC (INTVES6, 26 January 2011). Specifically, our attention was drawn to the section on the rights and duties of research personnel and the introduction of a four-year employment contract (replacing the '2+2' regime). The latter was, however, not in the original text; it was only introduced during parliamentary debates. To summarize, the promotion of the CC in Spain started as a bottom-up process to reform the working conditions of researchers; the Ministry attempted to steer this process by referencing the CC as inspiring national reforms and closer examination has shown that follow-up activities have not been fully realized. To what extent have the different promotional strategies affected the patterns of the CC endorsement and translation in these two countries?

## Endorsing the Charter and the Code

As of January 2013, 18 Norwegian institutions have formally endorsed the CC. Amongst these organizations, higher education institutions constitute the majority and, together, they account for 76 per cent of all research and academic staff working in the higher education sector in 2011 (Statistics Norway 2013). In the case of Norway, we detected three distinct waves of endorsement: *pre-2009* (pioneer institutions); *post-January 2009* (after publication of the national gap analysis); and *post-2011* (when the second, third and fourth HRS4R cohorts convened). Their motivations for endorsing the CC were as follows. For the pioneer institutions, as we shall discuss in detail in the next section, endorsing the CC was part of their individualistic institutional decisions to participate in the HRS4R; put simply, the CC endorsement was not seen as a separate act to implementing these principles. For most institutions endorsing the CC in 2009, their decisions were attributed to the request that the UHR made in February: it asked the universities and university colleges to sign a 'Declaration of Commitment'. It was successful; as our UHR interviewee puts it, 'The UHR has very good network and links into the administration at major universities and university colleges' and was thus able to galvanize support (INTVNO1). For the post-2011 signatories, their endorsement was a 'prerequisite' to joining the HRS4R process.

There are 46 Spanish institutions that have formally endorsed the CC; after Italy, Spain has the highest number of signatories (10 per cent). At the same time, in contrast to Norway, these organizations account for only 13.5 per cent of all researchers in Spain in 2009 (Eurostat 2013). The Spanish endorsement pattern is as follows: most occurred in 2011 (20); there were 19 endorsements during 2006–2010, with 11 institutions declaring their support in 2008. In terms of their features, the Spanish institutions are a veritable mix: the smallest institution employs 11 researchers while the largest has 7,500 (Highest Council for Scientific Research); two are regional ministries (Madrid and Catalonia); 36 are promoted by public administrations; and the rest are the results of public-private partnerships. There are three common features, however, that are shared by the majority of Spanish institutions: they are financially dependent on the regional governments (24 institutions); they are very young (33 were created in the 2000s, only six before 1990); and they belong to two highly competitive research sectors (25 in biomedical and seven in high-technology research).

According to our Spanish interviewees, they decided to endorse the CC due to one of three following reasons. First, similar to the post-January 2009 Norwegian endorsers, they endorsed the CC as the result of a formal request from an authority outside of their institution. This was the case for centres associated with the Institute of Health 'Carlos III' (nine institutions), Madrid Institute for Advanced Studies (IMDEA) (nine institutions) and those dependent on the Catalan Department of Health (five institutions). Although these organizations relied on the support of the regional ministries issuing the request, not all interpreted the request as a direct imposition. For instance, two centres linked to the Institute of 'Carlos III' (on epidemiology and neurodegenerative diseases) have yet to formally endorse at the time of writing.

Second, endorsing the CC was the result of an endogenous process triggered by exogenous factors. According to our interviewees, the most powerful exogenous factor was competition for EU funds: six organizations explicitly mention this as a reason and two cite it as the *only* motivation (the Valencian Institute for Small and Medium Enterprise and the Catalan Agency for Competitiveness). In this respect, EU funding conditions are particularly significant in triggering compliance. We should clarify, however, that this is only linked to the Marie Curie Co-Fund scheme which establishes the CC compliance as a desirable quality institutions could evidence in support of their application (European Commission 2010, p. 17). A total of 19 out of 46 Spanish endorsers are recipients of the Marie Curie Co-Fund, while none of the Norwegian institutions are grantees (European Commission 2013). Another exogenous factor, according to the Deputy General Director of Research from the regional Ministry of Education of Madrid, was the FJI's campaign supporting the CC implementation (INTVES3, 13 December 2010). We were told that the regional Ministry endorsed the CC as a symbolic gesture to show how they were improving research trainees' working conditions (INTVES3).

Third, the remaining Spanish institutions decided to endorse the CC as a result of endogenous processes within their organizations. Here, the decision was spearheaded by someone in a (high) decision-making position or within the HR department. We asked our interviewees how they became aware of the CC and were told that most of them found out via contacts from organizations with which they were formally linked (13 interviewees); five interviewees mentioned informal and personal contacts with other signatories. For these institutions, the CC endorsement was a tool to showcase the attractiveness of their HR policy to potential candidates (17 interviewees mentioned this); indeed, 13 interviewees even asserted that the CC principles are the very ones their institutions applied in HR management. Amongst these institutions, it should be noted that eight interviewees also stated that they anticipate the CC endorsement to improve their capacity to compete for EU funding vis-à-vis non-complying institutions.

**Participating in the HRS4R and Achieving the Logo**

There are 21 Spanish institutions participating in the HRS4R; this means that Spain has the highest participation rate amongst all countries (9.2 per cent of all participants). In terms of organizational characteristics, the HRS4R participating institutions mirror those that have endorsed the CC ('a veritable mix'): 12 belong to the biomedical sector and 11 have been awarded a Co-Fund project. Despite this high participation rate, only two Spanish institutions have received the 'HR Excellence in Research' logo at the time of writing: IMDEA Water (cohort 1) and the Basque Foundation for Science (cohort 2). An interviewee from the Institute of Health 'Carlos III' informed us that this institution has also been recognized by the European Commission in September 2012 and is awaiting formal confirmation when we carried out the interview in November 2012 (INTVES29, 27 November 2012).

According to interviewees from the Spanish HRS4R participant institutions, the decisions to translate the CC were natural 'follow-ups' to endorsement. Put simply, after initial decisions to endorse the CC were taken, implementation was merely an extension – 'continuity' as an interviewee from IMDEA Water puts it (INTVES4, 17 January 2011) – of the same decisional process. Hence, their rationales for implementation are the same as those for endorsement: nine interviewees cited increased capacity to recruit internationally, while six interviewees referred to the complementarity between their HR policy and the CC principles. Only three interviewees said that they were motivated by the potential to increase their institutional capacity to compete for EU funding.

There are eleven Norwegian organizations participating in the HRS4R process; they are fairly evenly spread across four cohorts (two in the second cohort and three in all the other cohorts). There are five institutions that have received the logo: Norwegian University of Science and Technology (NTNU), University of Oslo, Norwegian Research Council, University of Tromsø and Vestfold University College. As mentioned earlier, this study focuses on the first cohort and the following discussion will revolve around the motivation of NTNU, the Research Council and the University of Oslo to participate in the HRS4R and achieve logo status.

The Research Council of Norway was the first to sign the CC, but it was the last Norwegian institution in the first cohort to be acknowledged – in January 2011 – due to internal approval processes according to our interviewee in the Research Council (INTVNO2). Its motivation to participate in the HRS4R is rooted in the very complex roles that the Research Council plays in carrying forward the domestic policy agenda to internationalize Norwegian research. As we were repeatedly told by interviewees, for example such as another interviewee in the Research Council, Norway is a small country and its strategy to remain competitive is to internationalize its research (INTVNO7, 8 February 2012). The European arena is *the* gateway for this purpose: 'Participation in the EU Framework Programmes for research is essential as an instrument for the internationalization of Norwegian research' (St. meld. nr. 30 2009, p. 109). A major funder of research in Norway, the Research Council is also the Norwegian delegate to the EU in the research policy domain. It acknowledges this complexity in its gap analysis: the Research Council has 'three roles in relation to the Charter and Code' – 'a funder, employer and advisor' (Research Council of Norway 2010, p. 5). More specifically, its 'advisory function will entail pointing out deficiencies and challenges that need to be solved outside the Research Council' (ibid.).

We asked interviewees to explain why the Research Council has a role that one would usually expect the ministry to play in other countries. Most interviewees, such as the speaker from the Ministry of Research, referred to Norway's special relationship with the EU as a starting point (INTVNO4, 6 February 2012). Having twice rejected membership, its dealings with the supranational entity are politically sensitive; Norwegian policy-makers have sought to manage this relationship through the very complex institutional infrastructure erected by the European Economic Area (EEA) agreement (Chou and Gornitzka 2011). The Research Council, officially an independent agency, is given the tasks to represent Norway, alongside ministry officials, in various European research policy committees and to ensure that national institutions are fully informed of the most recent developments. Hence, its full participation in the HRS4R process also signals the political attention and seriousness that Norway devotes to EU research policy cooperation – even for voluntary measures.

The NTNU, the largest university in the country, was the third to endorse the CC and the first Norwegian organization to receive the logo in February 2010. According to the senior adviser in the HR department (INTVNO13, 29 February 2012) and its official report (NTNU 2010), it was motivated to participate in the HRS4R for two interlinking reasons: to attract international staff (33 per cent of Ph.D. and 25 per cent of researchers are non-Norwegians) and to use the CC as a tool for promoting its reputation amongst target recruits. An interviewee from the NTNU explained that the CC has been implemented 'as a bureaucratic exercise, to fulfil our requirements externally' and has not been 'used as an instrument for change as such' (INTVNO13). This is because of the 'administrative boundary-crossing' nature of the CC principles. As this interviewee put it: 'I've found it difficult to get attention to the Charter and Code at the bigger universities like ours. What's given attention are projects [for example quality development, well running receptions, service for international researchers], not the Charter and Code' (ibid.).

The University of Oslo, the oldest university in the country, was the second to obtain the logo in June 2010. According to interviewees in the HR department (INTVNO3, 3 February 2012; INTVNO5, INTVNO6, 6 February 2012), it was a 'lucky' coincidence that the momentum for translating the CC gathered in 2009 when the University of Oslo began an internal university-wide revision of the ten-years strategy. Participating in the HRS4R and implementing the CC principles were therefore considered primarily in light of how they may contribute to achieving the ambitions of the university. While interviewees at NTNU (INTVNO11, 23 February 2012) and the University of Oslo pointed to the 'ease' of accepting the CC principles due to existing Norwegian law, an HR official from the University of Oslo emphasized that this institution was attracted to the CC because it was sold as a tool for enabling researcher mobility and internationalization (INTVNO3). This interviewee explained how this became problematic during translation when it was not obvious how the CC contributed to encouraging Norwegian researchers to go abroad and to attract foreign researchers when national regulations were at an equivalent, if not higher, standard (ibid.). In the next section, we offer a more systematic interpretation of the empirical findings and show how they support the different explanations highlighted in the compliance literature.

## ACCOUNTING FOR VARIATION IN ENDORSING AND TRANSLATING THE CC

To offer a more structured explanation, we will consider the rationale behind compliance and the institutional conditions under which organizations decide to endorse the CC and proceed with its translation. Here, rationale refers to the logics behind voluntary compliance – the logic of expected consequences and the logic of appropriateness (March and Olsen 1984). In terms of the explanations discussed earlier, these logics point to the 'enforcement' and 'culture' mechanisms, but, as we shall show, the logic of appropriateness reveals aspects of the enforcement mechanism than are implied in compliance studies. The institutional conditions relate to the account based on a 'management' approach, which emphasizes organizational structures in inducing and ensuring compliance.

## The Logics at Work

Our findings reveal that both logics (the logic of expected consequences and the logic of appropriateness) have a place in accounting for institutional decisions to endorse and implement the CC in Norway and Spain. The logic of expected consequences – or anticipated future returns – is observed in cases where the institutional decisions to endorse and translate are made following that institution's positive evaluation of the CC. In Norway, the national gap analysis has greatly facilitated this calculation by demonstrating how existing laws and regulations already uphold the CC principles. In this way, Norwegian institutions in the first cohort were able to concentrate on analysing the benefits that translating the CC principles would bring; both the NTNU and the University of Oslo saw the CC as an instrument to raise their respective international profiles. This was also the case for the Spanish institutions; interviewees from nine HRS4R participant institutions pointed out that endorsing and implementing the CC contributes to the same goal.

Compliance, most interestingly, does not depend on direct negative institutional incentives. Our findings show that, in line with the enforcement thesis, it is feasible to trigger compliance by means of indirect institutional incentives such as introducing endorsement as a 'merit' for accessing EU research funds. This was the case for many Spanish institutions we studied; indeed, 41 per cent of these institutions were hosts of EU Marie Curie Co-Fund projects which consider the CC compliance as a positive feature of applicant institutions. While none of the Norwegian institutions we examined were Co-Fund recipients, the Research Council has started to insert the CC references into funding calls to 'stimulate research institutions to implement measures that improve working conditions and career opportunities for researchers' (Research Council of Norway 2010, p. 4).

What we have observed in many instances is an alignment of both logics, where the logic of appropriateness reinforces the logic of expected consequences. For instance, in Norway we were told by an interviewee from the University of Bergen who was involved in disseminating the CC in Norway that promoting the translation of the CC principles was 'solidarity work with the rest of Europe. We had secured social rights and rights for the students in Norway, why shouldn't we support the Ph.D. students in Germany, in Spain, in Italy, in England?' (INTVNO9). The overall sentiment is that Norway is a case of 'best practice' and therefore it should actively lead the process of endorsing and implementing the CC. This goes hand-in-hand with the consequentialist goal of raising institutional profiles and the strategy cultivated in the Norwegian system to internationalize national research through the EU framework. The convergence of both logics is also evident in Spain. In ten institutions, interviewees told us that complying with the CC was coherent with their organizational history and beliefs in human resource management while contributing to achieving their strategic goals such as increasing international competitiveness.

The non-convergence and co-presence of the two logics, quite interestingly, can help us shed light on non-endorsement. In principle, endorsing the CC should imply 'net gain' – all the advantages of branding without further costs – for signatories. This is due to the lack of an enforcement regime for penalizing violators. It follows that one would expect this cost-benefit outcome to resonate with a consequentialist logic which, in turn, would encourage institutions to endorse. Yet we know that only *four* out of 48 Spanish public universities have endorsed the CC; uncovering factors leading to this would show another way that 'cost' is measured. The Spanish Council of Universities, as discussed earlier, has yet to establish a unit within its secretariat to coordinate the CC promotion and compliance. The reason for this, in addition to the administrative capacity issue discussed below, is because some of the CC principles are in direct conflict with the HR policies in most Spanish universities. According to Fernández Esquinas et al. (2006), this includes lack of transparency and prevalence of non-merit criteria in the recruitment process. Similarly, the 2009 ERAWATCH report for Spain explicitly links low levels of the CC endorsement with the predominant selection practice in most research institutions (Heijs 2010, p. 30).

For these Spanish institutions, endorsing the CC is costly not because it directly and immediately entails adjusting to the CC principles; it is costly because the CC endorsement is a potential source of internal conflict. The HR practices at most Spanish universities are results of a historical process in configuring Spanish research and academic systems; they are reproduced by current incentives and governance structures. When the CC was adopted in 2005, the FJI immediately seized these principles and transformed them into a powerful 'dialectical weapon' to extract social security benefits and labour contracts for pre- and postdoctoral researchers (Real-Dato 2012). The gradual reforms in the last decade resulting in the abolition of grants without social security rights testify to their success. It is hardly surprising that few Spanish universities have endorsed the CC. For them, endorsing is inappropriate; the wrong thing to do. This is a crucial insight because it points to how powerful the perception of appropriateness is in determining behaviour even when symbolic, albeit formal, support could generate reputational benefits. As we shall now discuss, this was a non-starter for many when combined with low institutional capacity to manage the CC translation.

**Institutional Context and Organizational Capacities**

Our findings point to the importance of the institutional conditions in explaining variance in endorsement and implementation patterns amongst Norwegian and Spanish institutions. At the systemic level, the institutionalized pattern of cooperation between the Norwegian Ministry of Education and Research, the Research Council and the UHR has been crucial in forming a consensus regarding the CC endorsement and translation. This consensus is manifested in the production and dissemination of a national gap analysis and the creation and continual operation of a national HR Strategy Group. We asked an interviewee in the Research Council to account for the overall success and quick uptake of the CC and was told that 'maybe part of this is that we do have this close relationship with the ministry. . .we have this support, the political support is in place and I think that's important for a country to have that' (INTVNO7). This is an interesting insight for compliance studies: active support and close collaboration between institutions and the ministry encourage compliance with non-binding measures.

The decentralized set-up of the Spanish political system and the autonomy that the state and regions have in regulating this policy domain explain the CC endorsement and translation pattern in this country. Only one Spanish institution amongst our interview sample confirmed that they became aware of the CC through the national government despite federal efforts to promote these principles. According to the General Director of Research at the Ministry of Science and Innovation during 2008–2010, the CC was not considered 'a key paradigm for defining the research career framework' in Spain, it is 'just one reference among others' (INTVES6). The regional governments appear to share this attitude: only two (out of 17) are participating in the HRS4R. Although the 2009 Law of the Valencian Research and Development system has explicitly committed to applying the CC, no implementation measures have been taken as of time of writing. For compliance studies, the Spanish case offers this insight: active opposition is unnecessary to block compliance to voluntary measures; lack of enthusiasm is sufficient.

Turning to the individual institutions, we find that strong leadership in favour of the CC implementation was constant in all Norwegian and Spanish institutions participating in the HRS4R. While this is hardly surprising, it is remarkable that in the Spanish case this feature is found amongst research institutions with a particular structure: foundation created by the public administration. Hence, in terms of human resource management and their internal structure, these institutions could act as private entities with flexible regulations than those applied to public administration institutions such as universities.

## CONCLUSIONS

In this chapter, we set out to explain why national actors voluntarily comply with EU measures that may seek to change existing procedures, rules and practice. The case study offers interesting insights on this subject. Norwegian and Spanish institutions comply with the 'European Charter for Researchers and the Code of Conduct for the Recruitment of Researchers' for overlapping reasons. On the one hand, in line with a consequential logic, the formal endorsement of the CC and its translation depended on the extent to which institutional decision-makers perceived these activities as a source of immediate or future benefits – in political, reputational and/or financial terms. On the other hand, according to the logic of appropriateness, when the CC principles resonated with the organization's identity (beliefs, underlying histories, policies and practices), the more the institutions actively engaged in their translation. Conversely, when the CC was in conflict with these organizational aspects, the more reluctant the institutions were with formal endorsement, let alone actual translation, even when this symbolic gesture was very likely to produce reputational benefits. In addition, we also saw that the activation of the logics or the final realization of the intentions relied on the institutional context (such as the existence of institutionalized coordination/communication patterns between potential adopters) and internal capacities (regulatory autonomy, leadership, resources); these are key mediating factors in voluntary compliance.

The CC case also suggests that standards do have a role to play as tools in the European integration process, which has long been depicted as one that follows organizational and procedural hierarchy, and is characterized as 'integration by law'. The voluntary feature of the CC has managed to stimulate compliance by national funding agencies, universities and research institutes and, consequently, has positively contributed to the politically set goal of constructing a Europe of Knowledge. Yet, beyond this, the role of standards is also rather ambiguous. For instance, the European Commission only launched the HRS4R to assist national organizations in translating the CC when there was insufficient interest amongst governmental actors – the primary audience as originally stated in the CC – to do so. This can be interpreted as the European Commission's failure to promote the translation of the CC in the traditional (that is, 'hierarchical') manner: from the EU executive to the member states. However, it can also be interpreted as a sign of the 'flexibility' that standards as a policy tool offers to the European Commission – standards allow standardizers to use a variety of additional instruments to promote voluntary compliance without losing their non-binding character. Therefore, the 'roles' standards play in the integration process very much depend on how they are instrumentalized and reinstrumentalized.

This study shows that, in general, regulating through standards allows for a seemingly continual exploration of the regulatory boundaries of what is acceptable that follows a different pattern than the one associated with 'hard law'. The standardization process enables new alliances to form/reform without repeating the identifiable steps of the legislative process associated with legal integration. This approach may appear to be more conducive for addressing issues or areas where there are numerous dimensions of contention and questions of autonomy or 'regulatory ownership'. At the same time, this study also reveals that new expectations emerge from this process and on which the future operation of this voluntary mechanism may hang, that could be challenging for the standardizer to meet. For instance, would the European Commission be able to reform the EU funding programmes to offer more favourable treatments for those organizations that have achieved 'logo' status? If not, what would be the European value-added for 'logo' recipients when these organizations have completed the translation process? While we have an improved understanding of why some national actors comply with voluntary EU measures, the sustainability of these developments remains an open question.

## NOTE

1. Since the interviews were carried out under conditions of anonymity (Chatham House Rule), we provide only the country of the speakers in the text along with the date of the interview.

## REFERENCES

Angelova, M., T. Dannwolf and T. König (2012), 'How robust are compliance findings? A research synthesis', *Journal of European Public Policy*, **19**(8), 1269–1291.

Austrian Presidency of the EU (2006), 'A Researchers' Labour Market: Europe – a Pole of Attraction? (1–2 June)', Austrian Presidency of the EU, Vienna.

Berglund, S., I. Gange and F. van Waarden (2006), 'Mass production of law. Routinization in the transposition of European directives: a sociological-institutionalist account', *Journal of European Public Policy*, **13**(5), 692–716.

Börzel, T.A. (2010), 'European governance: negotiation and competition in the shadow of hierarchy', *Journal of Common Market Studies*, **48**(2), 191–219.

Börzel, T.A. and T. Risse (2012), 'From Europeanisation to diffusion: introduction', *West European Politics*, **35**(1), 1–19.

Börzel, T.A., T. Hofmann and D. Panke (2012), 'Caving in or sitting it out? Longitudinal patterns of non-compliance in the European Union', *Journal of European Public Policy*, **19**(4), 454–471.

Brunsson, N. and B. Jacobsson (2000a), 'The contemporary expansion of standardization', in N. Brunsson, B. Jacobsson and Associates (eds), *A World of Standards*, Oxford: Oxford University Press, pp. 1–20.

Brunsson, N. and B. Jacobsson (2000b), 'Following standards', in N. Brunsson, B. Jacobsson and Associates (eds), *A World of Standards*, Oxford: Oxford University Press, pp. 125–137.

Chayes, A. and A. Handler Chayes (1993), 'On compliance', *International Organization*, **47**(2), 175–205.

Checkel, J.T. (2005), 'International institutions and socialization in Europe: introduction and framework', *International Organization*, **59**(4), 801–826.

Chou, M.-H. (2012), 'Constructing an internal market for research through sectoral and lateral strategies: layering, the European Commission and the fifth freedom', *Journal of European Public Policy*, **19**(7), 1052–1070.

Chou, M.-H. and Å. Gornitzka (2011), 'Den femte frihet og Kunnskapens Europa: Konsekvenser for Norge (Rapport #6)', Europautredningen, Utvalget for utredning av Norges avtaler med EU, Oslo.

Consejo de Universidades (2008), 'Resolution of the Council of Universities, of 16 September 2008, on the Recommendation of the European Commission of 11 March 2005, on an European Charter for Researchers and a Code of Conduct for the Recruitment of Researchers', Ministry of Science and Innovation, Madrid.

Downs, G.W., D.M. Rocke and P.N. Barsoom (1996), 'Is the good news about compliance good news about cooperation?', *International Organization*, **50**(3), 379–406.

Duina, F. and F. Blithe (1999), 'Nation-states and common markets: the institutional conditions for acceptance', *Review of International Political Economy*, **6**(4), 494–530.

ERA-SGHRM Working Group (2012), 'Final Report on Human Resources Issues, Including the HRS4R and Other Examples of Good Practice not Directly Linked to the Charter and Code', ERA Steering Group on Human Resources and Mobility, Brussels.

Euraxess (2009), 'Norway: Competing for the Best and Brightest', in *Europe4Researchers/Newsletter*, Commission, Brussels.

European Commission (2001), 'Communication on a Mobility Strategy for the European Research Area (331 Final)', Commission, Brussels.

European Commission (2003), 'Communication on Researchers in the European Research Area: One Profession, Multiple Careers (436 Final)', Commission, Brussels.

European Commission (2005), 'Recommendation on European Charter for Researchers and on a Code of Conduct for the Recruitment of Researchers (251 Final)', Commission, Brussels.

European Commission (2006), 'Mobility of Researchers and Career Development Implementation Report 2006 [SEC(2006)971]', Commission, Brussels.

European Commission (2007), 'Mobility of Researchers and Career Development Implementation Report 2006 [SEC(2007)1074]', Commission, Brussels.

European Commission (2009), 'Mobility of Researchers and Career Development Implementation Report 2007 [SEC(2009)354]', Commission, Brussels.

European Commission (2010), 'People: 2011 Work Programme, Decision C(2010)8947, 14 December 2010', Commission, Brussels.

European Commission (2013), 'Community Research and Development Information Service (CORDIS)'. Seventh Framework Programme projects, available at: http://cordis.europa.eu/fetch?CALLER=FP7_PROJ_EN&QZ_WEBSRCH=COFUND&QM_EP_PGA_A=FP7-PEOPLE&QM_EN_OC_A=SPAIN&USR_SORT=EN_QVD+CHAR+DESC (accessed 4 January 2013).

Eurostat (2013), 'Statistics on Research and Development: Total Researchers (Head Count)', available at: http://epp.eurostat.ec.europa.eu/tgm/table.do?tab=table&init=1&plugin=1&language=en&pcode=tsc00003 (accessed 4 January 2013).

Falkner, G., M. Hartlapp and O. Treib (2007), 'Worlds of compliance: why leading approaches to European Union implementation are only "sometimes-true" theories', *European Journal of Political Research*, **46**, 395–416.

Falkner, G., O. Treib, M. Hartlapp and S. Leiber (eds) (2005), *Complying with Europe. EU Harmonisation and Soft Law in the Member States*, Cambridge: Cambridge University Press.

Fernández Esquinas, M., M. Pérez Yruela and C. Merchán Hernández (2006), 'El sistema de incentivos y recompensas en la ciencia pública española', Working Paper IESA 1-06, Instituto de Estudios Sociales Avanzados-Andalucía, Córdoba.

Gornitzka, Å., P. Maassen, J.P. Olsen and B. Stensaker (2007), '"Europe of knowledge": search for a new pact', in P. Maassen and J.P. Olsen (eds), *University Dynamics and European Integration*, Dordrecht: Springer, pp. 181–214.

Heijs, J. (2010), 'ERAWATCH Country Report 2009. Analysis of Policy Mixes to Foster R&D Investment and to Contribute to the ERA: Spain', Commission, Joint Research Centre – Institute for Prospective Technological Studies, Brussels.

Hoareau, C. (2014, this volume), 'Economic shocks, federalism and redistribution: exploring the future of Europe through a comparison of the evolution of student financial aid in the United States and the European Union', in M.-H. Chou and Å. Gornitzka (eds), *Building the Knowledge Economy in Europe: New Constellations in European Research and Higher Education Governance*, Cheltenham, UK and Northampton, MA, USA: Edward Elgar, pp. 219–244.

Kane, E. (2005), 'Report of proceedings', in *UK Presidency Conference on the European Charter and Code for Researchers*, London: UK Research Office.

March, J.G. and J.P. Olsen (1984), 'The new institutionalism: organizational factors in political life', *American Political Science Review*, **78**(3), 734–749.

Mastenbroek, E. (2005), 'EU compliance: still a "black hole"?', *Journal of European Public Policy*, **12**(6), 1103–1120.

Mastenbroek, E. and M. Kaeding (2006), 'Europeanization beyond the goodness of fit: domestic politics in the forefront', *Comparative European Politics*, **4**, 331–354.

Mbaye, H.A.D. (2001), 'Why national states comply with supranational law: explaining implementation infringements in the European Union, 1972–1993', *European Union Politics*, **2**(3), 259–281.

Ministry of Science and Innovation (2011), 'Official Communication on the Institutional Monitoring of the European Charter and Code of Conduct', Ministry of Science and Innovation, Madrid.

NTNU (2010), 'NTNU Status Report (updated May 2012)', Norwegian University of Science and Technology, Trondheim.

Ostrom, E. (2005), *Understanding Institutional Diversity*, Princeton: Princeton University Press.

Perkins, R. and E. Neumayer (2007), 'Do membership benefits buy regulatory compliance? An empirical analysis of EU directives 1978–99', *European Union Politics*, **8**(2), 180–206.

Quintanilha, A. (2004), 'Summary report of discussions on the code of conduct for the recruitment and career development of researchers', in *Brain Gain: the Instruments*, The Hague: Dutch Presidency Conference, available at: http://old.certh.gr/libfiles/PDF/MOBIL-26-Reports-workshops.pdf (accessed 28 December 2012).

Real-Dato, J. (2012), 'Mechanisms of stability and change in public policy: research training policy in Spain, 1999–2006', Ph.D. dissertation, Department of Political Science and Public Administration. Granada: University of Granada.

Research Council of Norway (2010), 'The Research Council of Norway's Self-Assessment of the Charter and Code', The Research Council of Norway, Oslo.

Sanz, L. (1997), *Estado, ciencia y tecnología en España: 1939–1997*, Madrid: Alianza Editorial.

St. meld. nr. 30 (2009), 'Klima for forskning (2008–2009)', Kunnskapsdepartement, Oslo.

Statistics Norway (2013), 'StatRes. Universities and Colleges. Resource data. Contracted man-years adjusted for long term leaves, by educational institution', available at: https://www.ssb.no/statistikkbanken/selectvarval/Define.asp?subjectcode=&ProductId=&MainTable=RessUniv3&nvl=&PLanguage=1&nyTmpVar=true&CMSSubjectArea=utdanning&KortNavnWeb=uh_statres&StatVariant=&checked=true (accessed 4 January 2013).

Sverdrup, U. (2004), 'Compliance and conflict management in the European Union: Nordic exceptionalism', *Scandinavian Political Science*, **27**(1), 23–43.

Tallberg, J. (2002), 'Paths to compliance: enforcement, management, and the European Union', *International Organization*, **56**(3), 609–643.

Thomson, R. (2010), 'Opposition through the back door in the transposition of EU directives', *European Union Politics*, **11**(4), 577–596.

Thomson, R., R. Torenvlied and J. Arregui (2007), 'The paradox of compliance: infringements and delays in transposing European Union directives', *British Journal of Political Science*, **37**(4), 685–709.

Tortosa, E. (2006), 'La I+D en el marco autonómico', in J. Sebastián and E. Muñoz (eds), *Radiografía de la investigación pública en España*, Madrid: Biblioteca Nueva, pp. 71–95.

Toshkov, D. (2008), 'Embracing European law: compliance with EU directives in Central and Eastern Europe', *European Union Politics*, **9**(3), 379–402.

Treib, O. (2008), 'Implementing and complying with EU governance outputs',

*Living Reviews in European Governance*, **3**(5), available at: http://www.livingre views.org/lreg-2008-2005 (accessed 19 September 2012).

Universitets- og Høgskolerådet (UHR) (2008), 'Charter and Code, Avviksanalyse for Norge', Universitets- og Høgskolerådet, Oslo.

Yin, R.K. (2009), *Case Study Research: Design and Methods (Fourth Edition)*, London: Sage.

# 4. Dynamics of institution building in the Europe of Knowledge: the birth of the European Research Council

## Åse Gornitzka and Julia Metz

## INTRODUCTION[1]

Institutions in a political system have effects for political life. Institutions comprising 'a relative enduring collection of rules and organized practices, embedded in structures of meaning and resources' (March and Olsen 2006, p. 3) matter for the decisions that are made, how these are implemented and what kind of effects they have. Institutions are also consequential for political systems' capacity to create and maintain a political community (Olsen 2010). Hence it is relevant to ask where institutions come from, why and how they take the form that they do and what it is that makes them viable. This is what will be referred to in this chapter as institution building. For a relatively new polity like the European Union (EU), processes of institution building are particularly important to investigate given that new institutions seem to be perpetually added to its institutional landscape as part of centre formation at the European level. The European Research Council (ERC) is one of these recent additions and the process that led to its establishment is the case of institution building examined in this chapter.

Why is this case of interest? Formally established in February 2007, the ERC is the EU's first funding body set-up to support fundamental investigator-driven research with academic excellence as the funding criteria. In this way, the ERC embodies a break with established principles and rules of resource distribution in the EU's research policy domain. During a relatively short time the ERC developed from being an 'idea' and vision of the few, to becoming an institution with a considerable staff and budget, with fairly established procedures and rules, and gaining a recognized position within European research governance.

The next section outlines four theoretical perspectives on institution building. Then the process that led to the establishment of the ERC is traced going from its prehistory, decision-making stage on to its

establishment and the period when the ERC attained an operational definition of its primary objectives and developed, adapted and implemented its
rules and procedures. The chapter then extracts some possible lessons on
the dynamics of institution building in the Europe of Knowledge from the
case of the ERC. We then conclude the chapter.

## ACCOUNTING FOR INSTITUTION BUILDING

Institutions very rarely arise from a clean slate but come about via institutions and might build on and challenge existing institutional arrangements.
In this respect theories of institution building are essentially also theories
of institutional change, the difference being the analytical focus on creation
processes (see Scott 2008, pp. 94–120). Consequently, theoretical diversity
is as paramount when it comes to accounting for institution building as
it is for institutional change in general. Theories of institution building
provide varying expectations as to what the sources of institutions are, how
the process of institution building unfolds and what the effects of creating
new institutions are likely to be. Theoretical diversity covers theories that
assume that institutions can be wilfully designed as well as theories that
highlight the limits of intentionality, rationality and control in creating
new institutions (Olsen 2010).

A *first perspective* sees institution building as driven by functional
requirements. The consequences of an institutional arrangement are
used to explain its existence and persistence (Scott 2008; Tallberg 2008).
The roots of such arguments are within economic organization theory
assuming a rational foundation of institutions. The structure of firms, for
instance, can be explained by their functional efficiency, a choice between
'markets and hierarchies'. Choice of organizational forms reflects the need
to minimize transaction costs in economic exchanges (Williamson 1981).
In the study of international relations the argument is that 'states create
international institutions in attempts to resolve problems they cannot solve
alone' (Mitchell and Keilbach 2001, p. 891) and that the structure of the
cooperation problem defines the institutional solutions.[2] In the study of the
EU the functional perspective has in particular been deployed to account
for the structural choice involved when authority is delegated to EU institutions (Tallberg 2002). As noted by Egeberg et al. (2009), this argument has
also been prevalent in the literature on the creation of EU level agencies.

Introducing actorhood to this argument incorporates the idea that the
creation of institutions is the result of instrumental action taken by political administrative executives to further collective goals through institutional design (see Olsen 1997; 1992 for an examination of this account).

Single or collective actors design new institutions in order to achieve fairly well-defined goals. New institutions emerge in response to new problems that confront political and administrative leadership and the process of crafting new institutions is marked by problem-solving. Leaders in control have insight into the relative problem-solving effectiveness of alternative institutional design solutions.

A *second perspective* sees institutions as the reflection of the power constellations of actors. Similar to a 'problem-driven' account of institution building, it is essentially an instrumental view but one that underlines the political nature of such processes and the multiple and conflicting interests that are involved in the design of institutions. Building institutions is a matter of choice made by actors who know what they want (fixed preferences), have the insight into the factors that realize these interests and the control over the factors that can realize them (power). In a power-oriented perspective a new institution represents the elongation of the most powerful and resourceful actors' interests. Institutions are 'the structural means by which political winners pursue their own interests, often at the great expense of political losers' (Moe 1990, p. 213). They come about through the politics of structural choice and a process where actors struggle to control the exercise of public authority. Inherent in such an idea is that institutions are 'designable', the creators will have sufficient resources and insight to be able to anticipate what kind of structure will enhance their interests. The structure of an institution can be deduced from the interests and insights of its creators and from the bargains struck between contending parties and the actors that mobilize around different interests. Power play among actors will be the most visible aspect of the process of institution building. Hence asymmetrical power relationships will shape the design. Institutions are, by the same token, changeable and expendable. Once the interests change or there are power shifts among those who created them, institutions will cease to exist or be redesigned in order to accommodate such changes. They will be sustainable only to the extent that their proven effects serve the interests of their creators. For institution building in the context of the EU, this perspective sees *member states* as the key actors (McNamara 2001, p. 157), along with other key EU level actors with conflicting interests and competing alternatives for institutional design (see Gornitzka and Metz 2014, this volume, for an elaboration of this argument). New institutions will be structured in ways that support the interests of the dominant states or coalition of states. Actors with conflicting interests and in a position to block the preferred institutional design are dealt with through bargaining and side-payments. The main factor accounting for institutional design is the expected *distributional* effects of institutions and how they serve or not serve powerful actors' interests (Tallberg 2010).

A *third perspective*, a diffusionist perspective, sees the shape of organizations as the adaption to environmental pressures underlining the imperative of hegemonic templates and scripts. General rules and norms in the larger cultural environment are seen as the source of new institutions (Meyer and Rowan 1977). Rather than seeing institutions as solutions to functional problems, or driven by bargaining among actors, their establishment is 'solution driven' and reflects the adjustment to such widely held ideas and a normative-ideational pressure within an organizational field (Strang and Meyer 1993; Tolbert and Zucker 1983). In particular under conditions of ambiguity and uncertainty the creation of a new institution will reflect the creator's symbolic need to dress the political order with certain types of institutions according to 'waves' of prelegitimated institutional forms. It is not actors with interests attached to substantive and distributive consequences of alternative institutional designs that push through the birth of new institutions, but powerful norms and ideas about institutional structure. *Mimetic* and normative diffusion are two main explanatory ideas (DiMaggio and Powell 1983) that we can expect to be particularly relevant to institution building in the EU. This perspective is likely to be an apt account of how ways of organizing political sectors spread internationally via and between international organizations and national political systems. Although a diffusionist perspective has been under attack for not paying analytical attention to the role of agency, several scholars have developed the overall argument to include the role of actors that carry formal institutional models, such as professional organizations, consultants and international organizations (for example, Finnemore 1993). These kinds of actors are likely to be present in institution building processes according to this perspective. Significant symbolic and legitimizing effects from adopting particular formal structures are likely to ensue irrespective of substantive, distributive effects or lack thereof.

Although empirical work within this perspective tends to focus on diffusion at a system's level, the relevance of such forces are found in accounting for the shape of single institutions in the context of the EU. For instance, McNamara (2001) argues for factoring in such ideational and normative forces in her account of the establishment and structure of the European Central Bank, and Groenleer (2009) finds that the creation of EU agencies also has elements of such a dynamic pointing to how EU level agencies are part of a general wave for creating (semi)independent regulatory agencies, a trend that has travelled among national polities through public sector reforms.

However, this perspective accords considerable weight to what can be seen as environmental deterministic forces (March and Olsen 1998). It does not square easily with an understanding of institutions as 'relatively invariant in the face of turnover of individuals and relatively resilient to the idiosyncratic preferences and expectations of individuals and changing external circumstances' (March and Olsen 2006, p. 3).

A *fourth perspective*, an institutional-cultural perspective, highlights how new institutions do not arise automatically as a response to environmental demands, or from choices made on a clean slate, but from processes that are impacted by institutional robustness (Olsen and Peters 1996). Institutions are likely to be moulded by the pre-existing institutional arrangements that exist in the close context within which institutional birth processes take place. Yet, institutional resilience does not equal institutional inertia. Institutions enable and capacitate institutional change. Actors build new institutions through (re)interpreting existing arrangements, clarifying vague ones and exploiting institutional voids (Caporaso and Stone Sweet 2001, p. 235). This implies that we have to take into consideration the institutional context and history from which new institutions arise and expect to see *incremental processes* of institution building that use established institutional arrangements to create new ones. The possibility of design from such a perspective requires the actors' attention to the legitimacy of institutional forms: being sensitive to traditions of the past and perceptions of what is reasonable, legitimate and appropriate (Olsen 1997). Furthermore, if 'history matters' then path dependencies, sequencing and timing of events prior to formal decisions to establish new institutions will be crucial in accounting for their shape and form (see Gornitzka and Metz 2014, this volume, for more on the path-dependency argument). This also implies paying attention to contingent events that can trigger change (Pierson 2004, p. 18).

Likewise, a proper account of institution building cannot stop at the point of formal decision. Here the classic formulations in institutional and organization theory are very clear. Institutionalization, according to Selznick, is the process where formal structures are given life and come to be infused with value 'beyond the technical requirement of the task at hand' (Selznick 1966, p. 17). Selznick's distinction between institution and organization rests on this insight. Also Simon (1976[1945]) demonstrates how a new organization can grow quickly and assume a reasonably coherent form without having been planned or subject to a deliberate choice. The structure and identities of a new organization are moulded by internal conditions and the interaction the institution has with its environment. The initial period in the life cycle of institutions is the stage where a new body is in search of its own mission, form, role and identity and a time when it develops routines and capacity for handling contingencies and for learning from its own experiences. The process of giving life to the organizational skeleton then takes the form of a learning process: a 'learning process in which growing insights and successive restructuring of the problem as it appears to the humans dealing with it, reflect themselves in the structural elements of the organization itself' (Simon 1976[1945], p. 334).

Handling theoretical diversity represents some challenges for exploring empirical cases of institution building. Such processes commonly span years and a number of events. Hence they are unlikely to be subject to one dynamic alone and be accounted for by one single perspective. The four accounts of institution building sketched out above may be more or less relevant at different stages of this process. Tallberg (2010) sensibly suggests taking on a domain of application approach rather than competitive testing of alternative explanations. Different accounts can be expected to be more or less relevant for some aspects and stages of institution building over others. Tallberg argues with respect to the foundations of the EU's negotiating institutions that *functional* demands are likely to have the most explanatory power for institutional creation, while *ideational diffusion* is central to the institutional structure, and *power differentials* are vital for the organization's distributive terms (Tallberg 2010). These considerations have implications for how to study institution building also in the case offered here. We then would expect that the ERC as a new type of institution to be brought to the agenda of the EU through the identification of a particular and new common action problem. The ERC would be matched with this problem as an institutional novelty through an instrumental process of problem-solving (pre-decision phase). The structure of the ERC on the other hand would be influenced by hegemonic ideas of how to organize distributive institutions, whereas the actual rules of distribution would be determined by the bargaining of self-interested actors with their eyes on the foreseeable distributive consequences of the new institution (decision stage). The institutional-cultural perspective is expected to account for how the practices of the ERC took shape in the post-decision stage. Expecting the relevance of theoretical accounts to vary according to different stages of institution building, we use a process approach to identify how institution building has happened over time in a series of occurrences. The evidence of how the processes have evolved is drawn from nine in-depth informant interviews (Commission officials, Council officials and stakeholders), the study of official documents and other written data sources, as well as data provided by other studies of relevance to this case.

## 'RESEARCH COUNCIL' – A CONCEPT WITH A HISTORY AND LEGACY

The research council as a model for how to organize public funding of research spread across Europe in the post-war period – a model that was intricately linked to the public involvement in national systems of science and research. Most commonly national research councils tended to have three tasks: quality control, allocation decisions and a research policy advisory function. Beyond these characteristics there was considerable variation in terms of organizational structures, institutional roles, disciplinary scope, the autonomy of its operations and how activities were funded (Braun 1998; Caswill 2003). Most commonly, research councils were positioned as intermediary bodies between government and research with considerable involvement of the academia in the governance and distributive practices of these bodies. Funding agencies tended to represent a combination of 'parliaments of the scientific community' and 'governmental bureaucracies' at (varying) arm's length from direct political and ministerial intervention (Van der Meulen 1998). Consequently, establishing a research council involves specialization of research policy functions where funding decisions are neither directly in the hands of a ministry nor left to the research performing institutions themselves. A main change in national research operations was the introduction of large scale research programmes as an additional and core way of organizing funding in national research councils in the 1980s (Benner and Sandstrom 2000). With these programmes an additional role of research councils was to identify a priori the research topics that should be given priority in their funding decisions (Most 2009, pp. 2–3). These developments made the research council as an organizational concept multifaceted with few unique instructions for how to build such an institution.

The international and European funding mechanisms for research have deep roots. Various initiatives were introduced especially in the 1950s that entailed some measure of resource allocation beyond the nation state level. The main model was not supranational but intergovernmental, also for the big basic science organizations such as CERN (The European Organization for Nuclear Research) and EMBL (The European Molecular Biology Laboratory).[3] In the long prehistory that ran up to the establishment of the European Science Foundation (ESF established 1974), the Nordic countries and the Netherlands voiced ideas about establishing a European organization modelled on the US National Science Foundation (US NSF), that is some version of a European research council. However the national research councils established the ESF as an alternative consensus-oriented coordinating body that did not challenge their own prerogative in funding basic research in nationally diverse ways (Gronbaek 2003). In effect the ESF as a funding body had a scant basis for acting relatively independently from national research funding bodies. The idea of a 'European NSF' or European Research Council had thus hovered in the ideational landscape for decades without materializing (Darmon 1997).

The organizational model for European funding for research which did materialize in the 1980s picked up the spirit of the time: the establishment of large research programmes. The multi-annual research programme (Framework Programmes, FPs) in 1984 made the European Commission a significant research funding agent in Europe. The European Commission's Directorate-General for Research and Technological Development (DG Research or DG RTD) became the FPs' main organizer, in charge of preparation and implementation. It provided permanent administrative capabilities to the distribution of research money and administration of research programmes directly and not via the national ministries/funding agencies. The FPs grew in scale and scope and became a major factor in European research. The FP model and administrative machinery became heavily institutionalized practices for funding research and development (R&D), a path dependency from which it was difficult to escape (Banchoff 2002). The member states were involved in decision-making on the shape and profile of the FPs through the Council of Ministers. The European Parliament's (EP) formal involvement increased along with the overall empowerment of the EP in EU decision-making. Member states could also oversee the implementation through the many FP comitology committees. The FPs further triggered and sustained the mushrooming of transnational organizations. Having an FP to administer and implement, the Commission became the main access point for stakeholders and transnational actors, for non-governmental organizations (NGOs) and lobbying groups from academia, business interests and research funding agencies (Grande and Peschke 1999). In particular, with an extensive use of its expert group system, the DG Research coupled such organized groups and independent experts to research policy development (Gornitzka and Sverdrup 2008).

The structure of the FPs was supranational (its profile, scope and scale decided by the EU institutions under 'the first pillar' with a dense set of decision-making and executive rules), no *juste retour*, geared toward applicability and stimulation of transnational cooperation and 'European added value'. The priorities were set a priori and according to the EU's thematic emphases. Hence the FPs were institutionalized with an elaborate set of rules defining appropriate behaviour in how to implement the programmes and how to change and adapt them. It embodied a specific understanding of the rationale and problems/solutions underpinning EU research policy and was geared towards economic and social applicability of research. Moreover, there were administrative and financial resources to uphold these rules, norms and ideas. These traits would lead us to expect that the major actors in EU research policy would resist ideas to establish the ERC, an institution that represented 'contrary' rules of distribution and different understandings of what constituted Europe's policy problems and solutions, an idea that in addition was marred with a history of failure.

# BUILDING THE EUROPEAN RESEARCH COUNCIL

### The Pre-Decision Stage and Initial Conditions

The odds were stacked against any radical institutional break with the FP concept. Nonetheless, under the Swedish Presidency in spring 2001 European level discussions on a European research council became audible. A community of elite European scientists and science policy-makers with ideas for a radical change of European research policy found the Nordic states as coalition partners at the political level who formally launched the ERC on the political agenda (Interview EURAB, 1 February 2011). In April 2002 an international meeting in Stockholm of leading scientists and administrators started the sketching out of what an ERC could be. The radical idea of a new independent denationalized research council had already gained support from leading science policy voices in France and Germany in this early period. The initiative was ideationally underpinned by the arguments provided by a leading professor of science policy, Ken Pavitt, for why Europe needed an entirely new EU level funding of academic research (Pavitt 2000). Under the Danish Presidency in October 2002 – the Danish Research Councils, cooperating with the ESF, the Swedish Research Council and the Commission, organized a conference entitled 'Towards a European Research Area: Do we need a European Research Council?'. The conference organizers concluded that an ERC was backed by a broad majority of the participants and was given careful support from the Commissioner for Research Busquin[4] (see Gronbaek 2003 for an in-depth description of the actors' arguments and positions in the pre-decision stage). The idea was established at the time that the new funding structure would cover all fields of knowledge, including the humanities and social sciences. In the Council of Ministers, under its then President, Danish Minister Helge Sander, European research ministers agreed to continue the discussion on an ERC and announced at the Council meeting on 26 November 2002 to 'explor[e] the options for its possible creation'.[5] The Council in the same meeting recognized some of the early defining characteristics of a future ERC: the proposal entailed 'scientific excellence' and that '[f]unding decisions would be based exclusively on scientific criteria'.[6] For the academics pursuing the ERC the developments during the Danish Presidency in 2002 presented 'the first political breakthrough for the ERC' (Interview EURAB, 1 February 2011). From then on the ERC was on the official EU agenda. An expert group established by the Competitiveness Council and led by Spanish Professor Mayor worked on elaborating what this idea could contain.[7] Presented in December 2003 the Mayor Report laid down what was seen as a central principle for the new construction: its main task should be to support investigator-driven research of the highest quality selected through European competition.

So what had happened for this idea to penetrate the agenda of the EU in an area that had seemingly been hostile to a new institution of this kind? First, we should be attentive to the contingent events: an opportunity presented itself in what the EU institutions were busy doing at the time. The new Commissioner for Research, Busquin, had come with another relaunch of an 'old' Community idea: establishing the European Research Area (ERA) (see Chou 2014, this volume). This was coupled to the Lisbon Strategy by timing and ideational congruence. R&D investment and area construction were heralded as a key to a competitive Europe by the heads of states. Yet the member states' interests were not dominant in the launching of the ERC idea. Far from it. The heads of states, aiming to keep the funding of basic research at the national level, were in the beginning not attentive to this idea (Interview DG RTD, 27 May 2009). There were no identifiable shifts in power constellations or changes in political preferences over European research policy in this early stage that can account for the ERC ending up on the EU decision-making agenda. National distributional consequences of an ERC were also not in the focus at this stage. However, the ministers of research acting in the role as Council Presidents were essential, as was the backstage work of national bureaucrats in Northern Europe. The ERC entered into the decision-making machinery of the EU. Once on the agenda, it stuck.

Nor was there an obvious 'new' collective action problem that needed a new institutional solution. The list of needs that the ERC could accommodate was long. Changing interpretations of what was the European predicament came to the surface. The ERC came with an ideational contestation, especially triggered by Ken Pavitt's publication from 2000. He challenged the idea of the 'European paradox', the widely held EU policy theory of the time, namely that Europe performs better relative to the US in academic research but is nonetheless unable to translate scientific advances into marketable innovations (Pavitt 2000). European academic research is not equal to the state of academic research in the US, Pavitt argued. His solution was the following: copy the way the US federal level organizes its funding. If so, the argument went, Europe could make a radical and necessary break with the EU research policy and its (dysfunctional) institutional legacies for the funding of research. A similar ideational shift was also promoted through organized policy/expert communities. Alternative beliefs contesting the usefulness of the practices and distributional principles of the FPs were for instance also held by the Swedish Committee for the Reform of European Research Policy (CNERP) established in 2001. This high profile Committee consisting of basic science funders, the Nobel Foundation and top-notch scientists[8] were instrumental in bringing the ERC onto the Swedish Presidency agenda and in carrying the idea over to the Danish Minister and Danish research councils.[9] Also the Dutch Ministry for Science and Education in preparation for the Dutch Presidency (autumn 2004) worked on the ERC idea and on establishing support for the ERC in member states capitals. Next to the strong supporters of the radically new ERC idea at national level, there were initially several actors sceptical towards establishing a big independent research council (see Gronbaek 2003).

The emerging new understanding of Europe's needs spread via the extensive consultations with stakeholders held by the Council's expert group on the ERC (Mayor Group). This unleashed considerable energy and attention among prestigious expert communities and organizations for European science in support of the need for an ERC. In the front line were the ESF[10] and the European Life Sciences Forum (ELSF), covering key life science organizations in Europe (the European Molecular Biology Organization, the European Molecular Biology Laboratory and Federation of Biomedical Societies), followed by other organizations such as the All European Academies (ALLEA), Academia Europaea and the European Research Advisory Board (EURAB). Both the ELSF and EURAB were key organizations in generating support for the ERC, developing its idea and mustering political-administrative support for an institution like this to see the light of day. The ELSF hired a coordinator that organized meetings in 2003 to discuss the shape of the ERC.[11] The ELSF also worked to bolster support for the ERC from other scientific fields. EURAB, a central European level stakeholder expert group, played an important role as the main driving force in promoting the idea of the ERC 'in the discussion, in the political debate, in the acceptance, in the way of how this thing would be structured, etc.' (Interview DG RTD, 10 November 2010).

These organizations brought to the table a full menu of European problems for which the ERC could be the solution: deep societal and economic problems of the EU, problems of academic quality, problems of European coordination and global competitiveness. The US federal funding agencies were again widely promoted as the object of emulation.

Yet at the pre-decision stage these organizations and individuals linked to them produced an array of different visions of what the structure of the ERC should look like. (1) What should be its task structure? (2) How should it be funded? (3) What kind of formal autonomy should it have from other EU institutions, from member states and from stakeholders?

(4) How should it relate to existing funding institutions at the European and national levels? The Mayor Report also lined up the full panoply of problems that an ERC could solve. But the solutions to these problems were weakly reflected in this Group's proposal for how to structure the new institution. One of the more prevalent concerns in this Report was nevertheless how to create a structure that could 'exploit the capacity for self-government of the research community',[12] hence secure agency autonomy and the legitimacy of the new institution in the European academic community. However, the Report left the question of legal status open but proposed the setting up of an independent European fund as the basis of the ERC.

Through ideational shifts and coinciding events, and several actors working for the idea both within the scientific community and within the administrative sphere, these streams of participants met in the pre-decision stage. As such, an idea with an ill-fated past thus made its way into the EU's decision-making resources and gained support from the scientific elites of Europe, national agencies and the EU institutions in the policy field. Actors in the ERC inception acted on an organized basis and also actively created capacity for action in order to promote the idea. The EU member states' political leadership were not prominent as proponents or as veto-points in this early stage. On the contrary, by 'skilfully circumventing the political actors, and most importantly [most] member states' (Interview Council, 4 November 2010), the scientific community managed to set the ERC on the EU decision-making agenda. Neither was there an automatic translation of a vague and partly conflicting idea of the ERC at the time, although some of the actors presented this as a necessity carried 'by time'.[13]

**The ERC Decision**

Like many of the actors in the research policy field, the Commission was in a state of conditional support, not resistance, and uncertain about what the ERC actually entailed. Some parts of the Commission had concerns as the ERC 'was really complicated also from a legal point of view', given that basic research does not fit into the Community's mandate, which is primarily to support European industry and European policies (Interview DG RTD, 27 May 2009; Interview DG RTD, 26 May 2009). Again others 'saw it more as a taxation: The more the ERC got, the less they would get' (Interview DG RTD, 26 May 2009). However, given the growing support for an ERC in the academic world, also the Commission gradually adopted the idea. In 2003 Commission President Prodi's Committee on 'An Agenda for a Growing Europe'[14] was aware of the ERC idea and recommended an agency modelled on the US NSF and Nordic countries/UK research councils. Consequently, the broad ERC idea had been legitimized outside the more narrow circles of the research policy elite in Europe. Judging from the documentary evidence, in this initial stage the role of the Commission's DG Research was not a frontline defender of the institutional innovation that the ERC represented. The Commission's Research Director General had already in 2002 expressed support for the ERC 'to the great surprise' of a smaller audience at a meeting organized by the ELSF. Initially the Commission DG Research's position had been perceived as hostile[15] given the scientific community's demand for autonomy from the Commission in running the ERC (Interview DG RTD, 27 May 2009). The Mayor Report invited the Commission to join in the preparations for setting up the ERC together with the member states. By 2004, DG Research clearly supported the process.[16] The idea meshed with the Commission's intensified attention to university policy and carving out a role for the EU in basic science as part of the ERA.[17] From 2004 onwards the DG Research used its own policy development capacity and brought the process further into the political domain as a tangible proposal. The other Commission services now perceived the introduction of an ERC as a 'fait accompli' (Interview DG RTD, 26 May 2009) or an 'inevitableness' (Interview DG RTD, 27 May 2009).

DG Research approached this in a consultative manner, especially drawing on its core group of experts (EURAB), the European Heads of Research Councils (EUROHORCs)[18] and science policy experts. First, it produced a Communication on Europe and basic science featuring the ERC idea. The Commission then set-up a High Level Group for the ERC in 2005 using its standard operating procedure for how to establish new proposals and anchor them in the respective stakeholder and expert communities. The Commission endorsed the ideational and normative underpinnings that had come during the pre-decision stage. Following the ERC High Level Group the justification for the ERC was linked to a change in terminology: what Europe needed was an institution supporting 'frontier research', rather than basic research. Moreover, member states' subsidiarity concerns were met by arguing that the ERC created added value by stimulating competition at the supranational level (Interview EURAB, 1 February 2011; Interview EURAB, 28 February 2011). The Commission proposed to make the *ERC part of the FP7* as a separate programme (the 'Ideas' programme within FP7).

This had implications for the process of institution building and the ERC's institutional design. When the ERC idea became part of the FP7 proposal from the Commission it was carried into the large and highly complex, regulated decision-making of the FPs that operated with a strict timetable. The link to the FP7 made the biggest impact on the funding base of the ERC – money was entirely supranational drawn from the general FP budget, and not conditioned by contributions from national funding bodies or industry sponsors. Although the Commission did not get the substantial increase in the overall budget for R&D it initially had proposed, there was fresh money added to the coffers of the FP through the EU's financial perspective. The budgetary increase was sufficient for the ERC to be funded without directly impinging on other parts of the FP. This was undoubtedly a path setting connection and one that created a very different funding structure to the ones that had been envisioned earlier in the process. The principle of 'excellence only' as a distributive rule was left untouched by the FP7 connection. This was confirmed by the Commission's proposal, as were the need for institutional independence and the arguments for such independence. The first sign of institutionalizing the ERC's academic autonomy and governance structure came before the Council and the EP formally decided on the FP7: 22 researchers were selected as the founding members of the ERC Scientific Council – in part recruited from the community that had initially promoted an ERC (Interview EURAB, 22 December 2010). ERC Scientific Council met for the first time in October 2005. The ERC now had its own institutional defenders.

**The Politics of the ERC Decision**

The discussions over the ERC moved into a different setting. Yet the spillover from the preparatory phase lingered on with an aura of appropriateness around the ERC idea. Discussions and papers prior to 2005 had massaged some of the key actors into support of the idea (Interview EURAB, 22 December 2010; Interview EURAB, 1 February 2011). The British parliamentary debate over the FP7 is illustrative in this respect. Several British actors had been sceptical, partly from the EU-sceptical reflex also in this policy domain. However, the British Under-Secretary of State for Science and Innovation, Lord Sainsbury, clearly promoted the ERC domestically. Hearings in Parliament reported that the ERC could be modelled on the best UK and US NSF practice of peer review.[19] In line with a power-oriented perspective on institution building, the member states with the stronger research base clearly anticipated the distributional effects of the fundamental principle of the ERC – 'excellence only' – and this argument was used on the national arena.[20]

In the political discussion on the ERC at the EU level the Italian government voiced the strongest objections against the basic principles of the ERC as proposed by the Commission. The territorial conflict line was activated. The Italian ministry described the ERC as 'perplexing'[21] objecting to the ERC excluding transnationality (multinational research teams) as a funding criterion. Here Italy joined a group of member states

(Spain, Greece, Portugal and Slovakia, the 'southern' member states). But on this issue the Commission and the 'northern' flank of member states (Denmark, Germany, France, Austria, Netherlands and Sweden) did not compromise. The 'excellence only' criterion had an overwhelming majority and with little prospect of gaining much leeway in the EP, the southern member states did not pursue their initial position (Muldur et al. 2006). In the ERC's rules of distribution, national concerns were excluded altogether.

The discussions over the ERC *administrative* structure and legal status pitted the supranational against the intergovernmental perspective. How should the ERC be structured in order to ensure the ERC's autonomy from member states and from the Commission respectively? The Commission proposed setting up the administrative side of the ERC as an executive agency – a legal body ultimately answerable to the Commission. Some member states favoured establishing the ERC as a legal entity entirely separate from the Commission (Article 171 TEU entity). This position was supported by the main scientific organizations from France, Germany, Poland, Spain and the UK and by some members of the EP. The Commission argued that an independent ERC, separate from the Commission, could be vulnerable to the principle of *'juste retour'*, thus weakening the criteria of scientific merit.[22] The then recently appointed President of the ERC Scientific Council also supported the Commission's proposal on the ERC's status. Some member states, in turn, feared the ERC to become devoid of any political influence whatsoever, which would carry risks in the long run (Interview Council, 4 November 2010). The compromise entailed that the ERC initially would become an executive agency answerable to the Commission but with the option of it becoming an independent structure.

The FP7 decision turned out to be a highly nationally sensitive issue. However, the overt conflict between member states as well as between the Commission and some of the member states, was not in the end over the path-breaking decision to establish the ERC, but over European funding of stem cell research (Interview DG RTD, 4 September 2009). On 18 December 2006, following its adoption by the EP, the Ideas programme and its seven-year €7.5 billion budget got the formal stamp of approval[23] and the day after the Council left it to the Commission to formally establish the ERC.[24] For the ERC the FP7 decision implied that it did not become an institution in legal terms but that the financial basis of the ERC was a reality, at least until the end of 2013. The Commission decision formally established the ERC on 2 February 2007 specifying the main organizational structure and principles for its operation. Table 4.1 shows the ERC's organization structure.

*Table 4.1 ERC's organizational structure*

---

ERC Scientific Council
- 22 members on four-year terms (renewable), appointed by the Commission
- Composed of 'scientists, engineers and scholars of highest repute'
- Task I: establish overall strategy and work programme, responsible for scientific operations and control of quality, and 'have full authority over decisions on the type of research to be funded'
- Task II: communicate with scientific community
- Elects President of the Scientific Council and two Vice-Presidents amongst its members
- Shall operate in an 'autonomous and independent manner'
- Where appropriate shall consult with scientific, engineering and scholarly community
- Is accountable to the Commission
- Commission is the 'guarantor of the Scientific Council's autonomy and integrity'
- Commission adopts annual work programme established by the Scientific Council

ERC Board*
- Consists of the ERC President, two Vice-Presidents, Director of (DIS)ERCEA and Secretary General
- Monitoring implementation of strategy and work programme of the ERC

Secretary General of ERC
- Selected by the Scientific Council, which also determines the Secretary's tasks
- Be a link between the Scientific Council and the ERC Executive Agency (DIS)

ERC Executive Agency (until July 2009 Dedicated Implementation Structure, DIS)
- Based in Brussels (Covent Garden building, Place Rogier)
- Set-up like all Executive Agencies by a specific Council Regulation
- Manages exclusively the Ideas programme (part of the EU's FP7), in line with the requirement to establish a 'Dedicated Implementation Structure' for the ERC
- Executes annual work programme
- Implements calls for proposals and organizes peer review evaluations
- Establishes and manages grant agreements
- Information to applicants and grant holders
- As for all Executive Agencies, it is managed by a Director and a Steering Committee (five members), Director and Committee members are appointed by the Commission

---

*Note:* * Not specified in the Commission decision of February 2007.

# FROM DECISION TO LIFE – THE ERC IN OPERATION

## Developing Rules for Academic Excellence

The challenges that the new institution had to face in a highly institution-alized European and national research policy arena and research system were considerable. The FP7 decision set out its overarching principles (scientific excellence only, no transnationality requirement), but did not provide an exhaustive template for how to organize the funding of excel-lence in research in practice, nor for the formulation of its specific mission. Yet the ERC's Scientific Council had already been put in place and had started acting on the ERC's behalf specifying its mission and modus oper-andi. It had already worked on the basic principles of the ERC peer review structure[25] and the first work programme of the ERC,[26] determining among other things the distribution of the budget over the main research domains[27] and the rules for the two types of grants with which they started out. The Scientific Council and the Board of the ERC continued to establish the rules for the scientific operations of the new institution (a Board had subsequently been added, see below). Much of the meetings and energy of the Scientific Council went into specifying the rules and terms of its scientific activity and adjusting its instructions and work pro-gramme to the experiences of the ERC's first months and semesters.[28] This included developing rules for handling the unanticipated, such as the flood of applications (9,000) that it received in the first call of the starting grants, and smaller additions to its policy, such as developing a policy for how to define what qualifies as the equivalent of a Ph.D.,[29] what the ERC should do with the money when a Principal Investigator dies.[30] The Scientific Council developed a pattern for how to interact with external constituen-cies – also addressing for instance its relationship to industry, the major FP7 stakeholder whose concerns were not directly reflected in the organi-zational structure of the ERC, and how to position itself to external events, such as the launch of the 'Innovation Union'.

This gradual process of specifying rules, tasks and procedures was a combination of learning from experience and borrowing from practices of peer review processes elsewhere[31] with reference to what were academi-cally appropriate procedural norms. The Scientific Council built on these and translated them into its own procedures. And it had leeway to do so: the actual process of project selection was indeed a clean break with the FPs traditional model. In these terms the new entity had considerable independence. *Vis-à-vis* the Scientific Council and Board, the Commission was seen to act according to a norm of non-intrusion (Vike-Freiberga et al. 2009).

The *governance structure* underlined the absence of national representation, both of the political level and from the national funding agencies. The ERC as the FP7 Ideas programme 'inherited' a programme committee (Comitology) with member state representation that oversees its implementation (all FP subprogrammes must have one). Yet this programme committee had, as it turned out, no say in how the ERC was run and in its allocative decisions. The ERC had managed to establish and demarcate its role *vis-à-vis* the nation state level from the start. The Scientific Council in its structure was 'nation free'. As pointed out by the first Secretary General of the ERC, Winnacker, the number of members of the Scientific Council (22) already implied autonomy from the member state constituency in so far as all 27 EU member states could not have a seat (Winnacker 2008, p. 126). Furthermore, the Scientific Council members are not representatives of specific organizations or interests groups but elected on the basis of their academic merits by an independent Selection Committee.

## Developing an Institutional Identity and a Role in the Larger Order of European Research Governance

The ERC was expected and took it upon itself to do more than formulate distributive rules and execute them. The Scientific Council's own mission statement stated that it 'looks substantially to strengthen and shape the European research system'.[32] At stake was also the role that an EU institution could play in the distribution of academic reputation, in defining the criteria for scientific assessment and the potential impact on the normative structures in academia. The ERC voiced ambitions of becoming the 'gold standard' in Europe.

The reputation of the ERC, not only as a potential pot of money, but as a standard setter was established fairly quickly (EURECIA 2012). It attracted the scientific elite as panel members and peer reviewers. Review procedures came to be valued by the applicants. The ERC gained a status within the academic community as an institution representing due process and adhering to the appropriate standards of what a research council should be. Transnational scientific organizations saw the ERC as an institution that supported the values they believed in and shared (EURECIA 2012, p. 107). This is a clear indication of the ERC becoming institutionalized within the European (elite) academic community. It became a 'living institution', hence much more than a research policy instrument and an 'expendable tool'.

The national funding agencies had not been attributed a direct role in the running of this organization. In this respect the ERC represents a bypassing of the national agency level. Despite this, the ERC gained a recognized place in the world of funding agencies in Europe (Vike-Freiberga et al. 2009, p. 17). This external validation should be seen as key to the institution building process. Most telling is the fact that several national research councils instituted rules that implied automatic funding for the ERC runners up.[33] The selection criteria based on excellence only seems to have gained a taken-for-granted status among the major constituency of the ERC and the EU research policy, despite the blatant skewed distributive effects produced by the ERC if viewed from a national perspective. The countries whose academic and science policy elites had been central in the process leading up to the ERC establishment were indeed overrepresented as grant holders. But so were the ERC host institutions from countries that were outside the EU decision-making bodies with no formal power to determine the shape of the FPs, such as Switzerland and Israel. With the current structure, the member states have very little possibility of redressing this distributive effect and to make sure that they will 'have their money back' from the ERC. It was easy to identify which member states were the 'short-term losers' and which research systems and institutions were the winners. To the extent that this is even an issue in the public domain, winner versus loser discussions have not been phrased as an attack on the ERC's institutional legitimacy. Illustrative in this respect is Poland, one of the biggest member states without much success in the ERC so far: the ERC is the organizational model for the most recent reorganization of the Polish research council system.

## Administrative Path Dependency

The ERC as a work organization has two pillars: the Scientific Council/ Board and its administrative structure. The latter started out as a 'Dedicated Implementation Structure' (DIS) with about 80 people. By the time it became an Executive Agency in 2009, it had over 200 staff members and a considerable number of national seconded personnel. It had its offices in a building separate from DG Research, underlining its physical independence from its 'mother DG Research'. However, the DIS/ ERC Executive Agency carried with it an administrative legacy. The dual structure of the ERC created the most salient tensions in the infancy of the ERC as a result of its administrative path dependency. It seemed that this part of the administrative structure of the ERC straddled two institutional allegiances, as a Research Council (institutional innovation) versus a Commission Agency (the path carved out). The attempt to reconcile the two parts of the ERC was soon reflected in its governance structure. The *ERC Board* had not been formally a mandated part but developed to help keep the dual structure of the ERC together.

The dual construction relied on the strict demarcation of a scientific domain versus a managerial/administrative domain. This turned out to be hard to maintain. The ERC Executive Agency is formally responsible for all aspects concerning programme implementation and execution. A core task of the Agency is to implement the peer review and selection processes according to the principles established by the Scientific Council and ensure the financial and scientific management of the grants. However, EU Executive Agencies are Community bodies with legal personality established by the Commission in order to implement by delegation EU spending programmes. Their main purpose is to alleviate the Commission of its administrative tasks and to save costs (European Court of Auditors 2009). In the case of the ERC the expectations of what an executive agency is and does clashed with what is deemed *appropriate* for a research council. The Review of the ERC from 2009 made it clear that the structure of the ERC Executive Agency and the way it was staffed was inappropriate: 'At the most fundamental level there is an incompatibility between the current governance philosophy, administrative rules and practices and the stated goals of the ERC' (Vike-Freiberga et al. 2009, p. 40).

Now the price to be paid for linking the ERC to the FP structure with its established rules and traditions became evident: the administrative lightness that was premised in the ERC visions was caught up in regulations that were general for the spending of EU funds. More than political pressure and expectations of national fair distribution, the administrative requirements were seen as a main threat to the ERC's sustainability as an institution that could attract the best scientists. This was especially true in the case of procedures for reimbursement and remuneration of panel members and reviewers. The institutionalization process was in the ERC's early days affected by the tension between the academic community's perception of due procedures and the formal administrative requirements and the way in which they were practised across the range of EU spending activities. The ERC was in the area of tension between the rules and regulations of the Commission and the academics' expectations of a light-footed, trust-based administrative system (Macilwain 2010). For an institutional account such observations are of relevance – the organizational form (Commission Executive Agency) and type of staff (Commission officials 'borrowed' from DG Research) can make one part of the institution operate on the basis of one set of norms of appropriate conduct that are at odds with other parts of the institution and with its environment. Stepping down as President of the ERC Scientific Council, Kafatos (2010, p. 1) commented:

> An overly strict control culture permeates the Commission. We continuously had to spend energy, time and effort on busting bureaucracy roadblocks that

kept appearing in our way. At best, this costs us precious energy and resources. At worst it may hamper our zeal to inspire and continuously improve the ERC strategy, it can damage the morale of our staff and discourage the top talented researchers from applying to or reviewing for the ERC.

Yet, this might not be a permanent state of tension, but alleviated over time as the institution gains experience, adjusts and even exports administrative rules to other parts of the FP (see EURECIA 2012). Despite these internal tensions occurring in a process of institutional change the ERC and the warning set out by its scientific promoters, in practice the ERC more generally has not failed to live up to the many expectations that were attached to the newborn institution. So far, the ERC is still considered as a symbol of European excellence in science.

## LESSONS ON INSTITUTION BUILDING IN THE EUROPE OF KNOWLEDGE FROM N = ERC

What then are the lessons to be learned about the dynamics of institution building and institutionalization from the analysis of the ERC case? As an institution the ERC has several transformative dimensions. It is a tangible expression of a change in *ideas and norms* (the kind of research policy that is appropriate and acceptable for the EU level to be concerned with), change in *rules* ('excellence only' principle), the structure of *resources* (placing about 15 per cent of the FP budget in the hands of the academic community, away from national political steering and out of reach from business and industrial stakeholders), and it is an institutional innovation with distributive consequences. Its governance structure grants considerable leeway for the academic community to conduct its operations independently from national concerns and interests and has been able to maintain and develop these structures (relatively) independently of personal idiosyncrasies and changing external demands. These characteristics of the ERC case challenge some of the theoretically anchored ideas about institutional inertia, or actors that represent veto points cemented by their vested national or other interests in status quo. Institutions can be built also in areas where we would predict preferences for status quo to prevail (cf. Banchoff 2002). The ERC was established despite involving the supranationalization of nation state prerogatives (funding of fundamental research run as a member states' domain) and despite breaking radically with the principles of the existing EU institutions.

Returning to our first theoretical argument on institution building:

can the creation of new institutions be accounted for by a functional-instrumental perspective? In this case concerns for functional efficiency, the needs of Europe and the inadequacy of the existing institutional arrangements, were a driving element in the call for a new institution, especially in the pre-decision stage. Actors presented their arguments for the new institution as a 'functional need' – the following quote is illustrative: 'The ERC is already a success. Why? Because Europe desperately needs it'.[34] There was also an important ideational shift and contestation that identified the 'need' in a new way. The fundamental principle of scientific independence for the ERC was argued on the basis of functional requirements. The pre-decision stage was heavily laden with several actors with high levels of expertise and reputation in the relevant policy domain, working on promoting the ERC as a solution to the problems of European research system(s) and on possible alternatives for structuring the new institutions. Building institutions in this case has clear elements of problem-solving and the matching institutional structures to several common European problems. Yet, its structure cannot be read as the consequence of an automatic and unique match to particular functional needs and functional needs cannot in themselves explain the building process. It was certainly not a case of instrumental design instigated and controlled from the top political leadership of the EU. Although the label 'excellence'/'research council' activated some actors (elite scientific communities) more than others (for example, industry), in the pre-decision stage the process was open for a range of problems, needs and solutions to be tossed into the process, and link between institutional format and the goal of 'excellence' and 'frontier research' was uncertain. Moreover, the concerns for the legitimacy of the innovation as well as the instrumental problem-solving value of it were present all along. Hence, *lesson number 1:* building an institution requires more than actors who identify a need; and the study of it requires taking into account how the shape of institutions reflects shared ideas and norms of what constitutes appropriate and legitimate institutional structures. Both causal and normative ideas are developed and massaged over time in collective processes that are unlikely to be controllable by one coherent set of actors.

*Lesson number 2:* in institution building powerful actors are *confined* by context and norms. The power-oriented perspective sees institution building as a matter of deliberate choice with distributional effects as the dominant concern. This process cannot be accounted for by reference to strong member states' will and control over institutional creation, or by pointing to the Commission as the engine of supranational institution building to increase its remit of responsibility. The role of transnational actors, notably academic elites and basic science spokespersons, in the inception of the ERC and after its establishment tells another story. This is particularly the case in the pre- and post-decision stage. Yet, stakeholders had little control over the factors that could realize their overarching idea, implying that the member states and the Commission had an important role to play in the decision stage of the ERC story. Also in the pre-decision stage stakeholder groups liaising with national research ministries was undeniably a key explanation for why it came in the EU agenda. Later on the member states with the prospect of winning the European level excellence competition continued to be (or became) supporters of the ERC. In the decision stage those member states were important for getting the ERC idea past formal decision-making hurdles. Whereas a majority of the member states and candidate countries had good reasons to expect to be ERC losers, only a limited set of them actually voiced their concern. Why? Their formal position papers indicate that national distributive concerns were deemed to be subordinate to the value that the new institution represented. In highly normatively laden policy domains the display of national interests is curbed by norms of what is appropriate: for potential 'losers' among the member states it seems to have become unacceptable to argue against the ERC by playing the short-term national interest card. For Ministers of Research and national research administrators/funders it is hard to argue on paper and in public against 'excellence'. Furthermore, in a process such as this, actors' interests seem not to have been exogenous but shaped by the process itself – from when the idea landed on the agenda of the EU, all the way to the stage when the new institution established itself within Europe's larger research policy order. A layering mechanism, rather than direct side-payments or overt exercise of the power of the strong member states over the weak, is central for understanding how promoters of the ERC got past the potential veto-players. In the decision stage opposition from the 'losers' and defenders of status quo (both among the member states, within the Commission and among FP stakeholders) could be circumvented by *adding* the new institution to the institutional landscape rather than replacing the old distributive institutions.

The diffusionist account alerts attention to how models of emulation serve as external reference points in institution building. The matching of the new organization to a *normative* environmental imperative has bearing on this case – the US NSF model's superiority was an important leitmotiv, especially in the pre-decision stage. The shift in the normative and ideational climate at the time, with the 'glorious return of peer review' and new excellence initiatives at the national level, seems to be a factor in accounting for how ERC autonomy was accepted and promoted. This was also a climate shift the ERC itself later on contributed to, by turning into a role model for national funding agencies. Consequently, *lesson number 3* is the following: new institutions can both ride larger winds of institutional pressures and become an active part in shaping such pressures. Yet, some reservations to the diffusionist account are in order. First, building institutions in a case such as this cannot be understood as automatic adaptation to institutional environments – hegemonic models for organizing competitive funding of academic research had been around for several decades without being diffused to the EU. Institutional pressures are not itself a sufficient condition for diffusion and the shape of the new institutions was not a reproduction of a hegemonic model. Clearly many actors have carried the idea of research funding on the basis of excellence and not only that, they have been interacting over how this solution could be coupled to the new definition of what was ailing European research and existing European research policy. The ERC's builders were exploiting the research council template and normative hegemony but also exploring new ways of defining its merits, rules and practices.

Drawing on the institutional-cultural perspective we can extract *lesson number 4:* established institutions strongly condition the process of building new ones. More than a mechanism of institutional inertia we observe how established institutions *enable* institutional innovation – a tangible expression of this is how actors are capacitated by procedures and resources of the EU Presidency and of the FP rules, FP administrative capacity/resources and its policy-making/administrative culture. The EU institutions and their established decision-making procedures in EU research policy, together with the transnational constituencies, incrementally developed the structures of the ERC, made sense of it and collectively matched the new institution to what was acceptable normatively for the scientific community, for institutions at the supranational level as well as the member states' policy-makers. In the decision stage the options were narrowed down by the formal rules that apply to the FPs. The traditions in the sector for interaction between administration/policy-makers and stakeholders groups are especially relevant as an explanatory factor. Without the activation of these formally powerless actors the ERC would not have been put on the agenda. These actors carried their ideas into the decision-making stage leaving it to formal institutions of the EU and their decision-making machinery to push the process further along. Without these formal institutions and established decision-making procedures of the EU the ERC would not have come about.

Finally, the remarkable post-decision life of the ERC, despite lacking a legal status as a permanent EU institution, is a lesson in quick institutionalization: institutions that are endowed with (relatively) independent resources, organizational structures and a formally sanctioned mandate are quickly able to fill out the blanks of the institutional arrangement, establishing its own institutional practices and starting the process of creating an institutional identity. More than through the material power (the power of the size of the funding purse) and proven instrumental value, a new institution can gain considerable independence through acquiring a *legitimate* status in its environment.

## CONCLUSION

In line with the domain of application approach, it appears that the diffusionist and functional perspectives highlight the dynamics at the *pre-decision* stage of institution building, whereas the power perspective has more bearing on the dynamics at the *decision* stage. An institutional-cultural perspective clearly is important for understanding the *post-decision* stage. *Context* (both existing institutional set-up and timing) appears to be consistently relevant at *all stages*. Overall our observations suggest that more than a domain of application approach, the interesting dynamic of institution-building is found in the interaction between context, cultural factors, environmental pressures and the power of actors. The ERC case underlines the need to contextualize institution building in time and space. This concerns not only the matching to normative environments, but it is striking how contingent events, timing and parallel processes are central to the story. The sequencing of the EU Presidencies, the EU's timetable for the revision of the FPs and the outcome of the negotiations over the EU's long-term budget were key opportunities that allowed the idea to get on the agenda, stay there, and eventually provide money and staff for the new institution. Context does not cease to matter when new entities start to live relatively independent lives – institution building is a continuous process also involving interpreting external events and expectations, and potentially translating them into internal structures. Hence, the sector-specific conditions of the European research policy landscape that are reflected in institutional arrangements shape how actors relate to each other, what kinds of interests and ideas are acceptable to promote within this setting, and what kinds of institutions it is possible to build.

It is too early to assess what kind of transformative power this innovation will have for the EU research policy portfolio over time and for the Europe of Knowledge more widely. It could be that the ERC gradually undermines principles of funding underlying the rest of the FP. Or the established practices of the FP/Horizon 2020 programme can over time 'invade' the newcomer and reduce the foreseen autonomy and mission of the ERC. So far there are very few indications that the latter will be the case. Even the highly skewed distributional effects of the new institution have not affected its acquired status and legitimacy. It may also be that the different elements of the EU research policy manage to live parallel, sustainable existences without one displacing the other. In any case, at present the ERC is an example of a new institution that breaks with, builds on, and affects established practices and dynamic relationships in the political order of the EU and in European science.

## NOTES

1.  Previous versions of this chapter have been presented as papers at the UACES Conference, September 2010 and at the Arena seminar, University of Oslo, June 2011. We thank the participants for comments and especially acknowledge the in-depth comments from Anne Corbett.
2.  This was the central tenet in the so-called 'Rational Design' project that researched the origins of the structure of international organizations in a number of issue areas (Koremenos et al. 2001).
3.  These influential organizations also have EIROForum, their own umbrella organization.
4.  Busquin's speech 7 October 2002, the Danish Research Councils' conference 'Towards a European Research Area: Do We Need a European Research Council?', Copenhagen.
5.  The 2467th Council Meeting (Competitiveness) Conclusions, 26 November 2002, 14365/02 (Press 360), p. 22.
6.  Footnote to minutes from Council Meeting 26 November 2002.
7.  The European Research Council – 'A Cornerstone in the European Research Area'. Report from an Expert Group. Published by Ministry of Science, Technology and Innovation, Copenhagen, 15 December 2003.
8.  The Bank of Sweden Tercentenary Foundation Annual Report 2002, pp. 40–44.
9.  Two of the members of CNERP were secretaries to the Mayor Expert Group on the ERC.
10. The ESF organized a High Level Working Group led by Richard Sykes of Imperial College London. It included Ken Pavitt who died during course of the work and one member who left the group to become the Spanish Minister of Research and Technology. The group also included the Director of the *Volkswagen Stiftung*, Wilhelm Krull, and Ernst-Ludwig Winnacker from the *Deutsche Forschungsgemeinschaft* who later became the first General Secretary to the ERC.
11. Kai Simons and Carol Featherstone, Cell 123, 2 December 2005.
12. Mayor Report 2003, p. 12.
13. The ELSF position document from 2003 uses the quote from Victor Hugo on the front page of their report: 'stronger than any army is an idea whose time has come'.
14. The Sapir Report July 2003.
15. Kai Simons and Carol Feartherstone, Cell 123, 2 December 2005.
16. 'The ERC itself is not the objective, it is the means – perhaps the indispensable means, but not the objective. Europe needs a system to promote basic scientific excellence based on scientific criteria, and if we focus on that we will identify the organisation that is needed' Director General of DG Research, Dr A. Mitsos, 25 February 2004.
17. See for example European Commission, Europe and Basic Research, COM(2004)9, 14 January 2004 and High Level Expert Group, 'Frontier Research: The European Challenge'.
18. Commission Interim Working Document on 'The Implementation of a Funding Mechanism for Basic Research', 29 September 2004.

19. Minutes of Evidence, taken before the European Union Committee (Sub-Committee B), Monday 13 February 2006, House of Lords, European Union Committee 33rd Report of Session 2005-06), June 2006.
20. See for example Dr Richard Dye's Memorandum to the House of Commons Select Committee on Science and Technology, 15 January 2003.
21. Italian contribution to the debate on the future of European Research Policy, Ministero dell Instruzione, dell Università e della Ricerca. October 2004.
22. Minutes of Evidence, taken before the European Union Committee (Sub-Committee B), Monday 13 February 2006, House of Lords.
23. Decision No. 198272006/EC European Parliament and the Council.
24. Council Decision 2006/972/EC.
25. ERC Scientific Council, Strategy Note 'ERC Peer Review Panel Structure – Fundamental Principles', initial publication 14 July 2006.
26. Agreed by the founding members of the ERC Scientific Council and transmitted to the Commission 17 January 2007.
27. Physical Sciences and Engineering, 45 per cent of the budget; Life Sciences, 40 per cent; and Social Sciences and the Humanities, 15 per cent. Interestingly enough this distribution is based on what the Scientific Council refers to as 'worldwide practice' (European Research Council Work Programme, 17 January 2007, p. 71).
28. Cf. EurActiv and minutes of the ERC Scientific Board meetings from 2007 to 2011.
29. See http://erc.europa.eu/sites/default/files/document/file/erc_policy_phd_and_equiva lent_degrees.pdf (accessed 12 February 2014).
30. Scientific Council meeting 13–14 October 2009.
31. The starting grant procedures were for instance modelled heavily on the EUROHORCs' Young Investigators Award, a scheme that was abandoned when the ERC came into operation (Langfeldt and Brofoss 2005).
32. See http://erc.europa.eu/ (accessed 12 February 2014).
33. The following countries and regions are among those having instigated such schemes: France, Hungary, Italy, Luxemburg, Spain, Switzerland, Sweden and Flanders.
34. Commissioner Potočnik (2009).

# REFERENCES

Banchoff, T. (2002), 'Institutions, inertia and European Union research policy', *Journal of Common Market Studies*, **40**(1), 1–21.

Benner, M. and U. Sandstrom (2000), 'Institutionalizing the triple helix: research funding and norms in the academic system', *Research Policy*, **29**(2), 291–301.

Braun, D. (1998), 'The role of funding agencies in the cognitive development of science', *Research Policy*, **27**(8), 807–821.

Caporaso, J.A. and A. Stone Sweet (2001), 'Institutional logics of integration', in A. Stone Sweet, W. Sandholtz and N. Fligstein (eds), *The Institutionalisation of Europe*, Oxford: Oxford University Press, pp. 221–236.

Caswill, C. (2003), 'Principals, agents and contracts', *Science and Public Policy*, **30**, 337–346.

Chou, M.-H. (2014, this volume), 'The evolution of the European Research Area as an idea in European integration', in M.-H. Chou and Å. Gornitzka (eds), *Building the Knowledge Economy in Europe: New Constellations in European Research and Higher Education Governance*, Cheltenham, UK and Northampton, MA, USA: Edward Elgar, pp. 27–50.

Darmon, G. (1997), 'European science foundation: towards a history', in J. Krige and L. Guzetti (eds), *History of European Scientific and Technological*

*Cooperation*, Luxembourg: Office for Publications of the European Communities, pp. 324–359.

DiMaggio, P.J. and W.W. Powell (1983), 'The iron cage revisited – institutional isomorphism and collective rationality in organizational fields', *American Sociological Review*, **48**(2), 147–160.

Egeberg, M., M. Martens and J. Trondal (2009), 'Building Executive Power at the European Level. On the Role of EU-Level Agencies', *Arena Working Paper*, 10(2009).

EURECIA (2012), 'Understanding and Assessing the Impact and Outcomes of the ERC and its Funding Schemes (EURECIA) – Final Synthesis Report', EURECIA May 2012, available at: http://erc.europa.eu/sites/default/files/document/file/eurecia_final_synthesis_report.pdf (accessed 25 November 2013).

European Court of Auditors (2009), 'Delegating Implementing Tasks to Executive Agencies: a Successful Option?', Special Report No 13/2009 European Court of Auditors.

Finnemore, M. (1993), 'International organizations as teachers of norms – the United Nations' educational scientific and cultural organization and science policy', *International Organization*, **47**(4), 565–597.

Gornitzka, Å. and J. Metz (2014, this volume), 'European institution building under inhospitable conditions – the unlikely establishment of the European Institute of Innovation and Technology', in M.-H. Chou and Å. Gornitzka (eds), *Building the Knowledge Economy in Europe: New Constellations in European Research and Higher Education Governance*, Cheltenham, UK and Northampton, MA, USA: Edward Elgar, pp. 111–130.

Gornitzka, Å. and U. Sverdrup (2008), 'Who consults? The configuration of expert groups in the European Union', *West European Politics*, **31**(4), 725–750.

Grande, E. and A. Peschke (1999), 'Transnational cooperation and policy networks in European science policy-making', *Research Policy*, **28**(1), 43–61.

Groenleer, M. (2009), *The Autonomy of European Agencies: A Comparative Study of Institutional Development*, Delft: Eburon.

Gronbaek, D.J.v.H. (2003), 'A European Research Council: an idea whose time has come?', *Science and Public Policy*, **30**(6), 391–404.

Kafatos, F. (2010), 'Interview "The labours of Fotis Kafatos"', *Nature*, **464**(20). Published online, available at: http://www.nature.com/news/2010/100301/full/464020a.html (accessed 12 December 2013).

Koremenos, B., C. Lipson and D. Snidal (2001), 'The rational design of international institutions', *International Organization*, **55**(4), 761–799.

Langfeldt, L. and K.E. Brofoss (2005), *Evaluation of the European Young Investigator Awards Scheme*, Oslo: NIFU STEP, Studies in Innovation, Research and Education.

Macilwain, C. (2010), 'Fork in the road', *The Scientist*, **24**(2), 30–38.

March, J.G. and J.P. Olsen (1998), 'The institutional dynamics of international political orders', *International Organization*, **52**(4), 943–969.

March, J.G. and J.P. Olsen (2006), 'Elaborating the "new institutionalism"', in R.A.W. Rhodes, S. Binder and B. Rockman (eds), *The Oxford Handbook of Political Institutions*, Oxford: Oxford University Press, pp. 3–20.

McNamara, K. (2001), 'Where do rules come from? The creation of the European Central Bank', in A. Stone Sweet, W. Sandholtz and N. Fligstein (eds), *The Institutionalisation of Europe*, Oxford: Oxford University Press, pp. 155–170.

Meyer, J.W. and R. Rowan (1977), 'Institutionalized organizations – formal structure as myth and ceremony', *American Journal of Sociology*, **83**, 340–363.

Mitchell, R.B. and P.M. Keilbach (2001), 'Situation structure and institutional design: reciprocity, coercion, and exchange', *International Organization*, **55**(4), 891–917.

Moe, T.M. (1990), 'Political institutions: the neglected side of the story', *Journal of Law, Economics, and Organization*, **6**, 213–253.

Most, F.v.d. (2009), *Research Councils Facing New Science and Technology. The Case of Nanotechnology in Finland, the Netherlands, Norway and Switzerland*, Enschede: University of Twente.

Muldur, U., F. Corvers, H. Delanghe, J. Dratwa, D. Heimberger, B. Sloan and S. Vanslembrouck (2006), *A New Deal for an Effective European Research Policy: the Design and Impacts of the 7th Framework Programme*, Dordrecht: Springer.

Olsen, J.P. (1992), 'Analyzing institutional dynamics', *Staatswissenschaften und Staatspraxis*, **3**(2), 247–271.

Olsen, J.P. (1997), 'Institutional design in democratic contexts', *Journal of Political Philosophy*, **5**(3), 203–229.

Olsen, J.P. (2010), *Governing Through Institution Building. Institutional Theory and Recent European Experiments in Democratic Organization*, Oxford: Oxford University Press.

Olsen, J.P. and B.G. Peters (1996), 'Learning from experience?', in J.P. Olsen and B.G. Peters (eds), *Lessons from Experience. Experiential Learning in Administrative Reforms in Eight Democracies*, Oslo: Scandinavian University Press, pp. 1–35.

Pavitt, K. (2000), 'Why European Union funding of academic research should be increased: a radical proposal', *Science and Public Policy*, **27**(6), 455–460.

Pierson, P. (2004), *Politics in Time: History, Institutions, and Social Analysis*, Princeton, NJ: Princeton University Press.

Potočnik, J. (2009), 'European Research Council – The Future Starts Today', Speech/09309, Brussels, 24 September 2009, available at: http://europa.eu/rapid/press-release_SPEECH-09-409_en.htm (accessed 13 December 2013).

Scott, W.R. (2008), *Institutions and Organizations: Ideas and Interests*, Thousand Oaks, CA: Sage.

Selznick, P. (1966), *Leadership in Administration: a Sociological Interpretation*, New York: Harper and Row.

Simon, H.A. (1976[1945]), *Administrative Behavior: a Study of Decision-Making Processes in Administrative Organization*, 3rd edition, New York: Free Press.

Strang, D. and J.W. Meyer (1993), 'Institutional conditions for diffusion', *Theory and Society*, **22**(4), 487–511.

Tallberg, J. (2002), 'Delegation to supranational institutions: why, how, and with what consequences?', *West European Politics*, **25**(1), 23–46.

Tallberg, J. (2008), 'Bargaining power in the European Council', *Journal of Common Market Studies*, **46**(3), 685–708.

Tallberg, J. (2010), 'Explaining the institutional foundations of European Union negotiations', *Journal of European Public Policy*, **17**(5), 633–647.

Tolbert, P.S. and L.G. Zucker (1983), 'Institutional sources of change in the formal structure of organizations: the diffusion of civil service reform, 1880–1935', *Administrative Science Quarterly*, **28**(1), 22–39.

Van der Meulen, B. (1998), 'Science policies as principal-agent games – institutionalization and path dependency in the relation between government and science', *Research Policy*, **27**(4), 397–414.

Vike-Freiberga, V. et al. (2009), 'Towards a World-Class Frontier Research Organisation'. Review of the European Research Council's Structures and Mechanisms. Following the Commission's decison of March 2009 (C(2009) 1871) to create 'Panel of Independent Experts for the Review of the Structures and Mechanisms of the ERC', 23 July 2009.

Williamson, O.E. (1981), 'The economics of organization – the transaction cost approach', *American Journal of Sociology*, **87**(3), 548–577.

Winnacker, E.-L. (2008), 'On excellence through competition', *European Educational Research Journal*, **7**(2), 124–130.

## ANNEX: INTERVIEW SOURCES

**European Commission:**

- DG Research, Policy Officer, Brussels, 26 May 2009
- DG Research, Adviser, Brussels, 27 May 2009
- DG Research, Adviser, Brussels, 7 July 2009
- DG Research, Cabinet Member, Brussels, 4 September 2009
- DG Research, Policy Officer, Brussels, 10 November 2010

**Council of Ministers:**

- German Ministry of Education and Research, Director General, and Unit for Education and Research at the German Permanent Representation in Brussels, Head of Unit, Berlin, 4 November 2010

**External Stakeholders:**

- Member of the European Research Advisory Board, telephone interview, 22 December 2010
- Member of the European Research Advisory Board, Berlin, 1 February 2011
- Member of the European Research Advisory Board, telephone interview, 28 February 2011

# 5. European institution building under inhospitable conditions – the unlikely establishment of the European Institute of Innovation and Technology

## Åse Gornitzka and Julia Metz

## INTRODUCTION[1]

Supranational institution building is at the heart of European integration. The dynamics of creating and designing new bodies is diverse, driven by functional needs, political motives, institutional fads and legacies (Groenleer 2009; Kelemen and Tarrant 2011). Some institutions have been established with relative ease, while others have come after protracted periods of struggles between main decision-makers, or have been proposed but never materialized. Particularly challenging to theories of European integration are the unlikely cases: if new European Union (EU) institutions are created when member states are unsupportive and historical legacies speak against them, how can this be accounted for and what can such cases tell us about the dynamics of supranational institution building?

In this chapter we argue that the establishment of the European Institute of Innovation and Technology (EIT) – a 'knowledge institution' under EU law that combines higher education, research and business activities – is such a crucial case. Its establishment provides an opportunity to study how new EU institutions are created and the nature of institutional design under inhospitable conditions. Several conditions have placed heavy odds against the establishment of this particular type of institution: in this area member states have been particularly reluctant to advance European integration, a high degree of national sensitivity to supranational involvement existed. The proposal for a European university as a supranational institution under Community law had for instance been enshrined in the European Atomic Energy Community (EURATOM) Treaty, but this provision was not implemented (Corbett 2005). In Europe the regulation of higher education has been the nation state's prerogative and EU member states have zealously guarded their authority in this sector. The EU has had few legal and financial resources, little legitimacy and no significant history of creation and maintenance of such types of institutions. The proposal for an EIT further presented a challenge for institution building, as it was a cross-cutting proposal integrating three distinct subpolicy areas: higher education, research and innovation policy. These three knowledge policy domains had so far been administered separately and displayed distinct policy patterns: education policy had developed its particular instruments, traditions and actor sets; research policy had its deeply institutionalized Framework Programme (FP) and a large administrative apparatus and stakeholder organizations; and innovation policy appeared as a third emerging policy domain struggling to find its own place in the EU policy landscape. It therefore had to overcome sectorally entrenched inertia. Yet, as of 9 April 2009 the EIT is in operation as an EU institution and a legal subject in its own right, with an administrative infrastructure, a geographical location and its own rules of operation. Hence its establishment leaves us with a puzzle: given these inhospitable conditions, why did the EU decide to establish it, how was institution building possible, and what shaped its design?

The chapter proceeds as follows. We start out by outlining four theoretical perspectives on institutional building in the EU and their main expectations. Following from this, the case of the EIT is chronicled in three main episodes: the pre-decision period, the decision period, and the period when the EIT began its operations after the decision to establish it was taken (post-decision period). Next we identify the main factors that account for how institution building takes place despite opposition of powerful actors and frictions created by path dependencies of political-administrative systems: where powerful opposition exists, it also needs powerful promoters of a new institution; these, however, need to relate their design to extant legitimate institutions, they depend on enabling temporal accidents, and have to be open towards unintended adjustments in the design. We then conclude the chapter.

## PERSPECTIVES ON INSTITUTIONAL BUILDING

We identify four perspectives on decision-making with the potential to explain the institutional design in the context of the EU (see Gornitzka and Metz 2014, this volume). These highlight different dynamics of institutional design: institution building as determined by the relative power of actors with conflicting interests, as shaped by path dependencies, as solution driven, and finally as temporal 'accidents'. Given the unfavourable conditions of powerful veto players opposing the creation of an EIT and institutional inertia in the area, we expect the last two perspectives to have more explanatory power than the former two in the pre-decision and formal decision-making stage.

**Power-Oriented Perspective**

From a rational institutional perspective institutions are instruments to solve problems and serve actors' interests. Institutions are intentionally designable (problem-driven) and are based on purposeful choices and actor interests. In situations where there are multiple actors with diverse interests, institutional design is seen as resulting from conflict. Thus, deciding to establish a new institution and how to structure it is essentially the outcome of the *politics* of structural choice. Actors bring their preferences into the process, and the most powerful actor will also have the power to *control* the process of design – including the resources to overcome veto points through side payments and bargaining power (Tallberg 2010). It follows that a new institution, such as the EIT, is created at the initiative of the most powerful actors in the system and its design represents the elongation of their interests. Precisely because new institutions will serve some purposes over others, that is, have distributional effects, there will be losers and winners associated with such choices (Moe 1990) and the design process takes place as confrontation, bargaining and coalition building among contending actors (March 1988, p. 170). In the EU we would expect two major conflict lines activated by the establishment of supranational institutions (institutions under EU law). First, structural choice is likely to mirror the fact that consequences of establishing new institutions are unevenly distributed between member states, which therefore have different preferences attached to them (Moravcsik 1998). Second, conflict between national and supranational interests is likely to arise, because member states and EU institutions have different interests attached to the expected outcomes of institutional design, as such outcomes concern the degree of delegation to the supranational level (Kelemen and Tarrant 2011; Tsebelis and Garrett 2000). While the Commission and European Parliament (EP) are expected to push for supranational solutions, member states in the Council would be promoting a design that allows them to retain control. Asymmetrical power among member states as well as between EU institutions (Commission and EP) and the member states, and the bargain struck between them, will thus shape design. Given the differences that prevail across national education policy systems and the strong member state control in this area, the establishment of a higher education institution, such as the EIT, appears to be unlikely – unless new actors with different interests gain power, or power constellations shift, leaving these new actors in control of the design.

**Path Dependency**

Taking issue with some of the assumptions of rational institution building, historical institutionalists make the argument that institutional design
takes place in an institutional context (Pierson 2004).[2] The reproductive
tendencies of social structures once in place shape institutional design
(Stone Sweet et al. 2001). Furthermore, there are other limits to the rationality of institutional choice: actors often act on the basis of their short-
term goals, being oblivious to or ignoring the long-term consequences of
the institutions they construct (Pierson 2004, pp. 109–115). In the EU's
institutional landscape short-term concerns of member states, unintended
consequences, institutionalized veto points, and resistance from actors
embedded in existing institutional arrangements constrain the designers'
control over institutional construction (Pierson 1996). Moreover, what
actors see as 'means and ends' relationships and what they want is defined
by their institutional context (March and Olsen 2006). As institutions
organize issues and actors, and endow them with resources to act, they
also structure patterns of conflict (Egeberg 2006) and the exercise of power
(Orren and Skowronek 2004). This is inherent in the way a polity is organized, as is the case in a highly institutionally structured decision-making
terrain such as the EU. We would expect proposals for new institutions
to be met with 'friction' in the established institutional orders (Mahoney
and Thelen 2010). Institutional creation processes may not only unleash
conflict among different member states and between member states and
supranational institutions, but also along non-territorial conflict lines, such
as sectorally and ideologically based patterns of cooperation and conflict
in EU decision-making (Curtin and Egeberg 2008) – which also prevail in
the area of knowledge policies. Here, we observe that the Commission's
administrative and political legacies and interactions with sector-specific
clients has become a source of resistance towards rather than an engine of
deeper European integration (Banchoff 2002). From the path-dependency
perspective we expect the three knowledge triangle trajectories of EU
involvement resulting from distinct sets of historical legacies engrained in
the Commission's organizational structure and differences in interaction
patterns to represent obstacles to cross-cutting initiatives such as the EIT.

**Solution-Driven Design**

While the path-dependence perspective underlines actors' institutional
'embeddedness' and frictions involved in institutional construction, socio-
logical institutionalism takes the queries on the assumption of instrumen-
tality in institutional design further: adoption of organizational forms can

have independent symbolic and cultural value as a signal of legitimate and appropriate behaviour (Meyer and Rowan 1977). In the provision of organizational solutions it might be more important to match prevailing ideas and norms for how to organize than to meet the substantive interests of powerful actors. The legitimacy and ideational hegemony of a particular form can account for an institution's establishment independently from its instrumental consequences. It is the social value of particular organizational forms that drives institutional design. Professionals, expert communities and associations are likely to act as carriers and purveyors of new conceptual systems and organizational solutions (Scott 2008, pp. 99–101; see also Gornitzka and Metz 2014, this volume). If such an argument can account for the design of the EIT, we expect the idea to establish an EIT and how to structure it to arrive at the decision-making process before the problems it should address are put on the agenda. The EIT structure would constitute a fairly stable solution that can be attached to varying sets of problems and structurally reflect normative hegemonic ideals and models.

**Temporal 'Accidents'**

One additional complication to any process of institutional design in complex settings that we so far have left untouched concerns what follows from attention scarcity. In information rich, complex settings with many parallel events and decision opportunities, attention is a scarce resource. Referring to decision-making in general, March claims that decisions happen the way they do, in large part, because of the way attention is allocated (March 1994, p. 24). In decision-making under such conditions, in combination with goal and technology ambiguity and fluid participation (conditions associated with organized anarchies), the temporal order *substitutes* a consequential order of means and ends (Cohen et al. 1972). Even in more structured decision-making situations, how decision-makers allocate their attention to some ideas, problems and solutions over others affects outcomes (Baumgartner et al. 2011). Kingdon stresses how the temporal configuration of factors is crucial in accounting for policy change in windows of opportunities (Kingdon 1995). These arguments underline the fact that institutional design cannot be adequately explained without taking into account other claims on the participants' attention. Timing and contingent events shape how some problems become prominent on the agenda and are eventually translated into concrete policies while others never do. Consequently, this perspective would argue for the EIT to have come about not because actors link problems to solutions or vice versa, but because streams of decision-making opportunities, decision-makers/participants, problems and solutions are connected in time, that is via concurrence. Attention scarcity affects both the patterns of participation in decision-making and the way in which problems and solutions are dealt with. From this perspective the EIT's design would present a result that had not been intended by anyone and perhaps running counter to the actors' initially stated interests.

## THE CASE OF THE EIT

These theoretical perspectives on institution building have implications for how to empirically approach the case included here. First, we focus on the accounting for the institutional structure of the EIT, its organizational framework, task structure, rules of operation, procedures, as well as its funding and governance structure.[3] We refer to this as *institution building*. However, by using this term we do not *a priori* privilege accounts of intentional far-sighted design, as evident from our discussion above. Second, we use a process approach where the emphasis lies in identifying how the process towards establishing the EIT happened over time in a series of occurrences, rather than accounting 'backwards' for the EIT by reference to its functions or distributional effects (see Hall 2008 on systematic process analysis). We identify the main actors, the problems and solutions that were brought into (and possibly taken out of) the design process, the decision-making opportunities in which this took place, and the main contingent events that surrounded the EIT decisions.

The empirical evidence of how the processes have evolved is drawn from 14 in-depth informant interviews (see annex to this chapter), the study of official documents and other written sources, including data provided by other studies of relevance to the case. Basing a qualitative analysis predominantly on interview material entails the risk that the conclusions drawn rely too much on the personal views of individuals engaged in the process. This caveat is addressed by interviewing several persons from different institutions on the same subject (Berry 2002), which are the Commission, Council, EP and stakeholders (interviewee's organizational basis is identified whenever we refer to interview data). By doing so, the risk of overestimating the perspectives of the individual parties engaged into the process is reduced. In addition, our additional empirical material cross-validates our interview data.

### The Pre-Decision Drafting Stage: Selling the Idea of an EIT

When the new Barroso Commission took office in November 2004 the EU was four years into the Lisbon Strategy. It had started its work towards a

competitiveness agenda, had institutionalized the heads of states' attention to socio-economic coordination through the 'Spring Council', and
had generated new activities to address the agenda. Coinciding with the
start of Barroso's Presidency, Wim Kok's High Level Group delivered a
bleak review of the Lisbon Strategy. Three months later, in February 2005,
Barroso announced his idea of a European Institute of Technology (EIT),[4]
a European university based on the model of the successful Massachusetts
Institute of Technology (MIT). By attracting the best researchers in
Europe, the EIT should become Europe's 'new flagship for excellence in
higher education, research and innovation' (Commission of the European
Communities 2006a).

The EIT thus emerged on the European agenda in response to Manuel
Barroso's political will to set his footprint as the new Commission President
(Interview Secretariat General, 8 July 2009), thereby evoking the ideals of
scientific excellence and mimicking the US institution as a role model.
Still, the idea of a 'European MIT' did not find much sympathy among
the policy community, and, as Barroso did not want to let go his idea, the
pre-decision stage of the EIT was defined by politically selling the idea
of an EIT. The Commission President was pushing for a supranational
institution as a solution to what he identified as a common European
competitiveness problem against member states' reluctance. At this stage
the classical tug of war between the supranational interest and the national
interests was clearly present. At the same time, however, several other
conflict lines were activated: the Commission's administration and stakeholders (universities, research organizations, industry or regions) almost
exclusively reacted with scepticism or even strong opposition.

Resistance primarily concerned the question of funding, because the
Financial Perspectives for the forthcoming years (2007–2013) did not
include a funding stream for the EIT (Commission of the European
Communities 2004). Given the painful discussions on the new financial
framework (Schild 2008), the creation of an EIT was perceived by national
and supranational administrations as threatening existing initiatives. This
particularly affected research and innovation policies, such as the FP7 or
the Competitiveness and Innovation Framework Programme (CIP) funded
under the 'Competitiveness' heading 1A of the Financial Perspectives, the
heading into which the EIT would also tap. Hence the *short-term* distributional consequences, more than the long-term consequences, underpinned
the opposition to the EIT idea. In addition, the DG for Research (DG
RTD) feared that an EIT would threaten the visibility of its recently proposed European Research Council (ERC) (Interview EURAB, 1 February
2011; Interview EP, 8 December 2009). Administrative resistance was
further problematic as the EIT aimed to integrate the three angles of the

knowledge triangle, which required the collaboration of the three DGs responsible: DG EAC (education), DG RTD (research) and DG Enterprise (innovation). The historically grown sectoral differentiation, which had led to diverging problem definitions and interpretations, caused reluctance of all three DGs to work together across organizational boundaries at the Commission's administrative level.

The questions of human resources devoted to the EIT and distinct EIT degrees and diplomas of a 'supranational standard of excellence' were also highly contested issues among universities and member states. Both actor groups feared losing their best researchers to a supranational competitor and existing national standards to be diluted. These concerns were largely present with well-established old universities (for example, Cambridge and Oxford) and technological and innovation-related universities (Interview DG EAC, 13 November 2009). National administrations referred to subsidiarity and emphasized that education and vocational training systems were under national responsibility (Interview DG EAC, 4 September 2009; Interview Council, 4 November 2010). Instead of establishing another university, as the Pro-Vice-Chancellor of the University of Cambridge argued, Europe should rather invest in existing world-class universities, such as Cambridge, Oxford or the Swiss Federal Institute of Technology in Zurich (ETH Zurich) (Leslie 2005). The European Research Advisory Board (EURAB) seriously questioned the whole organizational thinking underlying the proposal by saying that such an institution could not be created from 'top-down' (Interview EURAB, 1 February 2011).[5]

The fact that such a contested idea was not removed from the political agenda, but was instead further promoted and modified to meet all concerns, certainly owed to the fact that the EIT was the President's 'pet project' (Interview DG EAC, 4 September 2009). At its very apex the European executive kept its attention on the idea. After the initial resistance, this also raised the motivation of the entrusted administrative department in the Commission, the DG EAC. For the DG EAC, an otherwise relatively weak DG operating in areas with limited supranational competences, having responsibility over the President's 'baby' was a window of opportunity to raise its political profile (Interview DG EAC, 4 September 2009). Tasked with the job to guard the President's initiative, the DG EAC skilfully managed to overcome resistance within the Commission: by creating a small drafting group with the two other DGs of the 'knowledge triangle' a shared feeling of ownership developed (Interview DG RTD, 13 November 2009).

Under the premise that the President's initial idea would not be completely dismissed and at the end there would be a legislative proposal, the Commission's main task was now to adjust and promote the design of the

EIT in such a way that it was agreeable for important veto players, whose consent would be needed in the succeeding formal decision-making stage (Interview DG EAC, 13 November 2009). First and foremost, Barroso's vision of a single-site European university built of bricks and mortar – a truly 'European MIT' – had been abandoned. Step by step this idea was transformed into a networked structure of collaborations among already established institutes, so-called 'Knowledge and Innovation Communities' (KICs). Similar to the initial EIT idea, also here we can find emulation. The modified networked concept was modelled on existing arrangements at national level: KICs were 'extremely close' to 'Knowledge Integration Communities', also called 'KICs', experimented between 2000 and 2006 in the UK (Didier 2010, pp. 12–13). The KICs further displayed similarities to the Commission's 'Networks of Excellence' funded under its Research FPs (Interview DG RTD, 7 July 2009). Second, Barroso's plan to reallocate funds from existing research and innovation activities to the EIT was revised. In order to overcome the strong resistance from the DG RTD and the scientific community, the Commission finally proposed to finance the initial start-up costs of €308.7 million with 'unallocated margins beneath the ceilings of sub-heading 1A' (Commission of the European Communities 2006b, p. 8). Also the question of staffing was modified to meet member states' and universities' preferences, as the Commission did not demand the EIT's personnel to be seconded from national universities and research institutes anymore. Similarly the concept of distinct EIT degrees and diplomas was adjusted, and now allowed the participating universities to choose between joint degrees with other KIC members or their own individual degrees.

### The Decision Stage: Circumventing Veto Points in Decision-Making Opportunities

While the pre-decision stage of the EIT dealt with the transformation of an idea into a legislative initiative, during the decision stage an interinstitutional agreement had to be found among the European legislators. At this stage access to the choice opportunities followed the institutional procedures and the political 'office holders', not stakeholders, were the dominant actors (Interview Council, 4 November 2010). The major problem here was that the initial scepticism from the member states and the MEPs was now actually manifested in blocking veto points. Most troublesome in the process were large member states which hosted some important ancient universities, such as the UK, Germany, the Netherlands and Sweden (Interview DG EAC, 13 November 2009; Interview Council, 4 November 2010). As observed in the pre-decision stage, the administrative level of the Commission stuck to the status quo and was particularly reluctant towards this new cross-cutting initiative (Interview Council, 7 November 2011). Also the EP's Budget Committee, a veto player in EU legislation with financial implications such as the EIT, formed a blocking point. Continuing with the process that had started during the pre-decision phase, the institution's design was further adjusted to respond to diverging actor preferences.

To start with, when the Commission tabled its legislative proposal in October 2006 most political actors were convinced that it was doomed to fail (Interview Council, 4 November 2010). Not even new member states – which arguably could have benefited from the chance to host a new European university – showed an interest in an EIT (Interview EURAB, 28 February 2011).[6]

To the surprise of many the negotiations on the proposal made a substantial leap forward as soon as Germany took over the Council Presidency in January 2007. Whereas the German government had initially been a vehement EIT-opponent, as soon as it had taken over the Presidency, it announced the EIT as one of the Presidency's priorities. It was speculated that the Commission President had struck a political deal at the highest political level with the German Chancellor Angela Merkel to reach a political agreement on the EIT by the end of the Presidency in June 2007. This deal was viewed as the turning point in the EIT negotiations, as the initiative now had the support of a powerful coalition formed by the European Commission and the German Council Presidency (Interview Council, 4 November 2010).

However, this powerful alliance was still confronted with blocking member states in the Council and the EP's Budget Committee. Despite this, member states arrived at a political agreement on the legal design of the Institute on 25 June 2007 – something which had been unthinkable half a year earlier. One important reason for this outcome certainly was the favourable timing of the Germany Presidency: as one of the oldest and largest member states in the EU, Germany was a powerful and skilful negotiator for the EIT. A further window of opportunity opened with personnel shifts in the EP, which heaved German MEPs into key positions and provided the German Presidency with two national 'coalition partners' in the EP (Interview DG EAC, 4 September 2009). The chair of the EP's ITRE Committee (Industry, Research and Energy) was taken by Angelika Niebler (EPP, German) and in January 2007 the Budget Committee's Chairman changed to Reimar Böge (EPP, German). Thus, we see preference change through *replacement* as key positions in the decision process changed hands.

In addition, Germany revised the Commission's EIT proposal considerably – a procedure extremely unusual in European decision-making (Interview DG EAC, 13 November 2009; Interview Council, 4 November 2010), where the responsibility for legislative drafting lies with the European Commission and around 80 per cent of the legislation proposed by the Commission is adopted by the other institutions without revision (Hull 1993). Despite that, Germany took over the drawing board and based its new draft legislation on a number of conditional points which presented agreeable 'safety guarantees' for all participants, such as granting the KICs considerable operational autonomy (this made it more attractive for future participants, cf. BusinessEurope 2007) or integrating a 'sunset clause' – a two-step model consisting of an initial phase with three thematic KICs followed by an evaluation in June 2011, and the subsequent formulation of an ultimate Strategic Innovation Agenda (SIA), which made the regulation more flexible and less 'threatening' for the EIT-sceptics.

Moreover, the EIT's governance structure was modelled according to the normative *valeur* of 'excellence', which was the paradigm at the time and had already served as a reference point for the then recently established ERC. Emphasis was put on involving the top of the mark European business and academic community, leaving no room for national or supranational control in the governance structure of the EIT: the EIT's governing board in terms of representation was fully independent from both, member states and the Commission – an unusual governance structure in the landscape of the EU agencies (Groenleer 2009).

A further timely window of opportunity which facilitated negotiations appeared with the European Council Summit on 21–23 June 2007. Because Council President Merkel had managed to rescue the negotiations on the EU Reform Treaty at the very last minute (EurActiv 2007), member states were in an agreeable mood a few days later at the Competitiveness Council and supported Germany's draft EIT regulation without great debate (Interview Council, 4 November 2010). However, one point that could not be resolved by the end of June 2007 was the financing of the EIT's overhead costs. Reaching an agreement on this issue benefited from parallel political negotiations on the Galileo Satellite Navigation Project in March 2008, which demanded an extra €2.4 billion of Community funds. As discussions on finding additional Community funds for Galileo were taking place in the Council and the EP anyway, this last open point could easily be linked to the parallel debate and the respective solution, that is to draw on agricultural funds left unspent in 2007 (Europe Information Service 2007).

## Post-Decision: From Letter to Life?

The EIT regulation had established the rudimentary design of the EIT on paper (European Parliament and Council of the European Union 2008). It had a governance structure, a framework for how to conduct its business, and a geographical locus for its administrative unit. In principle it was set to lead an independent life when the spotlight of the EIT creators had moved elsewhere. This life began quickly, but was assisted by the DG EAC, which continued to be the responsible DG, whereas the other DGs did not attach much attention to the new institution (ECORYS 2011).

The EIT Governing Board played an important role in establishing the institution's independence, more so than the EIT administration and its headquarters. According to the rules of the EIT the Governing Board is composed of members from a mix of representatives from academia and business without any direct representation of the EU member states. In this sense member states had created an institution that they had few direct means to control. The same goes for the Commission (only an observer status in the EIT Board). Important for its operations was also the fact that the Board members were highly prominent figures, able to act on behalf of the new institution with self-assurance (ECORYS 2011). The Board soon established itself as the EIT's central rule maker. It is responsible for the overall steering of the EIT's activities, including the selection of KICs, appointing the headquarters' key staff, and establishing a SIA for the future. The autonomization of the Board was seen as problematic for the accountability of the new institution, as the Board seemingly acted without consulting when it developed the EIT's strategic agenda and it had *de facto* operational control of the EIT to the detriment of the EIT headquarters director (ECORYS 2011, p. XIV). The Board was seen by its surrounding institutions as taking 'liberties' in interpreting the EIT mandate (Interview Council, 4 November 2010). The decision-makers had partly taken the ERC as the model for the EIT's governance structure – that excluded both the representation of the member states and the Commission – and had not given much thought to the implications. In the post-decision stage member states wanted to rein in the autonomy of the EIT Governing Board, but with little avail (Interview Council, 7 November 2011).

In its initial period the EIT administration was within the DG EAC in Brussels. So when in April 2010 the headquarters were established in Budapest, this was also an important signal of administrative independence of the new institution. It had not become the bricks and mortar institution that Barroso initially had proposed, but the administrative side had a geographical locus. This made the EIT 'more real'. Yet the administration turned out to be problematic in the first stages. Although the EIT administration gained incrementally staff resources of its own, the first period was marked by high turnover and problems with acquiring and retaining qualified personnel. The first EIT director left after six months and it took one year to replace him – that is, in the critical initial stages the

EIT was without a stable directorship. The ambiguity of what it implied to 'act out' the EIT regulation was further related to the fact that what the EIT administration should do was not quite clear from the flexible legal text. Last, the first calls for the KICs were launched in April 2009 building on the criteria set out by the EIT regulation. But what this meant in practice was ambiguous and confusing to the potential applicants (ECORYS 2011, p. 28).

Despite these problems, the EIT managed to do what the regulation called for: deciding on establishing the KICs. The first three KICs were appointed in December 2009 as independent legal entities – on Climate, on Energy and on ICT. Through the activities of the Board and the formal design of the governance structure, the EIT started living an independent life, doing what it was expected to do but also taking a route that the member states and the Commission could not control. The first years of the EIT as a practice entailed that the Board carved out the role of the EIT and its KICs in the larger national and European innovation policy landscape without relating explicitly to other EU 'knowledge triangle' initiatives. Despite the EIT experiencing some teething troubles (Interview Council, 4 November 2010), in the post-decision stage it gained symbolic value: Ministers of Education have pointed to it as a 'model for the future' (Council of the European Union 2009: §7, p. 8), and it has symbolic export value as a reference point, being 'name-dropped' in new EU initiatives such as the new Competitiveness Strategy, Europe 2020 (European Commission 2010). Thus, the EIT now seemingly serves as a symbol of Europe as a modern knowledge system, and it has also found a place in the budget (about 3 per cent) of Horizon 2020.

## THE EIT SHAPED BY POWER, TEMPORALITY AND PATH DEPENDENCY

It took five years from one man launching an idea to having a new EU institution up and running, albeit in a feebler version than originally foreseen. The new institution has its headquarters staffed with more than 25 people and it has established three new EU legal entities with their own CEOs contracted for a period of seven years to be world-class European KICs. The EU's institutional landscape has a new, unique element added. Compared to what has been the case in similar institution-building attempts earlier in the history of the EU this is a case out of the ordinary. The institution that came about was also unconventional. Formally an EU agency, the EIT's structure and mission is unlike any other. How can we in theoretical terms account for this type of institution building?

The *will, power and control of core actors* over policy shaping loom large in accounting for how the idea of a new EU institution came on the agenda, with a Commission President championing a supranational instrument to address a common European problem. The initiative and the subsequent process triggered the classical conflict over EU jurisdiction that the creation of a new institution under EU law would entail, where actors' interests were pitched against each other. The Commission President promoted an institution for deeper European integration in areas where it had not been successful, whereas the member states favoured the status quo and to have the issue taken off the agenda, as establishing a new institution would not serve their interests. Consequently, the watered-down proposal carries the imprint of national interests. In this respect this case is very much in accordance with the power-oriented perspective. However, other than theoretically proposed, as much as powerful actors did appear as veto players in the process of institution building, one key *enabling* condition for establishment is the political attention at the highest level. Next to the attention from the Commission President, the role of Germany as a powerful member state has been essential for the establishment of the EIT, by rallying the largely negative member states to agree to an institution they did not want. Once Germany had changed its position in the decision-making stage, it used its status, Chancellor Merkel's personal support and the Presidency as a broker to 'giving' the Commission President parts of what he wanted. This underlines not only member state power but also the resources attached to the Presidency as an institution. Yet, the attention, position and will of powerful actors cannot alone account for the EIT coming into being.

First of all, *parallel events* are a key part of the dynamics of institutional design in this case. In the decision stage, the enabling condition for these powerful actors was the temporal order of opening windows of opportunity and the accidental concurrence of other developments. Examples are the timing of the German Presidency, the reshuffling of posts in the EP, the near failure of the European Council Summit in 2007 or the parallel Galileo budget negotiations, which were all crucial for the EIT's development. Actor preferences and power constellations have only been enabled by parallel events and windows of opportunity, as well as by existing norms to which actors could link their positions. The bargaining and politics of design took place in a larger flow of parallel decision-making processes and events.

Furthermore, not only the timing of these events shaped the design process, but also the EIT's *perceived appropriateness*, which allowed for 'legitimate linking'. In the initial phase the taken for granted character of an MIT-like institution was symbolically important: the MIT located in the US, the scientific superpower, made it difficult for opponents to dismiss the concept *per se*. Also part of the solutions proposed mimicked existing initiatives and concepts considered as legitimate among member states and stakeholders. This is especially visible in the organizational model of the KICs and the EIT governance structure. Over the different decision stages the EIT took a shape that no particular actor set had initially promoted, and various elements were assembled and combined in unpredictable ways in the creation of the EIT. The final resolution was far away from looking like the MIT, the iconic source of emulation. Hence, unlike what a 'solution driven' perspective on institutional design would predict, the reference to establishing a new institution by mimicking one particular role model was not in itself a driving force in the design process. Furthermore, the normative and ideational match with ideas dominant in the political economy in Europe, about innovation, cross-sectoral coordination and excellence, was *not* sufficient to carry the EIT proposal through the decision-making process. Symbols of action for the President of the Commission were more important in this respect. President Barroso being new in office did what most political leaders who have just entered office do: signal and affirm executive potency through institution building or reform (March and Olsen 1983). Hence, the argument of supply-driven mimicry in institutional design is only slightly relevant to this case.

From a path-dependent perspective on institutional design we had expected resistance to establishing institutions that upset the boundaries between policy domains. This came across especially in the early stage of the process, where we encountered *path-dependent conservatism at the administrative level* of the supranational and national executive, a conservatism that was confirmed by key stakeholder groups with established access to EU policy-shaping in the knowledge policy domains. As expected, establishing new supranational institutions can hence get entangled in 'sector segments' defending the status quo or parallel initiatives in other areas. This runs counter to the idea that depoliticization enables institution building. Quite the contrary, the political level was less committed to institutionalized ways of doing certain things, and more open towards innovative solutions. Yet, once the proposal was watered down, it became unsustainable for the relevant DGs and stakeholder groups to overtly oppose something that the Commission's political leadership obviously wanted, and over the different stages of the design process the DGs and stakeholders got used to the idea. As it turned out, under such conditions institutional lock-ins can be unlocked. A key lesson to be extracted from this case of institutional design in the EU is that resistance to establishing supranational institutions can come from within the administrative layer of the EU executive. Hence, viewing the supranational executive supported by powerful transnational stakeholders as the spark and engine of supranational institution building (see for example, Majone 1996) does not hold in this case.

Finally, the process of 'giving life to letter' is in its early days and the new institution is still in a fragile position. The preliminary evidence is, however, a reminder of how even smaller additions to the institutional landscape of the EU can have unanticipated consequences, gaining a life outside the immediate control of its creators. The novelty of the EIT's structure – its unique autonomy from its founders – could therefore be seen as an unintended outcome of hardened fronts between the Commission and member states. Both players preferred a flexible regulation, as this veiled clear winners and losers, and therefore handed over the task of giving life to the institution to third, non-political actors. The path that was set and the governance structure of the new institution brought in a new set of actors who aimed to make the best out of the political compromise. The structure contoured by the legal text was filled by actors who started to act independently on behalf of the new institution.

## CONCLUSION

The case of the EIT shows that institution building in nationally sensitive and path-dependent areas is possible within the margins of 'accidental policy-making'. In contrast to the ERC as a case of institution building in the European Research Area (see Gornitzka and Metz 2014, this volume), the EIT clearly demanded powerful promoters at the highest political level. However these promoters depended on seizing decision-making opportunities and had to be willing and able to make compromises that referred to existing legitimate institutions. Barroso wanted the EIT and got it, but not the kind of EIT he had wished for. The initiator of the institution in this case turned out to have very little control over how different elements of what would become the EIT were combined and moulded. A dominant element in the process of institution building in this case is that the EIT, initially received as a novel but unwelcomed idea by most actors, nonetheless survived and was formed by a mixture of actor preferences and concurrent events.

The analysis of the birth of the EIT shows that the creation of contested institutions in a multi-level polity like the EU demands a number of not easily controllable conditions for getting past institutional lock-ins and veto points. As theoretically expected, a proposal cutting across policy and administrative boundaries was hindered by institutionally entrenched inertia from national and supranational administrations, as well as from stakeholders. While power politics in the form of attention from the EU's executive's apex was a driving force throughout the process, national veto players first blocked decision-making, but subsequently served as promoters as soon as the institution had changed its shape. The EIT survived as a weaker reflection of the original idea – weak enough not to be an overt threat to anyone, yet tangible enough to serve as a symbol for reforming the European innovation landscape and for Barroso's legacy. These elements of the design process also were the factors that led to the EU erecting an innovative institutional construction. Theoretical perspectives emphasizing limitations on actors' will, knowledge and control can help account for institution building in this case. As an effect of accidental policy-making, after the decision had been taken, powerful veto players largely disappeared from the arena, giving way to actors who found their own way with the new emerging institutional structures.

## NOTES

1. We thank Miriam Hartlapp for constructive comments to previous versions of this chapter.
2. Addressing formal political institutions, Chapters 4 and 5 in Pierson (2004) are particularly useful as a summary of the main arguments on the limitations of rational design and functional explanations.
3. In our analysis we do not include the informal norms and cultures of the EIT that might have developed since its establishment.
4. At the request of the European Parliament the EIT was renamed from 'European Institute of Technology' to 'European Institute of *Innovation* and Technology' in 2007 during the interinstitutional negotiations.
5. See EURAB's opinion, http://ec.europa.eu/research/eurab/pdf/eurab_05_021_1_eit.pdf, April 2005 (accessed 9 February 2012).
6. Only later on, in 2008 after the decision had been taken, Poland and Hungary actually became enthusiastic competitors for hosting the EIT headquarters.

## REFERENCES

Banchoff, T. (2002), 'Institutions, inertia and European Union research policy', *Journal of Common Market Studies*, **40**(1), 1–21.
Baumgartner, F.R., B.D. Jones and J. Wilkerson (2011), 'Comparative studies of policy dynamics', *Comparative Political Studies*, **44**(8), 947–972.
Berry, J.M. (2002), 'Validity and reliability issues in elite interviewing', *Political Science and Politics*, **35**(4), 679–682.
BusinessEurope (2007), 'BusinessEurope's Views on the European Institute of Technology', Brussels, March 2007.
Cohen, M.D., J.G. March and J.P. Olsen (1972), 'A garbage can model of organizational choice', *Administrative Science Quarterly*, **17**(1), 1–25.

Commission of the European Communities (2004), 'Communication from the Commission to the Council and the European Parliament: Financial Perspectives 2007–2013', *COM(2004) 487 final*, Brussels, 14 July 2004.

Commission of the European Communities (2006a), 'European Institute of Technology: the Commission Proposes a New Flagship for Excellence', *IP/06/201*, Brussels, 22 February 2006.

Commission of the European Communities (2006b), 'Proposal for a Regulation of the European Parliament and the Council Establishing the European Institute of Technology', *COM(2006) 604*, Brussels, 18 October 2006.

Corbett, A. (2005), *Universities and the Europe of Knowledge: Ideas, Institutions and Policy Entrepreneurship in European Union Higher Education Policy, 1955–2005*, Basingstoke: Palgrave Macmillan.

Council of the European Union (2009), 'Conclusions of the Council and of the Representatives of the Governments of the Member States, Meeting Within the Council on Developing the Role of Education in a Fully-Functioning Knowledge Triangle', *14344/09*, Brussels, 20 October 2009.

Curtin, D. and M. Egeberg (2008), 'Tradition and innovation: Europe's accumulated executive order', *West European Politics*, **31**(4), 639–661.

Didier, A.-C. (2010), 'The European Institute of Innovation and Technology (EIT): A New Way for Promoting Innovation in Europe?', *Bruges Political Research Papers*, No. 13, May 2010.

ECORYS (2011), *External Evaluation of the European Institute of Innovation and Technology*.

Egeberg, M. (2006), 'The institutional architecture of the EU and the transformation of European politics', in M. Egeberg (ed.), *Multilevel Union Administration – The Transformation of Executive Politics in Europe*, Houndmills: Palgrave Macmillan, pp. 17–30.

EurActiv (2007), 'Summit Seals Mandate for EU "Reform Treaty"', available at: http://www.euractiv.com/en/future-eu/summit-seals-mandate-eu-reform-treaty/article-164917, Brussels, 23 June 2007 (accessed 25 November 2013).

Europe Information Service (2007), 'Budget 2008: Agreement at last on Galileo Funding', *European Report, No. 3421*, 27 November 2007.

European Commission (2010), 'Communication from the Commission: Europe 2020 – A Strategy for Smart, Sustainable and Inclusive Growth', *COM(2010) 2020 final*, Brussels, 3 March 2010.

European Parliament and Council of the European Union (2008), 'Regulation (EC) No 294/2008 Establishing the European Institute of Innovation and Technology', in Official Journal of the European Union (ed.) *L97*, Luxembourg, 9 April 2008.

Gornitzka, Å. and J. Metz (2014, this volume), 'Dynamics of institution building in the Europe of Knowledge: the birth of European Research Council', in M.-H. Chou and Å. Gornitzka (eds), *Building the Knowledge Economy in Europe: New Constellations in European Research and Higher Education Governance*, Cheltenham, UK and Northampton, MA, USA: Edward Elgar, pp. 81–110.

Groenleer, M. (2009), *The Autonomy of European Agencies: A Comparative Study of Institutional Development*, Delft: Eburon.

Hall, P.A. (2008), 'Systematic process analysis: when and how to use it', *European Political Science*, **7**(3), 304–317.

Hull, R. (1993), 'Lobbying Brussels: a view from within', in S. Mazey and

J. Richardson (eds), *Lobbying in the European Community*, Oxford: Oxford University Press, pp. 82–92.

Kelemen, R.D. and A.D. Tarrant (2011), 'The political foundations of the eurocracy', *West European Politics*, **34**(5), 922–947.

Kingdon, J.W. (1995), *Agendas, Alternatives, and Public Policies*, New York: Longman.

Leslie, I. (2005), 'Cambridge can hold its own against MIT', *Financial Times*, 8 February 2005.

Mahoney, J. and K. Thelen (2010), 'A theory of gradual institutional change', in J. Mahoney and K. Thelen (eds), *Explaining Institutional Change. Ambiguity, Agency and Power*, Cambridge: Cambridge University Press, pp. 1–37.

Majone, G. (1996), *Regulating Europe*, London: Routledge.

March, J.G. (1988), *Decisions and Organizations*, Oxford: Blackwell.

March, J.G. (1994), *A Primer on Decision Making: How Decisions Happen*, New York: The Free Press.

March, J.G. and J.P. Olsen (1983), 'Organizing political life: what administrative reorganization tells us about government', *American Political Science Review*, **77**(2), 281–297.

March, J.G. and J.P. Olsen (2006), 'Elaborating the "new institutionalism"', in R.A.W. Rhodes, S. Binder and B. Rockman (eds), *The Oxford Handbook of Political Institutions*, Oxford: Oxford University Press, pp. 3–20.

Meyer, J.W. and R. Rowan (1977), 'Institutionalized organizations – formal structure as myth and ceremony', *American Journal of Sociology*, **83**, 340–363.

Moe, T.M. (1990), 'Political institutions: the neglected side of the story', *Journal of Law, Economics, and Organization*, **6**, 213–253.

Moravcsik, A. (1998), *The Choice for Europe: Social Purpose and State Power from Messina to Maastricht*, Ithaca: Cornell University Press.

Orren, K. and S. Skowronek (2004), *The Search for American Political Development*, Cambridge: Cambridge University Press.

Pierson, P. (1996), 'The path to European integration: a historical institutionalist analysis', *Comparative Political Studies*, **29**(2), 123–163.

Pierson, P. (2004), *Politics in Time: History, Institutions, and Social Analysis*, Princeton, NJ: Princeton University Press.

Schild, J. (2008), 'How to shift the EU's spending priorities? The multi-annual financial framework 2007–13 in perspective', *Journal of European Public Policy*, **15**(4), 531–549.

Scott, W.R. (2008), *Institutions and Organizations: Ideas and Interests*, Thousand Oaks, CA: Sage Publications.

Stone Sweet, A., W. Sandholtz and N. Fligstein (2001), *The Institutionalisation of Europe*, Oxford: Oxford University Press.

Tallberg, J. (2010), 'Explaining the institutional foundations of European Union negotiations', *Journal of European Public Policy*, **17**(5), 633–647.

Tsebelis, G. and G. Garrett (2000), 'Legislative politics in the European Union', *European Union Politics*, **1**(1), 9–36.

# ANNEX: INTERVIEW SOURCES

## European Commission:

- DG Information Society, Policy Officer, Brussels, 6 July 2009
- DG Research, Adviser, Brussels, 7 July 2009
- Secretariat General, Policy Officer, Brussels, 8 July 2009
- DG Enterprise, Head of Unit, Brussels, 10 July 2010
- DG Education and Culture, Head of Unit, Brussels, 4 September 2009
- DG Education and Culture, Policy Officer, Brussels, 13 November 2009
- DG Research, Director, Brussels, 13 November 2009

## Council of Ministers:

- German Ministry of Education and Research, Director General, and Unit for Education and Research at the German Permanent Representation in Brussels, Head of Unit, Berlin, 4 November 2010
- German Ministry of Education and Research, Director General, Berlin, 7 November 2011

## European Parliament:

- ITRE Committee, Assistant to German MEP, Brussels, 8 December 2009

## External Stakeholders:

- Member of the European Research Advisory Board, telephone interview, 22 December 2010
- Member of the European Research Advisory Board, Berlin, 4 January 2011
- Member of the European Research Advisory Board, Berlin, 1 February 2011
- Member of the European Research Advisory Board, telephone interview, 28 February 2011

# 6. Dynamics of voluntary coordination: actors and networks in the Bologna Process

## Mari Elken and Martina Vukasovic

## INTRODUCTION

The Bologna Process is a Europe-wide initiative of voluntary policy coordination with its main aim to construct what is called the European Higher Education Area (EHEA). Along with the European Research Area (ERA) initiative led by the European Commission, it forms the two main pillars of the Europe of Knowledge (Maassen and Musselin 2009).

The Bologna Process has received much scholarly attention thus far, primarily focused on the national impact and implementation processes, in addition to aspects such as the institutionalization of the process and the role of prominent policy entrepreneurs (Corbett 2005, 2011; Haskel 2008; Hoareau 2012; Ravinet 2008b; Veiga and Amaral 2006). It has been characterized by its limited administrative capacity, general lack of legally binding instruments and a formally intergovernmental nature although the European Commission has a prominent role in the process (Corbett 2011). Nevertheless, it has been claimed to be a catalyst for wide reform processes across Europe, and despite its limitations it has led to the emergence of an additional governance layer.

Being a case of voluntary policy coordination, the process exhibits similarities with the European Union's (EU) Open Method of Coordination (OMC) approach, with focus on heterarchy, decentredness and dynamic aspects of the process (Hodson and Maher 2001) and has an emphasis on activities forming around targets, benchmarking, and 'naming and shaming'. Despite its loosely structured nature, the Bologna Process has become a platform for further European integration in an area where this was seen as practically impossible only a few decades ago. From being a declaration of intent, it has become regular and institutionalized (Beerkens 2008; Ravinet 2008a) and in addition to the participating countries, a number of European level organizations have become involved in the process. While inclusion of such stakeholder organizations does reflect domestic processes in many of the countries that are part of the Bologna Process it also seems to be taken for granted on the European level. Thus, the first puzzle is how we can account for the specific boundary rules of this process and the mechanisms that assured this gradual shift away from an intergovernmental process. This in addition implies that policy coordination in this case is not done just by a variety of actors, but by collective actors who have linkages to different governance levels.

This leads us to the basic question: who are these various collective actors, in what capacity do they participate and how can we explain their involvement in the process? An interconnected question is: how has the coordination and governance arrangement of the process developed over time? Further, what can be said about the relationship between various types of collective actors (including national authorities as well as intergovernmental and supranational bodies and transnational organizations) and the shifts in their relative power over time? Finally, how does this particular relationship between these collective actors contribute to the overall continuity, stability and openness of a voluntary policy coordination process such as Bologna?

We argue that adopting a network perspective allows us to shed light on the evolution of governance of the Bologna Process and highlight the dynamics and relative power between various types of actors, both collective and individual. We define actors as those who (through purposeful action) are attempting to affect the policy process and who are involved in this policy arena. In that sense, we can see both collective actors and individual actors in the Bologna Process. The collective actors include national ministries responsible for higher education, in addition to supranational, intergovernmental and transnational organizations that are part of the official Bologna Process structures. Individual actors take part in various capacities, but, as will be demonstrated later, enter the process through collective actors. And, it is the particular set of individual actors and their interactions that is of relevance for the stability of the process.

The following section will further explain the analytical starting point of this chapter, followed by an empirical examination of the developments in governance of the Bologna Process, with attention to the decision-making structures, inclusion of collective actors and the role of individuals. We conclude the chapter first by arguing that there is a specific set of collective actors involved in this process, which decreases the intergovernmental character of the Bologna Process and adds a transnational flavour to this particular case of voluntary policy coordination. Second, the individual actors who have entered the process through these collective actors have produced a network that is both stable and relatively closed, despite the lack of administrative capacity and loosely organized nature of the process.

# THE RATIONALE FOR AND IMPLICATIONS OF USING THE NETWORK PERSPECTIVE

Although broadly used, the network concept suffers from concept stretching (Sartori 1970): on the one hand it can refer to using networks as analytical tools to examine a particular process, while on the other hand it implies a more theoretical account of how governance is organized (Börzel 1997, 1998). While these two uses are not mutually exclusive, the clarification has important implications for levels of analysis and the analytical tools employed – where policy networks have a focus closer to individuals who form a particular policy network, network governance is focused more on the implications of these changing regimes on the level of societal systems.

Labelling the Bologna Process as a process of voluntary policy coordination, we presume a flat and loose structure for policy-making, as an alternative to the traditional hierarchy or market-like coordination. By focusing on the development of this network over time, we essentially also assume that voluntary policy coordination resembles an exercise of network governance when taking a macro perspective on the process. However, we use the network perspective as an analytical tool to gain a better understanding of the actor dynamics in the process – first on the meso-level where different kinds of collective actors have been included over time and furthermore on the micro-level in terms of the network of individual actors. As such, our focus is on examining the network itself and not the relationship to policy outputs or outcomes. A network perspective has rarely been applied to analysing the dynamic of the Bologna Process, and as such the analysis provides a novel lens to further understand how and why governance of voluntary policy coordination develops over time. We examine the existence and nature of a network on two separate but interconnected levels of analysis – between different kinds of collective actors in a context of voluntary international policy coordination, and how this is related to the set of individual actors participating in this arena.

## Policy Networks vs Network Governance

A number of different perspectives and theoretical implications can be linked to adopting a network perspective: they can exist on a number of levels and their conceptualizations vary depending on the disciplinary origins (sociology and political science). Comparing these two disciplinary traditions, on the macro-level one can find perspectives on the political economy of organizations and neopluralism; on the meso-level one can find interorganizational analysis and intergovernmental relations; and on the micro-level one can find group dynamics, social network analysis and various issue networks (Rhodes 1990). In recent years, two major research traditions focusing on the role of networks can be identified. One is the tradition on network governance that focuses on the state-society relationships, and the other is literature on policy networks that is more concerned with the structure of specific policy networks and their potential impact on outputs and outcomes (Fawcett and Daugbjerg 2012). These two traditions however imply a different level of analysis and a quite different use of the term network. The literature on policy networks is quite extensive but at times unsystematic, and there have been various attempts to create order in the myriad of labels available for various network perspectives in the policy literature: (1) according to discipline (Rhodes 1990); (2) chronological development over time (Dassen 2010; Jordan 1990); or (3) a set of characteristics (Jordan and Schubert 1992; Van Waarden 1992). Nevertheless, their common starting point is that they examine the interaction between various actors involved in a policy process. The network governance tradition is more focused on the horizontalization of governance arrangements, in essence referring to the inclusion of interest groups in policy processes (Gornitzka 2010). A significant part of this research tradition is focused on the democratic implications of such arrangements (Sørensen and Torfing 2003). However, both traditions suggest that applying a network perspective to explain the relationship between state and society has become a 'conventional wisdom' (Van Waarden 1992).

The increasing emphasis on horizontal coordination is especially noticeable in international policy arenas (Coleman and Perl 1999) in addition to the traditional lobbying and bargaining processes (Torfing and Triantafillou 2011, p. 6). This greater focus on horizontalization and focus on actors has also been referred to as decentred or 'interactive policy-making', implying a flatter and inclusive process of policy-making with a wide range of stakeholders included (Torfing and Triantafillou 2011). This conceptualization includes a number of various designs of these arenas with a range of formalization and institutionalization, from relatively loose discussion arenas to more formalized governance networks. The necessity for such arenas has increased due to the growing complexity of society that in turn leads to fragmentation (Torfing and Triantafillou 2011). As higher education in Europe consists of a diverse set of systems and given that higher education has traditionally been considered a predominantly national policy issue not suitable for an EU level decision-making (Gornitzka 2007), the way to develop a coordination structure for a process like the Bologna Process precisely requires such an interactive arena. In this, it is the horizontal interaction of various collective actors that makes action possible.

## Operationalizing Networks: Boundaries, Power Dependence and Stability

In order to study a network structure, a basic operationalization can be made, including actors, linkages and boundaries (Kenis and Scheider 1991). This means attention to the nature of the actors and their basis for participation, the boundaries that frame this network and the types of interaction between the actors. Being by definition non-hierarchical and horizontal, one places this perspective as distinctively different from the traditional hierarchical and market coordination perspectives, thus also highlighting the role of informal structures (Jones et al. 1997). However, being non-hierarchical does not presuppose that actors are assumed to have equal status in the network, either in terms of their formal or informal position. A network perspective can contain asymmetries, either based on power or on resources of various kinds. Therefore, an examination of the network would require attention to the power dependence between actors in terms of capacity to decide on legitimate action. Last but not least, we argue that a key concept overarching this debate is the overall integration and stability of the network.

### Setting boundaries and power dependency: exercise in meta-governance
Boundaries are not only defined by formal institutions, but are based on mutual agreement between actors (Kenis and Scheider 1991). This implies that in this perspective it is not only the formal boundary rules that specify the scope of a network, and that various constellations of actors and processes of inclusion can inhibit important informal aspects. Therefore, even when it is not the basis for formal decision-making, a network perspective implies that actors can exert influence by informal means (Börzel 1998). This highlights the need to examine the formal position and how this is linked to the relative power of the actors and whether some discrepancies can be identified. As such, one would need to examine the boundary rules that define membership, in addition to the general openness of the network and possibilities for entrance.

When examining the development of boundary rules over time, a core question becomes how rules that set a basis for governing this network are being developed and on what basis an agreement is reached. In essence, the process under scrutiny can thus also be seen as an exercise of meta-governance – initiatives by a certain number of actors to create and design a new governance arena through their formal or informal capacity (Torfing and Triantafillou 2011). Provided that our focus is on a voluntary coordination process, the use of the term resembles the one by Torfing and Triantafillou (2011) who examined meta-governance in the light of decentred policy processes. As such, our definition of meta-governance is the capacity to delineate boundaries for facilitation (what kind of incentives), regulation (who is included and how structured), and framing (what kind of measures are legitimate) of a policy process where actors voluntarily participate. The concept of meta-governance implies a certain element of design and purposeful action, despite variation in terms of hands-on and hands-off meta-governance (ibid.). In essence, any formal agreement on the rules of the game implies that there is some element of design in place to structure the governance arrangements of the process. The question thus becomes where do the rules of the game come from and to what extent have they been carefully planned or have they naturally emerged in the process (hands-on vs hands-off)? In addition, are there actors who appear to have a more prominent role in defining the rules? Furthermore, what is required to become a member? What are the formal and informal rules for this to occur and how stable is the membership? And not least, are the rules for membership clear?

**Focus on collective and individual actors**
By assuming meta-governance, this also implies a certain asymmetry between the actors power to push towards changing the rules. Therefore, power dependence between actors has important implications (Fawcett and Daugbjerg 2012), as the position of various collective actors can also have implications on overriding certain formal rules, and certain informal rules and individual actors can also have a powerful role in deciding legitimate and possible action. Even when one focuses on developments around collective actors, it is nevertheless individuals who are engaged in the process. While individual actors have their own preferences and opinions, they are also constrained by the organizations they belong to (Scharpf 1997) or arguably have belonged to previously. Having legitimized their role and position on certain issues as a representative of a particular organization, one can argue that that the sort of information they have been exposed to and the institutional environment as a whole has in turn had an impact on their preferences and orientations, that is, they 'went native' (Checkel 2005). Furthermore, one can thus question what kind of consequences this has for the participation of that individual actor in the network as well as how does this affect the stability and integration of the network.

## Stability of networks

Where earlier modes of coordination have been termed as rigid and formalized, networks are perceived as more fluid and less institutionalized in comparison (Lewis and Considine 2011). Stability is one of the key concepts in the literature about networks in general and the various classification systems that have been developed on policy networks (Coleman and Perl 1999; Jordan 1990; Marsh 1998a, 1998b; Van Waarden 1992). If a network does not have sufficient stability, it instead forms an issue network, a temporary structure that is focused on a very specific policy problem (Heclo 1978) and does not live past the resolution of said problem. The governance structures of the Bologna Process continued to exist beyond the self-imposed deadline of 2010 to establish the EHEA. One reason for this can be found in the partial implementation of some of the Bologna action lines (for example, qualification frameworks or student-centred learning). However, more important in the context of this chapter is the fact that there was continuous addition and further specification of action lines as the processes unfolded, suggesting that the process of Bologna policy coordination goes beyond addressing a one-time problem and that this added governance layer has become institutionalized. Therefore, examining the stability of this network gives important information about the opportunities to develop informal power dependencies between actors. Furthermore, an assumption can be made that the more closed policy networks are (with a low turnover of individual participants), the more stable and institutionalized they become. As such, the purpose is also to examine the role of individuals in interorganizational and intergovernmental policy-making and to what extent they act either as facilitators of stability or change in this network.

While distinguishing between levels of analysis is essential (Rhodes 1990), we argue that there are also important links between levels of analysis. When examining intergovernmental and organizational relations in these new policy arenas, the informal networks between individuals provide an important means for exchange of information and resources in addition to the more formalized occasions. Therefore, we argue that the inclusion of both individual and collective actors in the analysis allows us to better understand the dynamic of this process.

## Legitimacy

A number of the issues raised thus far are inherently linked to the concept of legitimacy. Legitimacy is another concept that often gets used, but rarely clearly defined, nor is it clearly identified why legitimacy matters to start with (Hurd 1999). A very basic definition would be that legitimacy as a form of power provides a source for order due to normative beliefs that a rule should be obeyed, and this goes beyond formal rules (coercion) and pure self-interest. As such, legitimacy, self-interest and coercion are the three basic mechanisms for compliance with a rule (Hurd 1999). For instance, in order for new collective actors to become a member of the process they have to be perceived as legitimate participants by existing members. In addition, when examining power dependencies between actors, the exercise of power has to be perceived as a legitimate one by others involved – especially in cases where this goes beyond formal rules (that is lobbying for new and other kinds of collective actors to be included). Not least, the Bologna Process as a whole is dependent on being perceived as legitimate on a national level, due to the sensitivity of education as a subject for European level coordination. This might hint that the inclusion of particular transnational actors can further provide legitimacy for the overall process and assure compliance on a national level (see below).

## Questions, Concepts and Methods of Analysis

The degree to which the governance arrangements of the Bologna Process were planned or emerged spontaneously is an empirical question. This implies an examination of the specific rules for participation that are set formally (who is allowed in?) and how have these rules evolved over time (have they changed, if so – when and why?). Overall, a core question becomes how a formally loosely coupled and weak coordination process can exercise meta-governance? Can we identify a purposeful process led by specific collective actors? And not least, how does one account for the gradual evolution away from an intergovernmental process, and the gradual involvement of a supranational actor (the European Commission) and various transnational organizations? Have particular actors had the role of gate-keepers and how have they exercised their (formal or informal) power to either prohibit or include new collective actors?

In order to examine policy networks, Coleman and Perl (1999) suggest a set of properties that in total give an indication whether the network is highly integrated and thus stable: (1) openness and boundary rules concerning membership; (2) size of the community and membership stability; (3) internationalization of interaction; and (4) the density and structure of information exchange. A stable network on an international policy arena would thus have relatively formalized rules for membership, have a stable and limited membership with internationalized interaction and high level of information exchange. Thus, we will focus on how the structural composition of the network developed on the meso-level (that is between collective actors), outlining the power division between various actors in terms of their opportunities to shape the network. Furthermore, we argue that the relative power of various organizations and individuals has not only been based on their formal competence, thus the role of the individuals acquires an additional dimension, given that according to Coleman and Perl (1999) their concurrent affiliation to collective actors puts them in a unique position to act as mediators. The role of mediators resembles somewhat of Sabatier's policy brokers (Sabatier 1988), but the role of a mediator can, in addition to active advocacy and conflict management to advance a policy process, have a much more soft nature where focus is on the translation of ideas and the development of common norms and values (Coleman and Perl 1999). In order to gain a deeper insight into the network structure on the individual level, we use the dimensions outlined by (Coleman and Perl 1999) – including factors related to the structure, interaction, membership and information exchange in this network.

The collective actors involved in the analysis include those who have been a part of the official decision-making structure (what came to be the Bologna Follow-Up Group, BFUG): European Commission (EC), Council of Europe (CoE), European University Association (EUA), European Association of Higher Education Institutions (EURASHE), European Students' Union (formerly known as ESIB – The National Unions of Students in Europe, ESU/ESIB), European Network for Quality Assurance in Higher Education (ENQA), pan-European structure of Education International (EI), United Nations Educational, Scientific and Cultural Organization (UNESCO, formerly as UNESCO/CEPES) and BusinessEurope (until 2007 called UNICE). The individual actors included in the analysis are actors who have at some point acted as representatives or worked for the aforementioned collective actors. As will be demonstrated later, some of these individual actors have been linked to several collective actors, and their movements between the collective actors have been traced on the basis of both organizational and individual biographical data.

The analysis is based on a qualitative analysis of official statements of the Bologna Process, various Bologna implementation reports, organizational data on collective actors, participation records of Bologna meetings (ministerial summits every two years, as well as BFUG meetings that take place at least once every six months with representatives from both full and consultative members), basic biographical data on individual actors collected from their personal or organizational websites, as well as secondary sources.

# POWER DEPENDENCE AND META-GOVERNANCE OF THE BOLOGNA PROCESS

Some authors refer to the Bologna Declaration as the beginning of the Bologna Process (Kehm 2010). Others, recognizing that the Bologna Process is only one aspect of building the Europe of Knowledge (Elken et al. 2011; Maassen and Musselin 2009), focus on the various European or transnational initiatives in higher education, and therefore indicate that the important events in this context were the Socrates-Erasmus decision in 1995 (Hackl 2001), signing of the Magna Charta Universitatum in 1988 (Neave and Maassen 2007), marketization turn in higher education in 1981 (Neave 2009, pp. 22–23) or even earlier initiatives within the EU framework (Corbett 2012). However, by many accounts (Corbett 2005; Faber and Westerheijden 2011; Hoareau 2012; Middlehurst and Teixeira 2012; Ravinet 2008b; Veiga and Amaral 2009; Witte 2008) the Sorbonne Declaration, signed in May 1998 by four ministers responsible for higher education in France, Germany, Italy and the UK, is a 'beginning of a new policy episode' (Corbett 2012, p. 52) and this is where our analysis of the governance of the Bologna Process will start. See Figure 6.1 for an overview of the evolution of the Bolonga Process governance arrangement.

**1998–2000: From the Sorbonne Four to the Question of the EU Commission and the University Associations' Involvement**

The Sorbonne Declaration, though listing a number of policy preferences related to mobility, recognition of qualifications, two main degree cycles, use of European Credit Transfer and Accumulation System (ECTS) and so on is rather poor with references to meta-governance, that is, how this process is to be governed, and how is membership in the process to be defined.

Ravinet (2008b) traces the origins of the Bologna governance arrangement to an Education Council meeting from early autumn 1998, that is quite quickly after the Sorbonne meeting and argues that the EU ministers took their own way of working as 'the first available satisfactory solution' (ibid., p. 359). The so-called Sorbonne Follow-Up Group (SFUG, see Figure 6.1) was put in charge of preparing the meeting in Bologna (including the drafting of the Declaration and contacting the participants). It was composed of the EU Troika (Austria, Germany, Finland), an Italian representative, and representatives of the EC, the Confederation of EU Rectors' Conferences and the Association of European Universities (CRE)[1] (ibid., p. 359), meaning that non-EU countries had no power to influence the

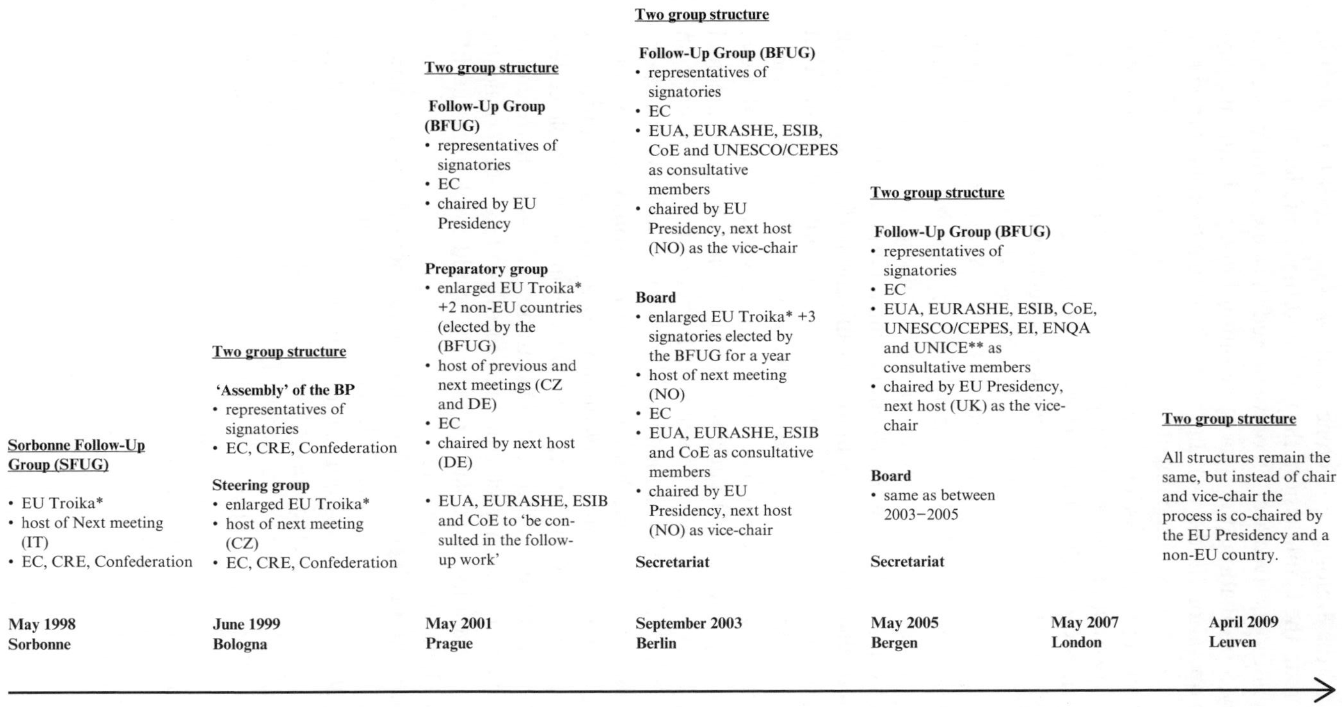

| May 1998 Sorbonne | June 1999 Bologna | May 2001 Prague | September 2003 Berlin | May 2005 Bergen | May 2007 London | April 2009 Leuven |
|---|---|---|---|---|---|---|
| **Sorbonne Follow-Up Group (SFUG)**<br>• EU Troika*<br>• host of Next meeting (IT)<br>• EC, CRE, Confederation | **Two group structure**<br>**'Assembly' of the BP**<br>• representatives of signatories<br>• EC, CRE, Confederation<br><br>**Steering group**<br>• enlarged EU Troika*<br>• host of next meeting (CZ)<br>• EC, CRE, Confederation | **Two group structure**<br>**Follow-Up Group (BFUG)**<br>• representatives of signatories<br>• EC<br>• chaired by EU Presidency<br><br>**Preparatory group**<br>• enlarged EU Troika* +2 non-EU countries (elected by the (BFUG)<br>• host of previous and next meetings (CZ and DE)<br>• EC<br>• chaired by next host (DE)<br>• EUA, EURASHE, ESIB and CoE to 'be consulted in the follow-up work' | **Two group structure**<br>**Follow-Up Group (BFUG)**<br>• representatives of signatories<br>• EC<br>• EUA, EURASHE, ESIB, CoE and UNESCO/CEPES as consultative members<br>• chaired by EU Presidency, next host (NO) as the vice-chair<br><br>**Board**<br>• enlarged EU Troika* +3 signatories elected by the BFUG for a year<br>• host of next meeting (NO)<br>• EC<br>• EUA, EURASHE, ESIB and CoE as consultative members<br>• chaired by EU Presidency, next host (NO) as vice-chair<br><br>**Secretariat** | **Two group structure**<br>**Follow-Up Group (BFUG)**<br>• representatives of signatories<br>• EC<br>• EUA, EURASHE, ESIB, CoE, UNESCO/CEPES, EI, ENQA and UNICE** as consultative members<br>• chaired by EU Presidency, next host (UK) as the vice-chair<br><br>**Board**<br>• same as between 2003–2005<br><br>**Secretariat** | **Two group structure**<br>All structures remain the same, but instead of chair and vice-chair the process is co-chaired by the EU Presidency and a non-EU country. |

*Notes:* * EU Troika – past, current and future EU Presidency; enlarged EU Troika – past, current and 2 future EU Presidencies; ** UNICE – changed its name in 2007 to BusinessEurope.

*Source:* based on official Bologna documents and Ravinet (2008b).

*Figure 6.1 Overview of the evolution of the Bologna Process governance arrangement*

preparation of the Bologna conference and the same goes for collective actors other than the Commission, the CRE and the Confederation.

In 1999 the Bologna Declaration only stressed the view of the process as one of policy coordination (Bologna Declaration 1999, p. 3) and intergovernmental cooperation (ibid., p. 4), and underlined that 'non-governmental European organizations with competence on higher education' (ibid., p. 4) would take part in this process. The latter in some ways legitimized the situation in which two academic associations (the CRE and the Confederation) were already involved in the SFUG. However, it also opened up the space for the inclusion of a variety of collective actors, such as the non-university counterpart of the CRE – the EURASHE,[2] as well student organizations operating at the European level, such as ESIB,[3] Association des Etats Généraux des Etudiants de l'Europe (the European Students' Forum, AEGEE), the Erasmus Student Network (ESN), discipline-based organizations and so on. According to this formulation, additional eligible collective actors were also teacher trade union organizations (for example, EI), organizations focusing on particular issues, such as the internationalization of higher education (for example, Academic Cooperation Association – ACA) or employers' associations. Other non-governmental collective actors that emerged somewhat later but would fit the 'non-governmental European organizations with competence on higher education' description include the ENQA, founded in 2000 and the Magna Charta Observatory (MCO), founded in the second half of 2001. For reasons discussed later, it is important to stress that the focus on non-governmental organizations implied that neither the CoE nor UNESCO were amongst eligible collective actors according to the Bologna Declaration. Finally, the reference to the intergovernmental character of the process and non-governmental European organizations, if adhered to strictly, would imply that the EC would not be eligible to participate.

However, despite the lack of official indication about meta-governance in the formal documents of the Bologna Process from 1998 and 1999, the process of institutionalization of the governance structure follows the pattern set immediately after the Sorbonne meeting (Ravinet 2008b). The EU Ministers met during the Finnish Presidency in Tampere in September 1999 and established two groups. The first one, responsible for steering the process, was restricted to the national representatives of the enlarged EU Troika (previous, present and two successive presidencies) and the Czech Republic (as the host of the then upcoming Prague Ministerial Summit in 2001) and the non-national collective actors: the EC, the Confederation and the CRE. The second group was the so-called 'enlarged' group composed of the representatives of all of the 29 signatory countries and the previously mentioned non-national collective actors.

The first puzzle emerges: if the aim was to limit EU involvement, how come a decision on the Bologna Process governance arrangement was made in an EU meeting in the first place and why in all of the governance arrangements in the Bologna Process is the EU rather prominent, through the Commission and strong involvement of the EU Troika and the EU Presidency? This has been extensively addressed in Ravinet (2008b) and Corbett (2011), showing a strong path dependence in reliance on the already tested community-like approach and underlying that none of the other collective actors had the financial and organizational resources to push the process further. In addition, as indicated by Corbett (2005), the bulk of the Bologna Process policy preferences were highly resonant with earlier EU activities in the area of higher education and included strong reliance on several instruments launched within the EU higher education initiatives and recommendations, such as the ECTS, focus on mobility and European cooperation in quality assurance.[4] The issue of how much the EU should feature in the Bologna Process has come to the fore several times since the meeting in Bologna in 2001 (see Figure 6.1). From 2003 onwards the Commission was a full member of the BFUG (the only full member that is not a national government). There are some indications that the Commission (or rather the DG responsible for higher education) did not manage to be as involved as it might have wanted: the proposal that the Secretariat of the process (in existence since the Berlin meeting in 2003) should not be rotating from one host country to another, but should be hosted by the Commission instead, was rejected twice: once in Berlin and then again in Bergen (Haskel 2008, p. 11).

The second puzzle is how the CRE and the Confederation joined. This takes us back to the immediate aftermath of Sorbonne. As indicated by Corbett (2005, p. 197), the CRE and the Confederation were 'the first to seize the chance to get a foot in the policy process. They gave Guy Haug, well known in the unofficial "Europe of Education" networks, the job of "improving" the Sorbonne declaration'. Furthermore, the CRE and the Confederation, and after 2001 their successor, the EUA, have supported the process actively, through the organization of seminars as well as the production of publications, not least the traditional 'Trends Report' series. Corbett (2005) also reminds us that the CRE has had a close cooperation with the Commission well before the Bologna Process began. In addition, the inclusion of the two academic associations in the follow-up of the process also decreased the strong governmental, top-down character of the process and therefore increased its legitimacy within the academic community, though the question remains whether these associations are representative of the academic community or of the universities as organizations (Neave and Maassen 2007). As indicated in Figure 6.1 and discussed in more detail later, the legitimacy with regards to the academic community was to be boosted again in 2005 with the inclusion of EI.

### 2000–2003: Enter the Council of Europe, Non-University Sector and Students

Neither of the groups established after the Bologna Ministerial Summit had the explicit mandate to include other countries or organizations as part of the enlarged follow-up group (Lourtie 2001). However as Lourtie (2001, pp. 2–3, added emphasis) says:

> ... it was the understanding of the groups that it would fall under the mandate of the enlarged group to *accept participation of other organisations as observers.* In 2000, *the Council of Europe, a Student Platform* and EURASHE were added, as observers, to the enlarged group. Any other decisions concerning the participation in the follow-up groups will have to be taken by the Ministers in Prague. *If the procedure adopted by the follow-up group is to be revised, an appropriate mandate from the Ministers is required.*

The Communiqué adopted at the Prague Ministerial Summit in 2001 clearly states that, apart from the EUA, the three other collective actors are to be 'consulted in the follow-up work' (Prague Communiqué 2001, p. 2).

What does the extension of the group to include the CoE, EURASHE and 'a Student Platform' tell us about the legitimacy of the governance arrangement thus far and the relative power of different collective actors?

With regards to the inclusion of the CoE, if the reference to non-governmental European organizations from the Bologna Declaration is adhered to strictly, the CoE, as an intergovernmental organization would not be eligible to take part. However, what seems to have worked to the CoE's advantage was first of all its pan-European coverage, with countries well outside of the EU as members (including Russia, the Caucasus countries and so on). The CoE was also heavily present in the EU candidate countries in the early 1990s through its Legislative Reform Programme (Fischer Appelt 1996) and the inclusion of the CoE took away the focus from the EU (even though the Commission and the EU Presidency continued to play a strong role). Furthermore, having in mind the formally rather weak EU capacity in the area of higher education, the CoE (together with UNESCO) had at its disposal the only legally binding instrument of relevance to the Bologna Process – the 'Convention on the Recognition of Qualifications Concerning Higher Education in the European Region' (the so-called Lisbon Recognition Convention, LRC) from 1997, already ratified by 33 European countries before the Bologna Ministerial Summit in 1999. Thus, the inclusion of the CoE boosted the legitimacy of the process by taking away the focus from the problematic EU involvement and by building on the already existing LRC and CoE presence in both the EU candidate and the so-called third countries on issues related to higher education.

When it comes to the inclusion of the EURASHE, it can be seen as 'the EUA of the non-university sector'. Therefore, given the Bologna Process' strong focus on employability and transferable skills as well as the fact that in many European countries a large part of the student population attends non-university higher education institutions (for example, polytechnics, university colleges), it could be said that the inclusion of the EURASHE was almost inevitable. However, the EURASHE remains less prominent in the process. It does not produce a counterpart to the EUA's 'Trends Reports', it organizes less events, produces less publications. Although it has existed since 1990, it was also much less visible in the European arena prior to the Bologna Process, unlike the CRE and the Confederation, the EUA's predecessors. Thus, the EURASHE's presence in the Bologna Process is weaker than the EUA's and is a reflection, first and foremost, of the differences in strength and prominence of the national organizations – university umbrella organizations and/or Rectors' Conferences are in many cases organizationally stronger within different countries than their non-university counterparts. In addition, this reflects more general developments in the higher education sector – while some countries seem to have erased their binary divide (for example, the UK), some maintain it (Finland).

With regards to the possibility of including a 'Student Platform' in the process, it is a part of a more general move towards including different stakeholders to boost the legitimacy of the process. No student organization was officially present when the Bologna Declaration was signed. However, the ESIB managed to secure access to the meeting through its member organization from Italy (Klemenčič 2011). As indicated earlier, the reference to a 'Student Platform' opens up the possibility to include a number of student organizations operating on the European level, including the aforementioned AEGEE and ESN, and initially there were attempts to form one platform out of these three organizations (Haskel 2008). However, the strength of the ESU/ESIB was its membership base. Unlike the AEGEE and the ESN, the ESU/ESIB members were national student organizations which, in order to be eligible for ESU/ESIB membership, needed to be representative within their national contexts, primarily in terms of the proportion of students they represent in domestic higher education policy arena. While the ESU/ESIB legitimacy stems from the legitimacy of its members in the domestic contexts, the AEGEE and the ESN are structured in a more top-down manner, with branches established in cities (AEGEE) or in relation to the EU Commission mobility programmes (ESN). The AEGEE does not focus on representing students in policy processes, while the ESN focuses only on international (mobile) students. Furthermore, the ESU/ESIB had student participation in higher education governance as one of its key policies and soon after the Bologna Summit established a specific committee[5] responsible for the Bologna Process who actively worked towards both inclusion in the process and uploading policy preferences. This was done through a combination of European level activities (participation in the official Bologna seminars and other European events), organizing high level events (for example, the Goteborg Student Convention sponsored by the Swedish EU Presidency in the run-up to the Prague Ministerial Summit), lobbying through national student unions which had good relationships with ministries responsible for higher education in their countries (again Sweden as one example, but also many Nordic, Benelux and French student unions), establishing close cooperation with other partners (at that time first and foremost the CoE and the EUA) and through developing policies and producing publications on the topic (Klemenčič 2011). Thus, the ESU/ESIB outran its competitors and already in the Prague Communiqué of 2001, the vague 'Student Platform' label is dropped and the ESU/ESIB (together with the EUA, the EURASHE and the CoE) is explicitly referred to as being 'consulted in the follow-up work' in the future, and students are seen as 'competent, active and constructive partners' (Prague Communiqué 2001, p. 2). Further recognition of the ESU/ESIB as the representative student platform came in Berlin when, this time together with the EUA, the EURASHE and the ENQA, the ESU/ESIB was put in charge of developing the European Standards and Guidelines for Quality Assurance in Higher Education (ESG).

### 2003–2005: Enter the ENQA, Teacher Trade Unions, Employers and the UNESCO

The inclusion of the European Network for Quality Assurance Agencies in Higher Education (ENQA)[6] in the BFUG as a consultative member is linked to the strong focus on quality assurance issues between Berlin 2003 and Bergen 2005 in terms of developing the ESG and defining quality assurance as one of the priorities to be addressed in the Stocktaking Report. The ENQA was furthermore connected to earlier cooperation in this area sponsored by the EU through large European Pilot Projects for Evaluating Quality in Higher Education in the mid-1990s that culminated with the adoption of the Council Recommendation of 24 September 1998 on 'European Cooperation in Quality Assurance in Higher Education'.[7] The EC was heavily involved in the foundation of the ENQA, including decisions concerning the organizational structure, operational objectives and financial support (ENQA 2010). The ENQA was launched in early 2000 in Brussels, at a meeting of quality assurance (QA) agencies and ministry representatives from the EU/European Economic Area (EEA) countries. It also established close cooperation with the EUA, the EURASHE and the ESU/ESIB early on in the Bologna Process, and included them in its Steering Group as well as large scale projects (the first being the so-called TEEP project, the Transnational European Evaluation Project[8]). It was very active, both publication and event wise, and provided significant input in terms of development of QA agencies in Central and Eastern Europe, given that membership of the national QA agency in the ENQA was a quality seal improving trust in a national agency in the domestic arena, but also boosting the trust in the overall quality of higher education in the said country internationally. The heavy focus on QA and the adoption of the ESG in 2005 eventually gave rise to the European Register of Quality Assurance Agencies (EQAR). Thus, a combination of: (1) cooperation with a number of other collective actors; (2) strong linkages with the Commission; and (3) importance of the QA action line in the Bologna Process, paved the way towards inclusion of the ENQA in the Bologna governance arrangement. This further boosted the legitimacy of the process from the point of view of QA agencies, which in turn were expected to facilitate implementation of QA-related action lines of the Bologna Process in the domestic contexts.

The inclusion of the UNICE[9] as a representative of employers and EI as a representative of academic staff took place at the same Bergen meeting in 2005, but for different reasons. The UNICE took advantage of the employability focus: the new Bologna degrees had to be labour market relevant and who better to consult about this relevance than employers. However, the UNICE's presence in the process has not been prominent. Similar to the EURASHE, the UNICE do not produce specific reports for the ministerial conferences and do not have particular policy statements on the Bologna Process or on higher education in particular, they focus more on lifelong learning and general (secondary and primary) education. They are also much less active than other collective actors in the Bologna Process working groups and networks: they are part of three groups, while other collective actors (in particular the ESU/ESIB and the EUA) are active in almost all of them.

The inclusion of EI as a consultative member of the BFUG in 2005 was partly connected to the fact that by that time the implementation in many signatory countries had progressed beyond just legislative changes, to include changes in study programme structure, curricula, teaching and learning approaches and so on, the support of the academic staff was essential. However, while the EUA and later also the EURASHE joined as representatives of higher education institutions and the ESU/ESIB as a representative of students, until 2005 there was no group representing the academic staff directly, which deteriorated the legitimacy of the process amongst those expected to implement changes at the grass-roots level (Neave and Maassen 2007, p. 140), in particular given the polarization of views on the Bologna Process amongst academic staff regarding the time spent on implementation and the added value gained (Gornitzka and Langfeldt 2005). It should be stated that, while the UNICE had a history of cooperation with the EC and could rely on this connection to secure their place in the BFUG, EI initially had only an informal connection to the ESU/ESIB, through regular annual meetings with the new ESU/ESIB leadership. The fact that both organizations are essentially umbrella organizations for trade or trade-like unions indicated shared interests and facilitated this bond. The communication and cooperation between the two organizations was intensified and further formalized between the Berlin Ministerial Summit in 2003 and the one held in Bergen in 2005 (when EI was accepted into the BFUG), through several joint projects (mostly funded by the EU). The trade union-like character of both organizations implies also similarity of norms and beliefs regarding higher education (in particular financing and governance). Of course, the ESU/ESIB, a consultative member itself, was formally a much weaker player than the Commission in terms of pushing forward particular policy preferences or the case of EI becoming a member of the BFUG. However, the ESU/ESIB could benefit from EI joining the BFUG because that would essentially introduce a potential ally on issues of financing and governance. Thus, building on the idea that the governance arrangement of the Bologna Process should essentially be inclusive in terms of the participation of different stakeholders, and making alliances with other collective actors (some national ministries and the CoE first and foremost), the ESU/ESIB contributed to the inclusion of EI in the BFUG.

The story behind the involvement of the UNESCO/CEPES is less clear. The UNESCO/CEPES was a European centre based in Bucharest part of the UNESCO structure, established in 1972 to promote cooperation between the UNESCO's member states from the so-called Europe Region (European countries, North America and Israel). Its activities, given its strategic placement behind the Iron Curtain, were mostly focused on Central and Eastern Europe. In its information gathering, consultancy and policy development support activities, the UNESCO/CEPES coordinated a number of projects, organized events and also published books and a journal (*Higher Education in Europe*[10]). Thus, the UNESCO/CEPES as a branch of an intergovernmental organization whose scope was worldwide, not only European, would not be eligible to take part if the initial Bologna Declaration reference to non-governmental European organizations was interpreted strictly. Furthermore, the UNESCO/CEPES did not really add further legitimacy to the process, since it did not bring significantly novel stakeholder perspectives that were not already involved through the CoE or national ministries. However, the UNESCO/CEPES was strongly connected to the CoE through the aforementioned LRC, since it acted as the secretariat of the network related to the implementation of the LRC and therefore was in the position to provide information as well as support further developments in one of the important Bologna areas – recognition of qualifications. The UNESCO/CEPES was also involved in several projects in a number of countries in South Eastern Europe, most of which were relative latecomers to the Bologna Process and had rather underdeveloped systems of QA. In addition, the UNESCO/CEPES was entrepreneurial in terms of linking the themes of the special issues of its journal to the Bologna Process as well as organizing seminars particularly focusing on aspects of implementation (for example, focusing on the impact of the Bologna Process on higher education policy and legislation in 2004). It is interesting to observe that the UNESCO/CEPES stopped working as a European UNESCO branch in 2010, so the participation in the Bologna Process went into the hands of the higher education division at the UNESCO headquarters in Paris.[11]

## Collective Actors in a Nutshell

As was demonstrated in previous sections, the meta-governance of the Bologna Process consolidated in terms of boundaries in the period between 1998 and 2005. Four rounds of enlargement of the decision-making structure took place, gradually including: (1) ministry representatives of the countries involved in the process; (2) the EC (DG Education) and universities; (3) the non-university sector, students and the CoE; and (4) the network of QA agencies, UNESCO/CEPES, trade unions and employers.

The clarification of boundaries of the governance arrangement also left some of the collective actors out. Some of the European student organizations that are either top-down organizations or focusing only on a small portion of the student population have been left out. Organizations providing necessary information for the implementation of the process (for example, the Academic Cooperation Association focuses on mobility), are not part of the formal structures either, even though they attend ministerial summits. The MCO, which is in charge of monitoring compliance to the Magna Charta Universitatum that contributed to the normative basis of the Bologna Declaration, is also not part of the governance arrangement.

The first enlargement round shifted the power balance from the Sorbonne Four to include all the EU countries. The second round gave the formal status to the EU Commission (despite initial attempts to avoid this) and stressed the importance of consultation of (but not direct participation in decision-making) to the EUA. The third and fourth enlargement rounds extended the consultation position to other transnational organizations acting on behalf of different interest groups (ESU/ESIB, EURASHE, ENQA, EI and BusinessEurope) and two intergovernmental structures (CoE and UNESCO/CEPES). While the formal decision-making power remains in the hands of the ministry representatives and the EC (given their full membership status in the BFUG), the consultative members exercise informal influence in the process, primarily in terms of providing information on implementation, drawing legitimacy from their membership base or intergovernmental character.

The inclusion of the transnational organizations representing different interest groups boosted the legitimacy of the Bologna Process. In a sector marked with significant professional autonomy, bottom-heaviness and loose-coupling (Clark 1983; Weick 1976) an intergovernmental basis for legitimacy of a European process was not sufficient, in particular because the process in its impact on national policy development went beyond mere voluntary policy coordination. The gradual clarification of boundaries in terms of participation of collective actors, including the rules related to decision-making structure, also meant that by limiting the number of new collective actors, the individual actors in the process would either remain stable or be dependent on turnover of individuals within these participating collective actors. A more stable set of individual actors could lead to a more closely integrated network as this would facilitate development of informal ties between collective actors. As we will now argue, the network of individuals that emerged around the Bologna Process showed both of these characteristics in a unique combination that proved to be essential for the level of integration of the overall network.

## INDIVIDUAL ACTORS: INCREASING THE INTEGRATION OF THE NETWORK

When examining the nature of individual actors who have been involved, the turnover amongst participants has been rather low, as entry for individual actors is granted only through the collective actors. Although few apparently non-affiliated individuals were prominent in the beginning of the process (for example, Guy Haug), their affiliations to some of the collective actors can be traced (in this case the CRE/EUA as well as the EC).

In the later stages of the process, the rules have become rather explicit (collective actors are indicated by name) and rigid (it is hard to change them), and as such, individuals are dependent on a limited number of collective actors to gain access. This in turn means that the community of people has become more stable through time, as the last additions to the BFUG in terms of collective actors were made only in 2005. As such, it is the limited number of collective actors that also stabilizes the individual participants.

While some of these individuals remain prominent and are not necessarily perceived as representatives of a particular collective actor (the aforementioned Guy Haug being one case in point), it should be stressed that once the rules on participation became more explicit, individual actors needed a clear affiliation to a collective actor to enter the arena. In addition, on several occasions the higher education research community was asked to contribute to the Bologna Process. The first major contribution of such kind was in 2008 in the run up to the Leuven Ministerial Summit when an edited volume was commissioned by the organizers (Kehm et al. 2009), but it seems that the researcher contribution did not have a major impact on the process given the lack of reference to the volume in the Leuven Communiqué (2009). The other major contribution was the Bologna Independent Assessment Report (Westerheijden et al. 2010), a large scale study commissioned by the EU Commission and conducted by a consortium led by two prominent research centres (CHEPS and INCHER)[12] and included a network of researchers and experts. This Report was referred to in the Budapest-Vienna Declaration (2010) although at this point it is not clear what impact the Report had on the process and the Declaration. In 2011 the first Bologna Researchers' Conference took place in Bucharest and resulted in two large volumes which included contributions by researchers and individuals representing collective actors alike (Curaj et al. 2012). However, at this point it is not clear whether such conferences will be organized in the future and what impact they will have in the policy process. Apart from the ESU/ESIB and some of the national collective actors, the other (transnational) collective actors have a rather stable situation with respect to individuals in leadership positions: those who participate in Bologna-related meetings change seldom, if at all. The most prominent examples of this are the EUA and the CoE which have been represented by the same individuals since the beginning of the process, as well as country representatives of Austria, Belgium (French community), the Czech Republic, Latvia, Luxembourg and Slovenia, according to official meeting participation records.

The ESU/ESIB is in this respect an interesting and outlier case given that, despite the turnover of individuals (new executive structures are elected every year), it manages to maintain prominence. While some would argue (including the ESU/ESIB representatives themselves) this is due to organized trainings and handovers between incumbent and newly elected individuals, the organization also has official policies on a number of Bologna-related issues that constrain individual actors and provide continuity in terms of policy preferences.

However, the ESU/ESIB is also an interesting case from another point of view. Between 150 and 180 individuals can be identified as have been, at some point, affiliated to one of the collective actors (excluding national ministries) and have participated in the Bologna meetings as part of the collective actors delegations (this does not include national government representatives). More than 50 per cent (closer to two-thirds) of the individuals that are part of this group have the ESU/ESIB as their initial affiliation. While this result is somewhat artificial since the ESU/ESIB has a much higher individual turnover (see above), it is interesting that more than 40 per cent of the ESU/ESIB individuals do not leave this policy arena after finishing their mandate or work in the ESU/ESIB, but stay involved through affiliations with transnational actors or national collective actors (ministries responsible for higher education). So far five individuals who entered this arena as the ESU/ESIB representative went on to work for EI, four for the CoE and three for the EUA. Ten individuals went back to the national level (working for ministries, QA agencies or Rectors' Conferences) or the university level. Seven individuals have gone into higher education research – having completed or currently working on their Ph.D.'s. Some of the ESU/ESIB individuals also stay involved as leaders of key Bologna Process structures: the BFUG Secretariat in the run up to the Bucharest Ministerial Summit in 2012 was led by a former ESU/ESIB Chairperson and both the current Director and the first President of the Executive Board of the EQAR have the ESU/ESIB as their initial affiliation.

Given that there are non-ESU/ESIB-affiliated individuals who have remained in the network (for example, one moved from the CoE to the EUA to Eurydice and one moved from the EUA to a national Rectors' Conference), we would propose to expand the view by Coleman and Perl (1999) who see *mediators* as actors who are simultaneously members of various policy communities at the same time and thus can function as 'translators' between these communities. We argue that also the individuals with consecutive affiliations with various collective actors can also act as translators – from one transnational actor to another, or from European to national level actors. Furthermore, the more they are socialized into the norms and values of the actors they are affiliated with, the more likely they are to transfer to a collective actor with similar policy preferences (see above for the examples of the ESU/ESIB representatives transferring to EI and the CoE). This has the potential to facilitate closer network ties and cooperation between the collective actors on joint projects and therefore also further convergence of policy preferences. While at the moment we do not have data to make a strong causal claim, an interesting case for further research is that the ESU/ESIB and EI intensified their project cooperation in late 2000s and that coincided with several ESU/ESIB individuals working for EI.

When it comes to interactions between individual actors, they are rather internationalized – transnational collective actors interact more intensively and more frequently than national collective actors interact amongst themselves or than national actors interact with transnational ones. The transnational actors participate in joint projects and meet more often in Bologna-related events, but also other events organized on the European level. These characteristics in terms of stability and also rather internationalized interactions within the network have the potential to expand the opportunities for exchange of information from only formal channels. Continuous presence of some individual actors (either through only one collective actor or through consecutive affiliations to several collective actors), coupled with high interaction between transnational actors in various forums provides an opportunity for a much livelier informal communication. This in turn can be the leverage of the collective actors who have only the consultative status in the Bologna decision-making structures, since it provides the opportunity to come to common policy preferences, form advocacy coalitions and elaborate lobbying strategies. One possible case for this, although more data are necessary to completely map the communication patterns, is the role that an informal coalition between the ESU/ESIB, EI, the CoE, the EUA and some national governments played in bringing the social dimension of Bologna (including specifications of what that actually entails) as one of the priorities of the process.

## CONCLUSIONS

As was demonstrated, the Bologna Process governance arrangement has its origins in the immediate aftermath of the Sorbonne Declaration of 1998. In the early years of the process, the governance arrangement did not have clearly defined boundary rules in terms of participation and there was an implicit shared understanding on the appropriate arrangement for the governance structure – expressed by the ambiguous official documents. As no other viable solution emerged and there appeared to be some need to structure the activities, the EC gained an opportunity to participate in setting the rules for the game, in essence a process of careful hands-off meta-governance (Torfing and Triantafillou 2011). As such, the development was perhaps not a conscious exercise of meta-governance or purposeful design, but more linked to existing path dependencies.

Since Bologna was quite early on framed as an intergovernmental initiative, the national ministries of signatory countries have an obvious place in the governance arrangement. However, as our earlier discussion indicates, other transnational actors gained access during the four waves of expansion. During this process, the boundary rules became more formalized, and clearer. Alongside, this has also meant that the membership has over time closed up and that it is increasingly difficult for new collective transnational actors to become a member.

What emerges is that the inclusion did not always follow strict formal rules and various strategies for membership can be identified. The EC used its history of supporting European cooperation in higher education, financial and administrative capacity. The two associations of universities – the CRE and the Confederation/EUA – boosted the legitimacy of the process, provided crucial expertise and also brought in a long history of European cooperation in this area, including cooperation and support to the EU activities. Similar to the EUA, the ESU/ESIB, as a student representative, provided an additional legitimacy boost, as did EI. The UNICE/BusinessEurope played the employability and linkages to the EC cards. The ENQA, also with strong links to the Commission, got in thanks to the strong focus on QA. The CoE brought in the only legally binding Bologna instrument (the LRC) and filled in the geographical gap to the East and South East of Europe. The UNESCO/CEPES also tied its participation to the LRC, as well as expertise and projects in higher education, in particular in Central, Eastern and South-Eastern Europe.

This indicates that the inclusion can be related to the rather instrumental needs, and at times the formal rules have been relatively creatively read by the actors involved to assure necessary resources – whether financial resources, information or legitimacy. While this has contributed to the integration of this network of actors, this has also diluted the intergovernmental character of the process, and introduced a significant transnational element. Although these transnational collective actors are consultative members, the rather closed group of individuals that has formed around the process, along with the high number of ESU/ESIB alumni indicates a number of possible arenas to deepen informal ties and further interests. It is especially the individual actors who remain in the process and travel between organizations that further bring stability, as they have in-depth knowledge and experience from different organizations, thus acting also as mediators between various kinds of collective actors on various levels. How these interests are linked to potential policy convergence is another avenue for further research, along with the potential for more detailed social network analysis of these actors and their trajectories.

Furthermore, the Bologna Process is usually set somewhere in the usual continuum of supranational vs intergovernmental, where it is either the nation states or the EC that is seen as being in the driving seat. However, we argue that the inclusion of transnational collective actors and their relative power over time has changed this balance. It points towards a rather unique setting of a formally intergovernmental process with supranational participation that in practice is much more influenced by transnational actors and sectoral interests.

## NOTES

1. The two organizations merged into the European University Association (EUA) early in 2001, a month and a half before the Prague Ministerial Summit. Further referred in the text as 'the Confederation' and 'the CRE'.
2. The International Association of Universities has a much wider coverage, given its worldwide membership.
3. In 2007 the ESIB changed its name to the European Students' Union (ESU).
4. The Council of Ministers adopted in September 1998 a recommendation on 'European Cooperation in Quality Assurance in Higher Education' (98/561/EC), which also served to launch the ENQA into existence.
5. The committee was first called the Committee on Prague 2001 and was later renamed the Bologna Process Committee.
6. In 2004 changed its name to the European Association for Quality Assurance in Higher Education.
7. Available at: http://eur-lex.europa.eu/LexUriServ/LexUriServ.do?uri=OJ:L:1998:270:0 056:0059:EN:PDF (accessed 14 January 2014).
8. See: http://www.enqa.eu/indirme/papers-and-reports/occasional-papers/TEEPmethod(1). pdf (accessed 14 January 2014).
9. In 2007 the organization changed its name to BusinessEurope.
10. Recently relaunched as the *European Journal of Higher Education*.
11. This division recently also ceased to exist, and higher education now is a section under the Division for Teacher Development and Higher Education.
12. CHEPS – Center for Higher Education Policy Studies from Enschede, the Netherlands and INCHER – International Centre for Higher Education Research from Kassel, Germany.

# REFERENCES

Beerkens, E. (2008), 'The emergence and institutionalisation of the European higher education and research area', *European Journal of Education*, **43**(4), 407–425.

Bologna Declaration (1999), *Towards the European Higher European Area*, Bologna: Italy.

Börzel, T.A. (1997), 'What's so special about policy networks? An exploration of the concept and its usefulness in studying European governance', *European Integration Online Papers (EIoP)*, **1**(16), 1–28.

Börzel, T.A. (1998), 'Organizing Babylon – on the different conceptions of policy networks', *Public Administration*, **76**(2), 253–273.

Budapest-Vienna Declaration (2010), *Budapest-Vienna Declaration on the European Higher Education Area*, Budapest, Hungary and Vienna, Austria.

Checkel, J.T. (2005), 'International institutions and socialization in Europe: introduction and framework', *International Organization*, **59**(4), 801–826.

Clark, B.R. (1983), *The Higher Education System: Academic Organization in Cross-National Perspective*, Berkeley, CA: University of California Press.

Coleman, W.D. and A. Perl (1999), 'Internationalized policy environments and policy network analysis', *Political Studies*, **47**(4), 691–709.

Corbett, A. (2005), *Universities and the Europe of knowledge: Ideas, Institutions and Policy Entrepreneurship in European Union Higher Education Policy, 1955–2005*, Basingstoke: Palgrave Macmillan.

Corbett, A. (2011), 'Ping pong: competing leadership for reform in EU higher education 1998–2006', *European Journal of Education*, **46**(1), 36–53.

Corbett, A. (2012), 'Principles, problems, politics ... what does the historical record of EU cooperation in higher education tell the EHEA generation?', in A. Curaj, P. Scott, L. Vlasceanu and L. Wilson (eds), *European Higher Education at the Crossroads*, Dordrecht: Springer Netherlands, pp. 39–57.

Curaj, A., P. Scott, L. Vlasceanu and L. Wilson (eds) (2012), *European Higher Education at the Crossroads: Between the Bologna Process and National Reforms*, Dordrecht: Springer Netherlands.

Dassen, A. (2010), *Networks: Structure and Action. Steering in and Steering by Policy Networks*, Enschede: University of Twente.

Elken, M., Å. Gornitzka, P. Maassen and M. Vukasovic (2011), *European Integration and the Transformation of Higher Education*, Oslo: University of Oslo.

ENQA (2010), *ENQA: 10 Years (2000–2010). A Decade of European Co-operation in Quality Assurance in Higher Education*, Helsinki: ENQA.

Faber, M. and D. Westerheijden (2011), 'European degree structure and national reform', in J. Enders, H. de Boer and D. Westerheijden (eds), *Reform of Higher Education in Europe*, Rotterdam: Sense Publishers, pp. 11–28.

Fawcett, P. and C. Daugbjerg (2012), 'Explaining governance outcomes: epistemology, network governance and policy network analysis', *Political Studies Review*, **10**(2), 195–207.

Fischer Appelt, P. (1996), 'Assistance in higher education legislation: the legislative reform programme of the Council of Europe', *Higher Education in Europe*, **21**(2–3), 82–89.

Gornitzka, Å. (2007), 'The Lisbon Process: a supranational policy perspective', in

P. Maassen and J.P. Olsen (eds), *University Dynamics and European Integration*, Dordrecht: Springer, pp. 155–178.

Gornitzka, Å. (2010), 'Bologna in context: a horizontal perspective on the dynamics of governance sites for a Europe of knowledge', *European Journal of Education*, **45**(4), 535–548.

Gornitzka, Å. and L. Langfeldt (2005), 'The role of academics in the Bologna Process – a survey of participation and views. Results from a survey among EI-member organisations in Europe', *Education International Working Papers*, **15**, Brussels: Education International.

Hackl, E. (2001), 'The intrusion and expansion of community policies in higher education', *Higher Education Management*, **13**(3), 99–117.

Haskel, B. (2008), 'When Can a Weak Process Generate Strong Results? Entrepreneurial Alliances in the Bologna Process to Create a European Higher Education Area', *Center for European Studies Working Paper Series*, **2008**(165).

Heclo, H. (1978), 'Issue networks and the executive establishment', in A. King (ed.), *The New American Political System*, Washington, DC: American Enterprise Institute, pp. 87–124.

Hoareau, C. (2012), 'Deliberative governance in the European higher education area. The Bologna Process as a case of alternative governance architecture in Europe', *Journal of European Public Policy*, **19**(4), 530–548

Hodson, D. and I. Maher (2001), 'The open method as a new mode of governance: the case of soft economic policy co-ordination', *Journal of Common Market Studies*, **39**(4), 719–746.

Hurd, I. (1999), 'Legitimacy and authority in international politics', *International Organization*, **53**(2), 379–408.

Jones, C., W.S. Hesterly and S.P. Borgatti (1997), 'A general theory of network governance: exchange conditions and social mechanisms', *The Academy of Management Review*, **22**(4), 911–945.

Jordan, G. (1990), 'Sub-governments, policy communities and networks', *Journal of Theoretical Politics*, **2**(3), 319–338.

Jordan, G. and K. Schubert (1992), 'A preliminary ordering of policy network labels', *European Journal of Political Research*, **21**(1–2), 7–27.

Kehm, B. (2010), 'Editorial', *European Journal of Education*, **45**(4), 529–534.

Kehm, B., J. Huisman and B. Stensaker (eds) (2009), *The European Higher Education Area: Perspectives on a Moving Target*, Rotterdam: Sense Publishers.

Kenis, P. and V. Scheider (1991), 'Policy networks and policy analysis: scrutinizing a new analytical toolbox', in B. Marin and R. Mayntz (eds), *Policy Networks. Empirical Evidence and Theoretical Considerations*, Frankfurt/Main: Campus, pp. 25–59.

Klemenčič, M. (2011), 'Europeanisation of the "European Student Movement"', Paper presented at EUSA 2011: Papers Archive from the Network of European Union Centres of Excellence, Washington, DC, available at: http://euce.org/eusa/2011/papers/7c_klemencic.pdf (accessed 14 January 2014).

Leuven Communiqué (2009), *The Bologna Process 2020 – The European Higher Education Area in the New Decade*, Leuven: Belgium.

Lewis, J.M. and M. Considine (2011), 'Network governance in the frontline', in J. Torfing and P. Triantafillou (eds), *Interactive Policy Making, Metagovernance and Democracy*, Colchester: ECPR Press, pp. 29–50.

Lourtie, P. (2001), *Furthering the Bologna Process: Report to the Ministers of Education of the Signatory Countries*, Prague: Czech Republic.

Maassen, P. and C. Musselin (2009), 'European integration and the Europeanisation of higher education', in A. Amaral, G. Neave, C. Musselin and P. Maassen (eds), *European Integration and the Governance of Higher Education and Research*, Dordrecht: Springer, pp. 3–14.

Marsh, D. (1998a), 'The development of the policy network approach', in D. Marsh (ed.), *Comparing Policy Networks*, Buckingham: Open University Press, pp. 3–17.

Marsh, D. (ed.) (1998b), *Comparing Policy Networks*, Buckingham: Open University Press.

Middlehurst, R. and P.N. Teixeira (2012), 'Governance within the EHEA: dynamic trends, common challenges, and national particularities', in A. Curaj, P. Scott, L. Vlasceanu and L. Wilson (eds), *European Higher Education at the Crossroads: Between the Bologna Process and National Reforms*, Dordrecht: Springer Netherlands, pp. 527–551.

Neave, G. (2009), 'The Bologna Process as alpha or omega, or, on interpreting history and context as inputs to Bologna, Prague, Berlin and beyond', in A. Amaral, G. Neave, C. Musselin and P. Maassen (eds), *European Integration and the Governance of Higher Education and Research*, Dordrecht: Springer, pp. 17–58.

Neave, G. and P. Maassen (2007), 'The Bologna Process: an intergovernmental policy perspective', in P. Maassen and J.P. Olsen (eds), *University Dynamics and European Integration*, Dordrecht: Springer Netherlands, pp. 135–154.

Prague Communiqué (2001), *Towards the European Higher Education Area*, Prague: Czech Republic.

Ravinet, P. (2008a), 'From voluntary participation to monitored coordination: why European countries feel increasingly bound by their commitment to the Bologna Process', *European Journal of Education*, **43**(3), 353–367.

Ravinet, P. (2008b), 'Analyzing the Institutionalization of Europe: Back to the Classics. The Case of the Bologna Process', *ARENA Working Papers*.

Rhodes, R.A.W. (1990), 'Policy networks: a British perspective', *Journal of Theoretical Politics*, **2**(3), 293–317.

Sabatier, P.A. (1988), 'An advocacy coalition framework of policy change and the role of policy-oriented learning therein', *Policy Sciences*, **21**(2), 129–168.

Sartori, G. (1970), 'Concept misformation in comparative politics', *American Political Science Review*, **64**(4), 1033–1053.

Scharpf, F.W. (1997), *Games Real Actors Play: Actor-Centered Institutionalism in Policy Research*, Boulder, CO: Westview Press.

Sørensen, E. and J. Torfing (2003), 'Network politics, political capital, and democracy', *International Journal of Public Administration*, **26**(6), 609–634.

Torfing, J. and P. Triantafillou (2011), 'Introduction to interactive policy making, metagovernance and democracy', in J. Torfing and P. Triantafillou (eds), *Interactive Policy Making, Metagovernance and Democracy*, Colchester: ECPR Press, pp. 1–25.

Van Waarden, F. (1992), 'Dimensions and types of policy networks', *European Journal of Political Research*, **21**(1–2), 29–52.

Veiga, A. and A. Amaral (2006), 'The open method of coordination and the implementation of the Bologna Process', *Tertiary Education and Management*, **12**(4), 283–295.

Veiga, A. and A. Amaral (2009), 'Policy implementation tools and European governance', in A. Amaral, G. Neave, C. Musselin and P. Maassen (eds), *European Integration and the Governance of Higher Education and Research*, Dordrecht: Springer, pp. 133–157.

Weick, K.E. (1976), 'Educational organizations as loosely coupled systems', *Administrative Sciences Quarterly*, **21**(1), 1–19.

Westerheijden, D. et al. (2010), *The First Decade of Working on the European Higher Education Area: Executive Summary, Overview and Conclusions.* Wien: BMWF.

Witte, J. (2008), 'Aspired convergence, cherished diversity: dealing with the contradictions of Bologna', *Tertiary Education and Management*, **14**(2), 81–93.

# 7. How strong are the European Union's soft modes of governance? The use of the Open Method of Coordination in national policy-making in the knowledge policy domain

## Åse Gornitzka

## INTRODUCTION[1]

The use of European Union (EU) hard law is a key component of European integration (Katzenstein 2005). Consequently, the implementation of law has been a major theme in studying how European governance output affects national level policies and polities (Treib 2008). However, softer modes of governance have been present in parallel to the use of hard law, and as European integration has developed and progressed in areas where there is little transfer of legal competencies to EU institutions new modes have been added to the hard vs soft law/ modes of governance continuum. The focus of this chapter is on the EU's Open Method of Coordination (OMC) that emerged in the framework of the EU's Lisbon Strategy. It is a poignant case of a kind of soft mode of governance[2] that does not establish precise, binding and enforceable rules (Abbott and Snidal 2000). This has begged the question whether and in what way European governance outputs can have an impact on domestic policies outside the incorporation of European legal acts into national legal corpus (harmonization) or without the recourse to material sanctions. This question also links to the parallel research in international relations where there has been an enduring interest in non-legal means of governance at the level beyond the nation state. The angle offered in this chapter is not about the (relative) effectiveness of the OMC as such. The question is then not only whether and under what conditions soft modes of governance have an impact but also what types of impact we can observe, or what in this chapter will be referred to as types of OMC *use*.

This chapter examines the scale and locus of impact of the OMC at the national level drawing on survey and interview data from policy-makers in national ministries and agencies. The country case is Norway, a non-member of the EU but strongly associated with the EU through the European Economic Area (EEA) agreement. The research follows a two-step strategy. First, it covers an analysis of the OMC usage in the central administrative bodies in general based on survey data covering officials from all Norwegian ministries and national agencies. Second, the OMC's multimodal use in domestic policy-making and the factors that affect utilization are further elaborated by drawing on a study of the role that the EU's 'Education and Training 2010/2020' (E&T) has played in domestic policy developments. The E&T has since the turn of the century been the mainframe for European cooperation in the education sector. Hence this chapter is also relevant for understanding the role of this type of soft mode of governance in the Europe of Knowledge.

Education and higher education are policy areas that have traditionally been regarded as domestically secluded, but have increasingly become internationally connected and connected to organized processes of European integration (see Chou and Gornitzka 2014, this volume). These are areas where EU institutions have little legal competencies to make binding rules subject to third party enforcement. Hence this case may contribute to the general understanding of how soft governance is used when the shadow of law is weak and add to our understanding of the interplay between domestic and European sources of policy change and continuity in education and higher education as policy areas.

## THEORETICAL PERSPECTIVES AND EXPECTATIONS

This chapter takes as a starting point that: (1) the impact of soft modes of governance can be seen as a case of information use in public policy-making; and (2) that such use can be fruitfully studied from an organizational perspective. An organizational perspective puts forward the idea that the organizational structure of government bureaucracy intervenes in the policy process and shapes its outcomes (Egeberg 2012). In particular the organizational contexts represent an organized informational 'bias' in policy-making (Thompson and Wildavsky 1986). Organizations may endow actors with interests and goals, but they are also information repositories – storing, communicating and filtering knowledge and information in their procedures, norms, rules and forms (March 1991, p. 73). Not only 'where you stand' (preferences) depends on 'where you sit' (Allison 1969, p. 711), but also what you see and when you see it (temporal sorting and sequential attention to problems). All of these aspects are significantly affected by the organizational structure and context within which policy-makers are positioned.

This chapter pays attention to two sets of organizational factors that can be expected to affect use of the OMC: the characteristics of the organization of the OMC processes at the European level and the domestic organizational factors. Below these two overall theoretical arguments are spelled out, but first the concept of domestic impact of soft modes of governance needs to be addressed.

**What is Impact and Use?**

The use of information in policy-making takes on a variety of forms. Grouped into broad categories we can distinguish between five utilization modes: (1) instrumental/substantive use, where information is used for problem-solving or policy learning, and implies change in policy agendas, priorities or instrumentation; (2) conceptual use; (3) monitoring/surveillance mode; (4) strategic use/legitimating action *post hoc*; or (5) as symbol and signal of appropriate organizational behaviour (Feldman and March 1988; Gornitzka 2003; March 1988; Rich and Oh 2000). Consequently the search for information in organizations does not only happen in a decision mode, hence organizations gather more information than they use instrumentally (Feldman and March 1988). Different forms of use imply varying links between information and decision, between information and change in decision-making behaviour. Similarly one could argue that utilization of soft law/modes of governance in domestic policy-making would also encompass such a range of use, and that this constitutes varieties of domestic impact. Hence the focus of this chapter is on the wider potential uses of the EU's soft modes of governance in domestic policy-making.

It follows that one cannot a priori equate impact with policy convergence. In this respect this chapter's focus and research question differs from those studies motivated by an observation that governments adopt similar policies. In such studies the analytical problem is to account for global or European policy convergence or policy clustering (Elkins and Simmons 2005) or for adoption rates and speed of particular policies (for example, Finnemore 1993). Also the idea that transnational spread leads to convergence is empirically and theoretically contested. This is evident in the literature on the spread of organizational forms and of the global spread of public sector reform concepts (Greenwood et al. 2008, p. 11; Pollitt 2001). This is especially the case when the object of diffusion or transfer is malleable, and characterized by low reproductive reliability (March 1999), as elements of public policies tend to be. They are subject to adaptations when they travel from one context to another. Also the implementation deficit of public policies could be framed as a question of context sensitive transformation, as policies travel 'from Washington to Oakland' (Pressman and Wildavsky 1984). It could be argued that even EU hard law is reproductively unreliable in so far as the implementation of EU law takes colour from the national or other conditions (Dimitrova and Steunenberg 2000; Eyre and Lodge 2000; Risse et al. 2001), compliance is ambiguous and takes shape in dialogue between governance levels and institutions (Katzenstein 2005, p. 73). In light of this, a good argument could be made for seeing the EU's soft modes of governance as dynamic (Abbott and Snidal 2000) and their use as multimodal.

The mechanisms that mediate soft modes of governance are associated with different types of impact. Take the concept of policy learning, a key assumed dynamic of the OMC (Radaelli 2008) and central to instrumental use of information (see above). A strict definition of policy learning limits learning to cases of substantial policy change: learning is 'a deliberate attempt to adjust the goals or techniques of policy in response to past experience and new information. Learning is indicated when policy changes as the result of such a process' (Hall 1993, p. 278). However, Hall's concept of social learning in policy-making entails that learning addresses different policy levels, or what he refers to as the three orders of policy change: change of goals, modification of instruments while keeping the goals and the overall policy paradigm intact, down to the modest degree of change when learning leads to fine-tuning existing policy instruments. Any of the three types of policy change can in principle occur as a result of learning from success/failure, from cultural reference groups or learning from increased interaction (Simmons and Elkins 2004). Different orders of policy change do not necessarily imply that learning is the underlying mechanism. In policy band-wagoning (Ikenberry 1990), goals, language, and instruments can be emulated without the deliberate attempt to adjust policy in the light of one's own experience or from the experience of others, but because it is taken for granted as the right thing to do, or because there are reputational or material costs/benefits associated with adoption. Rather than reserving the concept of impact to the reproduction of EU policies at the national level, this chapter unpacks impact in terms of different OMC use (see above) in national policy-making and probes the mechanisms underlying use.

**What Affects the Domestic Use of the OMC?**

Taking an organizational perspective on the use of information in policy-making – what factors can be expected to affect the use of the OMC? The first set of factors addresses the organizational features at the European level. Just as the study of international regimes attaches importance to the organizational infrastructure for regime effectiveness (Underdal 2008), we can expect that the qualities of the organizational architecture of the OMC at the national level will have an autonomous effect on its domestic impact.

When the focus is on soft law/soft modes of governance the interest is not in the EU as a law-making system, but as an organized 'transfer platform' (Bulmer and Radaelli 2005). The OMC literature points to considerable variation of the organizational architecture built up around the OMC. First, the various elements of the OMC as a concept are to varying degrees materialized in processes that carry the label 'OMC': specification and quantification of EU level goals; timetables for achieving the goals; establishing quantitative and qualitative indicators and benchmarks; establishing measures to compare and identify good practice; periodic monitoring, evaluation and peer review; and the organization of learning processes. The OMC exists in different blends. There are significant differences in how institutionalized OMC processes are at the European level, from loosely structured meetings, to full-blown organizational architecture with a specialized organizational set-up, with formal goals and benchmarks, established rules for reporting and monitoring, routines for information handling, rules for how to organize policy learning and information gathering/dissemination, and considerable administrative resources attached to uphold such rules and routines.

These features we can expect will affect information flows. They speak to the organizational capacity at the EU level for structuring the attention of domestic policy-makers; systematizing and certifying information, and identifying and promulgating normatively and cognitively appropriate good policy practice (Holzinger and Knill 2005). The organization of the OMC varies considerably in the extent to which resources are attached to it. Especially, the role the European Commission (Commission) is given or takes in coordination and communication tasks (Borrás 2009) we expect to be essential in structuring information flow. The more the OMC organization provides stable rules, timetables and reporting commitments, as well as routinizing and regulating interaction between member states and the Commission, the stronger impact we will expect to find. Consequently, there will be considerable variation between policy areas due to sectoral differences in how the OMC processes have been organized (Laffan and Shaw 2005).

Alternatively, the domestic impact of soft modes of governance might be conditioned by the presence of other harder governance arrangements within a policy area. If the OMC is the 'inferior cousin' to hard law and only will appear in areas where hard law is not practised, then a condition for soft governance to have domestic impact is the absence of EU hard law in a policy area.

## Domestic Factors and Impact of the OMC – Structure and Culture

For domestic policy-makers the OMC architecture at the EU level will (at best) be a *secondary* structure, and much less demanding than their primary affiliation, that is, the organization that employs them full-time (Egeberg 2004). The use of the OMC can be expected to depend on how the link between the European level governance arena and national policy-making processes is organized and institutionalized, and the organizational properties of national administrations. National political-administrative factors have been central in the literature on the implementation of EU hard law. In particular domestic *administrative capacities and cultures* have been documented to significantly affect the transposition process (Treib 2008; Treib et al. 2007). Consequently, domestic organizational factors should also be expected to play a central role in cushioning, fending off or accommodating the potential impact of the OMC in patterns of domestic resilience or adaptation.

One set of domestic factors concerns key organizational variables. First, we need to examine how domestic administrations organize their relationship to soft governance processes, and how these arrangements affect use. If specialized staff or units are set to handle the OMC processes, then that should be conductive to use. However, if these organizational arrangements are in turn decoupled from the regular policy-making processes the impact will be limited to international or European enclaves (Vifell 2006). Through 'enclaving' or decoupling, national administrations can filter 'Europe' into separate units or positions, but filter it out of established domestic policy-making. Then the OMC is likely to only affect those who are directly in contact with EU institutions in an organized manner. However, if we find that the higher echelons of national bureaucracies are 'OMC connectors' then the OMC will be attended to and filtered into the ministries' decision-making. It will then have penetrated close to the apex of domestic policy-making. Consequently, identifying the national OMC connectors and their position within national policy-making is a key to understanding domestic utilization.

Moreover, we can expect the task structures, their modes of decision-making within ministries and their function in the political-administrative system to affect their use of the OMC. We know information use in government organizations is affected by variation in how routinized its decision-making practices are. In task areas where there are established patterns of policy-making, information behaviour tends to be introvert, less susceptible to external and new information; whereas in areas that involve uncertainties and knowledge deficits, the information behaviour is more open (Gornitzka 2003).

In addition to task structures, we can assume that organizational culture and traditions affect information openness, rejection and use (Thompson and Wildavsky 1986). In hierarchical organizations the information style tends to be protective of the policy paradigm the organization embodies. The use of the OMC, we could expect in particular to be affected by organizational cultures and traditions for being internationally/transnationally oriented. Administrative units with a national orientation will see the OMC as irrelevant and inappropriate, irrespective of whether there are organizational links to EU soft governance arenas.

A focus on the structural properties and bureaucratic culture for the impact of the OMC will tend to mask other conditional factors that are highly relevant for understanding information use in public administration embedded in a domestic *political* order (Olsen and Peters 1996). First, political cleavages and conflict lines in domestic political life will have an impact on information utilization, *inter alia* on how 'usable' the OMC is. The level of political conflict and value incongruence in the wider policy area can affect the potential for softer instruments to be effective. In the context of public regulation, for instance, the argument has been put forward that soft instrumentation does not work in cases of high levels of political conflict (Pierre and Peters 2009, p. 342). Second, it is probable that *situational factors* (Olsen and Peters 1996, pp. 29–32) can facilitate or hamper the use of the OMC. In particular there is a need to examine how openness to OMC usage is more likely to be present in times of crises when policies are destabilized and their merits questioned.

## CASE SELECTION: WHY NORWAY AND WHY EDUCATION AND TRAINING 2010?

The EEA Agreement that came into force in 1994 facilitates first and foremost an internal market between the EEA countries and the EU, ensuring 'the four freedoms'. It also grants Norway participation in other policy areas, such as environmental protection, statistics, consumer affairs and social issues. Consequently, Norwegian legislation has been aligned with EU legislation in a number of areas to ensure a congruent legal framework. Norway has been a conscientious implementer of EU hard law within a Nordic 'culture of compliance' (Sverdrup 2004). Administrative observance of EU law is in the Norwegian context mixed with high public scepticism of the EU, and a political landscape where the issue of EU membership is poisonous, subject to a self-imposed gag rule among political parties (Fossum 2009). However, through the EEA agreement Norway practises what should be labelled as an active non-membership ('outside-ship') – an outsider to the EU by consequence of not having a formal membership while being closely associated with the EU in most policy areas. Studies have shown that the impact of the EU on national administrations is considerable, but less in the Norwegian case when compared to other Nordic states. This is attributed to Norway's membership status (Lægreid et al. 2004). EEA membership grants very limited access to the EU's political process, with the Commission as the main access point in the preparatory stages. Norway does not have access to formal Council meetings nor can it put its signature on the conclusions of the European Council meetings. Norway has formally not been part of the Lisbon Process, and is under no moral or other obligation to nationally organize and respond to the EU's voluntary policy coordination processes. In this respect the OMC processes are outside the realm of Norway's 'culture of compliance'.

For Norway the resort to the OMC could be seen as 'bad news' for its active outsideship, because it moved the centre of attention to a part of the political cooperation in Europe to which Norway does not have formal access. Yet the different sectoral versions of the OMC (both tightly or loosely coupled to the core of the Lisbon Strategy) pointed to above, created opportunities for Norwegian policy-makers to connect and adapt to the process. Such opportunities arose in the 'knowledge policy areas'. When the EU heads of state asked for a modernization programme for European education systems as part of the Lisbon Strategy, it supported the new kind of cooperation in education – based on the OMC – that eventually would be known as the 'Education and Training' programme (E&T). The EEA agreement had already coupled Norwegian knowledge policy to the European level through programme cooperation as the EEA agreement ensured Norway access to the EU education programmes and to the Framework Programmes (FPs) for research. On this basis Norwegian policy-makers also were exposed to a new set of governance arrangements at the European level when the connection between the OMC, the Lisbon Strategy and knowledge policy was made at the turn of the century. This makes it possible to use the case study of Norwegian policy-making and E&T as a basis for discussing how and through what mechanisms an OMC process makes its impact on national policy-making.

# DATA

The empirical analysis of domestic impact and use of the OMC follows in two steps. First, the OMC's impact on Norwegian ministry civil servants is analysed on the basis of data from a survey conducted in 2006 of all ministry officials with at least one-year tenure, from executive officers to top civil servants (18 ministries, 1,848 respondents, response rate is 67 per cent) (see Egeberg and Trondal 2009). This is a unique data-set with a survey addressing a range of issues covering decision-making behaviour, contact patterns, and values and opinions among Norwegian ministry officials. The survey also included questions specifically on the OMC's impact: 'to what extent has the use of the EU's OMC (characterized by peer review, benchmarking and soft law) led to changes in the following aspects of your own field of work?' Then ten different aspects were listed and respondents were asked to rate the extent of change on a five-point scale. These data can tap into the impact in national ministries with respect to instrumental/substantive use of the OMC and conceptual/monitoring use (see Table 7.1). In the analysis a simple additive index is used that combines the ten possible aspects of impact (OMC use index, 0 to 50 point scale, where 0 is 'no reported impact' to 50 as 'full impact' on all ten 'use indictors'). These data cannot tap directly the legitimatizing and symbolic uses of the OMC nor tease out the underlying mechanisms of use, but given the very comprehensive sets of variables in this survey, several variables that tap core factors expected to affect the use of OMC are used for bivariate and multivariate analyses. The survey data on OMC use in ministries are compared to data from a survey among national *agency* officials also conducted in 2006 covering the same questions (questionnaire was sent to a random sample of every third official, N = 1,452, response rate is 57 per cent).[3]

Second, the study of the impact of the OMC in the Ministry of Education and Research is based on an analysis of in-depth interviews (conducted 2005–2007) with 11 policy-makers who participated in the process,[4] together with the analysis of written sources such as national reports and other written documentation from Norway's participation in the E&T programme, as well as Ministry Green Papers and White Papers. In the present chapter these qualitative data are used for cross-checking and elaborating the results from the survey, and to go further into the different modes of using the OMC.

# THE OVERALL DOMESTIC IMPACT OF THE OMC

## Does the OMC Matter?

The results from the survey show that the majority of all ministry officials see no impact of the OMC in their own field of work (59 per cent). In national agencies the OMC's overall use is more widespread than at the ministry level (47 per cent of officials in national agencies report no use of the OMC).[5] The share of respondents who report a deep impact of the OMC is low, both within the ministries and agencies. There are no comparable quantitative data from other countries that allow us to check whether the impact of the OMC in the Norwegian central administration are above or below domestic effects in other contexts, whether these findings can be attributed to the professed feebleness of the method as such or are a consequence of the particularities of Norway's membership status.

As expected the impact of EU hard law goes beyond any reported use of the OMC: among ministry and agency officials only 13 per cent and 20 per cent respectively report that hard law originating from the EU is not practiced in within their own issue area. Yet, we find little overall evidence that practising EU hard law in a policy area drives out the possible use of OMC in the ministries. The opposite is the case (positive significant correlation Pearson's r 0.19). At the overall level the idea that the absence of hard law is a precondition for the use of the OMC is not supported.

What kind of use do we find? The use of the OMC according to these data is clearly multimodal, but some types are more prominent than others. Table 7.1 shows that the OMC's primary usage in the ministries is in the learning mode: the OMC has been instrumental in changing the ability to learn from the experience of other countries. But the OMC represents also significantly an opportunity to 'teach' their European peers, this mix of receiving and giving information implies that the OMC in deed works as a ' transfer platform'. Also the OMC seems to have changed the overall pool of knowledge and to a somewhat lesser extent the overall access to information (elaborated below). Hence the findings underline that ministry officials use of this method in a surveillance/monitoring mode. We note considerably less impact on national budgets and priorities (direct substantive impact) as well as on national policy agendas.

As we can see from Table 7.1 the use profile is fairly similar in ministries and national agencies, with one major exception: agency officials are more inclined to report that the OMC has had an impact on formulation and elaboration of regulations and standards than officials in the ministry.

*Table 7.1　Types of OMC use among ministry and agency officials. Share of officials who report some, high and very high degree of impact of the OMC ( values 3, 4, 5 on a five-point scale)*

| Use of OMC | Ministry officials | Agency officials |
|---|---|---|
| Instrumental/substantive use. The OMC has changed: | | |
| • Agenda | 14 | 13 |
| • Priorities | 14 | 15 |
| • Regulations and standards | 19 | **28** |
| • Budgets | 7 | 6 |
| • Ability to learn from the experience of other countries | **26** | **24** |
| Monitoring/conceptual use. The OMC has changed: | | |
| • Access to information | 17 | 17 |
| • Overall knowledge about own policy area | **21** | 18 |
| • Access to and use of quantitative indicators | 12 | 10 |
| • Spreading Norwegian experiences to other countries | **22** | **21** |
| *N (average)* | *1,023* | *777* |

*Table 7.2　Use of OMC according to ministry. Score on OMC use index and impact on 'learning'*

| | Share with high/very high degree of impact of OMC on ability to learn from other countries | OMC index mean score | N |
|---|---|---|---|
| Ministry of Education and Research | 41% | 17.7 | *94* |
| Ministry of Government Administration and Reform | 23% | 14.3 | *47* |
| Ministry of Trade and Industry | 20% | 11.0 | *62* |
| Ministry of Labour and Social Inclusion | 24% | 10.3 | *59* |
| Ministry of Health and Care Services | 10% | 9.3 | *64* |
| Ministry of Children and Equality | 22% | 8.3 | *35* |
| *Average for all ministry civil servants* | *14%* | *6.7* | *1,073* |

## Where do we Find the Use of the OMC?

Table 7.2 lists the six ministries that are top users of the OMC. This supports the basic idea that the nature of the OMC process also affects the use of it domestically. Not surprisingly the top OMC users are within the core 'Lisbon portfolios' (Ministry of Trade and Industry, Ministry of Labour and Social Inclusion, Ministry of Education and Research, and the OMC for 'better regulation' (Ministry of Government Administration and Reform)), but we also find that the more weakly institutionalized or nascent OMC processes for health care have had an impact to some extent. The OMC processes at the time of study (just one year after the relaunch of the Lisbon Strategy in 2005) were to a large extent organized according to a sector principle with disparate organizational set-ups. In this respect the OMC reinforced the 'silo' structure of EU governance organized according to a sectoral principle (Egeberg 2006), and amplified the sectoral division at the domestic arena. A caveat is of course the particular characteristics of the EEA membership, for instance, there is no requirement for Norway to organize the coordination of sector-specific contributions to and implementation of the Lisbon Strategy domestically as is the case for the EU member states (Borrás 2009).

The education and research policy portfolios' position as top users of the OMC is striking and indicates how the nature of development of European level matters to the domestic use of the OMC. As argued elsewhere the development of the OMC process at the European level in education should be seen as the evolution and partial institutionalization of a governance structure at the European level that represents a real addition to the existing forms of cooperation in this policy domain (see also Chou and Gornitzka 2014, this volume; Gornitzka 2007). The use of the OMC in this ministry is remarkably more widespread and intense compared to all other ministries (41 per cent report that the use of the OMC has to a high or very high degree changed their ability to learn from the experience of other countries). We cannot separate between subpolicy areas, so these data conflate the impact of the E&T and the OMC for research/the 3 per cent investment in R&D. We note nonetheless that the 'supply' of soft law/ modes of governance in this policy area covers basically the whole spectrum of the policy areas that make up the portfolio of this ministry (see case study below).

**A Domestic Structure for Use?**

What characterizes the OMC user in the ministries? How does the domestic organization affect the use of the OMC? First, we do not find evidence that the usage is most prevalent among the lower echelons of the ministry hierarchy. The main carriers of the OMC in the ministries are at the mid to higher level of the ministry (positive Pearson's r 0.17 significant at 0.01 level for 'OMC learning' and 0.18 for the OMC index). So it seems that the use of the OMC is connected to the ministries' hierarchical, decision-making lines. In this respect the OMC has penetrated to some degree the backbone of the domestic policy-making process. For instance, overall among 'rank and file' civil servants almost 75 per cent make no use of the OMC in order to learn from the experience of other countries, whereas for the mid to upper levels close to 40 per cent report that the use of the OMC affects transnational learning in their own field of work to some or high extent. This does not support the expectation that OMC usage is decoupled from everyday decision-making in the ministry.

However, it might be that the actual contact patterns of the OMC users are different than for the OMC non-users and that this represents a de facto OMC 'enclave'. However, a simple correlation analysis does not support this argument. The opposite seems to be the case. OMC users are better connected to political and administrative leadership within their own ministry and to the Parliament, as well as stakeholder groups compared to non-users (see Table 7.3).

*Table 7.3　Contact patterns and the use of OMC. Correlations (Pearson's r)*

|  | OMC index | 'Ability to learn from other countries' |
|---|---|---|
| Contact with political leadership of own ministry (Minister) | 0.16** | 0.14** |
| Contact with administrative leadership (Directorate General) | 0.11** | 0.10** |
| Contact with national parliament | 0.08* | 0.07* |
| Contact with national agencies | 0.06 | 0.04 |
| Contact with unions | 0.07* | 0.07* |
| Contact with other stakeholder organizations | 0.20** | 0.14** |
| Contact with European Commission | 0.39** | 0.37** |
| Participation in committees under the Commission | 0.36** | 0.34** |
| Number of travel days (international) | 0.14** | 0.16** |

*Notes:*　* Significant at $p < 0.05$; ** Significant at $p < 0.01$.

*Variable values:*
OMC index: 0 to 50: 0 = no impact on any aspect of own portfolio to 50 = full impact on all.
'OMC learning from other countries': five point impact scale from 0 = no effect/not relevant to 5 = very high.
Contact variable: five point scale from 0 = never to 5 = practically every week.
Participation in Commission committees during a year: 1 = never, 2 = once, 3 = several times.

Considering the contact with European institutions and civil servants' travel patterns we find some evidence in favour of the enclave-argument. There is a strong correlation between OMC usage and being directly in contact with the Commission/participating in Commission expert groups and committees. This correlation supports the idea that a prerequisite for using the OMC is being part of the process at the European level and being directly connected to a multi-level European administrative space. These contacts and participations are part of the civil servants' formal role (they are formally and organizationally linked). The personal interaction with the EU institutions that results from these contacts breeds use. It also shows how dependent the use of the OMC is on attributing organizational capabilities to the link with Europe.

**A Culture for Use?**

The ministerial overall international orientation seems also to be positively affecting the use of the OMC. That is more the case for those who have a multinational orientation (those who make it an organizational routine to copy from international organizations) than for those with a bilateral orientation (copying from other countries). This aspect is of particular consequence for the Ministry of Education and Research. Forty four per cent of officers in this Ministry have a strong multilateral international orientation in their decision-making behaviour ('very often' and 'fairly often' categories), and 55 per cent have a strong bilateral international orientation ('very often' and 'fairly often' categories) (see Table 7.4). When we

*Table 7.4   International copying in domestic policy-making in the Ministry of Education and Research and in all ministries (in per cent) 2006*

| How often civil servants copy models from international organizations or other countries in policy development | International organizations | | Other countries | |
|---|---|---|---|---|
| | Ministry of E&R | All ministries | Ministry of E&R | All ministries |
| Very often | 17 | 11 | 25 | 15 |
| Fairly often | 27 | 22 | 30 | 32 |
| Sometimes | 26 | 32 | 24 | 34 |
| Rarely | 15 | 21 | 13 | 12 |
| Very rarely/never | 15 | 14 | 8 | 8 |
| N (not 'EU filtered', 'missing' excluded) | 160 | 1,837 | 163 | 1,854 |

look at the general development of the Ministry's portfolio, the use of the OMC is one part of a much larger picture. This Ministry was ten years ago predominantly inward looking (Egeberg and Trondal 1997), but has now become one of the most internationally oriented of all Norwegian ministries. Of course, as the case study of the Ministry's use of the OMC will demonstrate, a confluence of international and European, and domestic developments has contributed to such a change in international orientation in this policy area. These developments are partly supporting the EU's soft governance processes and partly competing with them. This is particularly the case with Norway's participation in the Bologna Process for establishing the European Higher Education Area (EHEA). Also it is problematic to attribute causality to 'international culture' as a variable – it might be that the OMC's use has contributed to a change in international orientation, and not the other way around.

However, contrary to the evidence on other types of information use in public policy-making, the task structure does not significantly affect the OMC's use in the ministries. Officials with tasks related to policy development and acting as 'political secretariats', developing policies and rules rather than applying them, are equally inclined to use the OMC. Considering the documented effect of tasks for general reform orientation in government organizations (Christensen and Lægreid 2008; Pollitt and Bouckaert 2004), this is a surprising result. It suggests that the underlying mechanism of use is different in the case of EU soft law/governance than for other types of information behaviour.

Similarly, these survey data do not support the idea that the politicization of a policy area affects the use of the OMC; at least this is the case when the degree of politicization is measured as the civil servants' perception of the level of conflict in their own field. However, the OMC users tend to work in areas where there is little *public* debate ($r = -0.09$ significant at 0.05 level). Also we recall that government agencies are slightly more prone to use the OMC compared to civil servants in the ministries. These results could indicate that the use of the OMC finds a better breeding ground in a technical-administrative setting outside the public eye.

Table 7.5 sums up the results of the survey through a multivariate analysis that includes the main explanatory variables, organizational structure, contact and international orientation. (Since no significant bivariate correlation was found with respect to the task structure and the degree of politicization these variables were omitted.) Overall, multivariate control underlines the main results presented above. Yet, some additional points of interest come to the fore. First, we see that EU interaction has the strongest effect on the propensity to use the OMC. Second, two of the indicators

*Table 7.5    Summary of regression equations by factors affecting ministry officials' use of the OMC*

|  | OMC use index | Learning | Spread information |
|---|---|---|---|
| *Position* | 0.12* | 0.10* | 0.08* |
| *Contact patterns domestic* | | | |
| ● Minister | 0.01 | 0.01 | −0.01 |
| ● Administrative leadership | −0.01 | −0.01 | 0.00 |
| ● Stakeholder organizations | 0.08* | 0.03 | −0.06 |
| *EU interaction* | | | |
| ● Contact with European Commission | 0.18* | 0.19* | 0.21* |
| ● Committee participation | 0.24* | 0.22* | 0.22* |
| *International orientation in decision-making* | | | |
| ● Multilateral | 0.16* | 0.14* | −0.08* |
| ● Bilateral | 0.04 | 0.05 | 0.03 |
| ● Number of travel days (international) | −0.08* | −0.05 | −0.04 |
| *Policy area characteristics* | | | |
| ● Level of public debate | 0.02 | 0.03 | 0.02 |
| *$R^2$* | *0.25* | *0.22* | *0.23* |

*Notes:*    * Significant at $p < 0.05$; OMC use index; OMC as 'learning from the experience of other countries'; OMC as 'spreading information'; Standardized Beta coefficients; OLS regression; $N = 1006$.

of the overall international orientation (bilateral international policy copying and number of travel days abroad) have no significant effect on use in the multivariate model. This could indicate that the use of the OMC is not so much a case of general orientation towards what is happening in other countries, but a separate process that depends on a specialized organizational arrangement to take effect. If this is to be understood as an enclave, than it is not a general 'cosmopolitan' enclave, but a specialized EU enclave. Third, the domestic connectedness of civil servants has no independent effect on the use of the OMC when controlled for the effect of the hierarchical position of the OMC users. Still, the implications of the bivariate association between contact patterns and the OMC use are relevant – we know that the OMC users can potentially function as 'teachers' or sources of spread through their connections to domestic policy actors. But we also find that it is the hierarchical position that facilitates this connection.

# THE MULTIMODAL USE OF EU EDUCATION AND TRAINING 2010 IN NATIONAL POLICY-MAKING

## Organizing Connections to a European Soft Governance Experiment

Following the general Lisbon ambition, the Council of Ministers for Education agreed in 2001 on broad strategic goals for European education and training systems. The OMC-based E&T programme was a watershed EU cooperation in the field of education This work programme was developed further and reviewed in the 'Strategic Framework for European Cooperation in Education and Training' adopted by the Council in May 2009.[6] Contrary to what happened in several other sectors (Borrás 2009), the sector Directorate-General, DG Education and Culture (DG EAC), almost immediately orchestrated the OMC by attributing administrative energy and resources to get the work organization up and running.

As argued earlier in this chapter, such basic properties of this soft governance process (political endorsement, money and administrative resources) have implication also for its domestic use. In the case of Norway, the fact that the Commission took a leading role is essential. Being outside of the EU, Norwegian ministers and ministries could do little more than watch these changes taking place on the European political arena in the wake of the Lisbon Summit in 2000. Participating fully in EU education programmes, however, the Ministry had insights into the link that was in the making between education cooperation and the Lisbon Process. Domestically, internationalization of higher education had become a core policy objective in this period (Gornitzka and Stensaker 2004). And this international orientation could further benefit from Norway's participation in the intergovernmental Bologna Process to establish the EHEA. So, a confluence of developments contributed to the alertness of the Ministry towards the European arena. Also in 2002 the political leadership of the Ministry changed. The incoming Minister from the Conservative party had a clear profile as a pro-EU politician and was willing and able to connect to the European arena. At the administrative level the Ministry put time, effort and consideration into Norwegian participation. The Ministry argued vis-à-vis the Commission that since parts of the E&T activities were paid for through the education programme's budget to which the EEA countries also contributed, Norwegian participation in the E&T would be appropriate and not breaching the terms of the EEA agreement. Already here we can see the significance of domestic and supranational administrative resources in combination with political backing for securing an organized lifeline between European soft governance processes and domestic policy-making.

The Ministry's involvement was handled by the section for international affairs and the Ministry's 'EU team' that cuts across the various Ministry departments. The E&T also became a regular item on the agenda of the EU forum the Ministry organizes for core stakeholder groups. So some attention, especially among the leadership of the teachers' unions and secretariats, was directed towards the Education/Lisbon strategy link (Interview1205). The Ministry's involvement in the OMC process was also presented for the national parliament's Education Committee (Interview0405), but not as a regular report item from the Ministry.

**Monitoring the European Policy Environment Through the E&T**

As we have seen from the quantitative analysis, without direct interaction with the European level there is little use of the OMC among ministry officials. However, in the beginning the Ministry established this link without having a clear idea of what this new governance concept would entail – it felt like being part of an 'extreme sport event' (Interview0605). Especially in the beginning the national participants who were sent to Brussels for working group meetings described the experience as sitting there (in Brussels) with the OMC 'landing in their lap' (Interview0306). This initial response to the E&T is a foreboding of what the core use of the OMC would become in this case. The endeavour to be connected to the activities at the European level was not only a sign of the Ministry's identity ('we are after all Europeans') and international orientation (Gornitzka and Langfeldt 2008), the Ministry did not want to be left out of the education policy 'salons', even though the civil servants could not tell a priori where this process was heading. As long as the process was framed within an overarching consensual idea of the 'modernization of European education systems', latching on to the OMC process was within the political-administrative zone of acceptance. Consequently, a primary use of the OMC was as a way of *monitoring* the European policy environment and accessing information, and of being 'in the European loop'. Use of the OMC was in a 'surveillance mode', more than in a decision-instrumental mode.

**Conceptual use of the E&T**

In so far as participating in an OMC process shapes how domestic policy-makers see a policy field and the concepts and language that frame public policies, we can talk of a conceptual use. However, conceptual shifts are hard to unravel precisely because of the taken-for-granted nature of concepts and ideas that are integral parts of cognitive structures. Nonetheless, some general points can be made from the way in which national level policy-makers engaged in a conceptual use of the E&T.

First, E&T developed a standard that outlined what a good, healthy and modern education system should look like – it should, *inter alia*, focus on basic skills, and the teaching of foreign languages ('mothertongue+2'), on output and learning outcome rather than on input factors. It should have low drop-out rates, high mobility in tertiary education, a higher education system adjusted to the Bologna Process and to the EU's modernization agenda for its universities (see Chou and Gornitzka 2014, this volume). There should be high investment (including from private sources), and the education system should take a profiled and recognized place in the new economy, framed within a lifelong learning perspective.

As a political wish list, this standard did not represent a high level of adaptational pressure for Norwegian policy-makers. It matched central ideas in the domestic policy paradigms (with some notable exceptions discussed below). So a conceptual use did not imply many short-term overt changes in domestic policy. Core concepts central to the E&T were already an integral part of domestic policy. This was especially the case for lifelong learning strategies, where Norway together with other Nordic peers purportedly could upload their policy paradigms to the E&T platform. As for the higher education reform agenda, the Bologna elements were already well under way of being translated into the comprehensive national higher education reform that was implemented in 2004 ('Quality Reform' for higher education) (Gornitzka 2006). The conceptual impact of the E&T meant for the most part amplifying the existing tune more than introducing a new melody.

Second, the E&T's output orientation also matched the spirit of the comprehensive reform of the primary and secondary education sectors that was presented by the Centre-Conservative government in 2004 and prepared in parallel to the first stages of the E&T. The underlying premise of this reform was drawn from the international comparisons and the fundamental idea that Norwegian schools evidently failed to deliver on basic skills. Also later in the process the agenda of the E&T had a striking overlap with the main headlines of the government reform proposal. The latest example of an agenda overlap is the policy decision to introduce a teaching and learning component into pre-school childcare (2008), a concern that has also made it into the Common EU benchmarks for the renewed E&T programme adopted in May 2009. Of course, overlap does not constitute evidence of influence or emulation. Yet, it seems reasonable to argue that the language used is an indication of policy concepts that have been amplified domestically through the European E&T process.

Third, conceptual use is evident in the ideational hegemony of performance indicators and evidence-based policy-making. Here there was a considerable cognitive and partly normative match between 'European' and the domestic policy paradigm. The way that the E&T partly appropriated the indicators of the Organization for Economic Co-operation and Development (OECD), the Programme for International Student Assessment (PISA) study and the Trends in International Mathematics and Science Study (TIMMS), and started developing 'genuine' European indicators made the Norwegian participation in the E&T's work on indicators and benchmark all the more appropriate. Domestically, the use of performance indicators was being introduced at full speed in the governance and funding models for schools.[7] The development of education indicators is arguably a tangible expression of conceptual use of the OMC. The categories that were negotiated, argued and deliberated within the E&T process were deposited domestically as a set of hardened, quantified concepts, and some were highly politically salient. Here we see considerable domestic reproductive reliability of European level policy concepts. To the general public, however, the impact of indicators was perceived as a sign of an OECD-effect. The Ministry made references to the OECD and not primarily to the EU when using international comparisons to induce domestic change (strategic use). At the domestic arena the OECD had a different professional legitimacy and authority compared to the EU's overt political nature – 'saying "OECD studies show that . . ." carries a lot of weight. I don't think saying "EU studies show" does the same. People will see that as biased . . . EU is after all politics big time' (Interview0405).

Unpacking the impact of the EU's modernization agenda for European universities we see a different pattern of conceptual use. The overall agenda is an iconic part of a common European policy rhetoric that is most ardently promulgated by the Commission, also within the E&T. Parts of the national autonomy and governance reforms in higher education were couched in a similar language. But the national translation of this overall agenda is 'unreliable', marked by national filters, path dependencies and contingencies (see Gornitzka 2009).

**Learning From the E&T**

At the European level the organization and practices for learning and peer reviewing in E&T lived in a tensile balance between institutionalization, experimentation and disintegration. The learning element of domestic impact proved in this case to be more multifaceted than the strict definition policy learning suggests. The first learning outcome for the national administrations and the Commission was simply learning 'what is it that we don't know'. This is a kind of learning that national administrations could not have done single-handedly. Surveying the knowledge and information status, and identifying blind spots were central elements to the process. The thematic groups established at the EU level pooled information on national policy measures and experiences into compilations of 'soft facts'. In this respect the E&T made information more accessible and organized. The national progress reports that member states' ministries eventually made according to the time-rules and template produced by the DG EAC brought the E&T further towards giving an overview of policy developments in the member states' education systems. These reports contributed to laying the groundwork for mutual policy learning.[8]

A general conclusion from the Norwegian case, however, is that through the OMC process policy-makers learned more *about* their own system than directly *from* other countries' experiences. The comparisons prompted by the E&T both confirmed and seriously challenged the perception of the state of affairs in the domestic education sector. The PISA studies are of course the primary illustration of international surveys that destabilize the collective readings of the quality of national schools and students. As noted earlier, this boosted the national reform of primary and lower secondary education in the public eye and as a concern for the government. At the European level the informal rules of E&T toned down the reputational control (naming, shaming, faming) as the working ingredient of the method, but at the same time 'performance tables' were read as rankings in the European capitals, Oslo included. The special membership status for Norway had the effect that ministry representatives did not shirk potential shaming, but had to 'fight' to be included in the statistical tables and the member states' comparisons (Interview0405).

Why was it difficult to take cognitive shortcuts by learning directly from the experience of others through the E&T? The participants were in a European policy classroom where there was no obvious established and certified 'curriculum' when it comes to the more practical instrumentation of policy. Several of the interviewees pointed to how a lack of systematic assessments and peer reviewing made it difficult to establish 'good practice'. There were no ready-made and accepted criteria for certifying the experiences of other countries as good examples. Characteristics of information provided by national experts were also an impediment to transnational learning. National experts experienced at times cross pressure from being expected to present national measures as attractive ('bragging'), while having first-hand insight into the less attractive realities of prestigious policy measures (Interview05(1)05). Those actors who over time participated in common European OMC forums experienced that the organized venues for interaction reduced alienation and changed the actors' perceptions of cultural proximity and appropriate reference groups to some extent. Some of these venues even created more permanent communication networks with other sister/brother ministries in Europe ('knowing who to call') and even personal friendships (Interview05(2)05).

Limited transferability from one context to another also comes down to the characteristics of the 'learner'. Most of those who participated in the OMC process were national experts with very good insights into the institutional conditions of national educational policy-making. Practices from 'the best student in the class', such as Finland in the area of reading literacy/ teacher training, are not entirely replicable, not even for a Nordic neighbour. Furthermore, the experienced officials reviewed transnational lessons in light of what was politically acceptable domestically. A prime example is the Nordic countries' response to student fees as a European good practice to increase investments in higher education (Interview05(3)05).

Mutual learning within the framework of the E&T also stalled at other well-known barriers to learning, especially ruptures in the link between individual learning and organizational learning. All interviewees say they have learned a lot from participation in the OMC process and that the process has been open for sharing the experiences of a non-EU member. This underlines the fact that policy-makers understand learning as a process of circulating ideas. Yet several interviewees saw a weak link between individual learning and ministerial action. One of them said about the Ministry, 'I don't think anyone even read what we [the E&T working group] wrote. Only people like you read these things' (Interview05(1)05). Although the survey data clearly highlight the significance of the organized connections between the domestic arena and the EU soft governance processes, in practice the OMC connectors in the Ministry reported problems with diffusing, not so much information, but the learning experiences within the Ministry. This has also to do with the *timing* of learning from European lessons relative to domestic decision-making opportunities. Insights into the experiences of other education systems are – for many reasons – not readily translated into to domestic policy change and adjustments. However, we should not rule out that the kind of policy surveillance that the Ministry became engaged in could increase its absorptive capacity and in the long run be translated into domestic policy change.

## CONCLUSION

The development of the OMC is commonly staged as a drama between the strong integrative outcome of hard law and the weak or non-existent outcome of soft law/governance. In terms of overall impact on domestic policy-making, the evidence offered here supports this perception to some extent. The overall effect of the OMC on domestic policy-making is limited. Compared to the body of EU hard law that has been transposed soft governance is weak. A majority of Norwegian civil servants in ministries and government agencies see no relevance or a negligible importance of the OMC in their field of work. Yet, the use of the OMC is extremely unevenly distributed, and it is significant for some pockets of national administrations. We have seen in the Norwegian case that the impact is strongest in the Ministry of Education and Research. These findings clearly echo the response of the DG EAC to the OMC concept: 'This is a method for us' (Gornitzka 2007).

This chapter has argued for rephrasing the question of the strength of soft modes of governance in light of what we generally know about how policies are made, how administrative men and women in government organizations behave and how information is used in organizational decision-making. Then the pertinent question is not so much the impact of soft versus hard governance, but what the evidence on the use of EU soft modes of governance can tell us about 'how political and administrative institutions generate experience, how they monitor their environments, and how they interpret, store, retrieve, and act upon experience' (Olsen and Peters 1996, p. 4).

The data tell us that the OMC processes organized at the European level have become a transmission belt that has affected the generation and flow of policy relevant information. We also see that the OMC's use is multimodal and some types of use are more prominent than others. Civil servants use the OMC in a learning mode, that is the OMC affects the ability to learn from the experience of others and the opportunity to 'teach' their European peers (a mix of receiving and giving information). Also the OMC users report that it has changed the overall pool of knowledge and to a somewhat lesser extent the overall access to information.

The case study of the E&T's impact domestically shows that the instrumental use – plucking pieces of policy from the EU's OMC transfer platform and inserting them into national educational policy – is not the dominant use of the OMC. This direct instrumental use is not the strength of soft modes of governance. Learning about yourself through a comparison with others is more important than the clean-cut policy change via learning from the experience or success of others. This case study finds little evidence to support the argument that the impact of EU soft modes of governance runs in a straight line from country X's experience via the European organization to country Y's domestic policy change.

How domestic policy-makers act, or fail to act, on the basis of information generated and accessed through the OMC processes, partly has to do with how processes are organized and practised at the European level. Here we can see that policy-makers have considerable difficulties in finding generally acceptable and appropriate ways to review and 'certify' information and experiences that can be reproduced reliably in other domestic contexts. But there are also several prominent domestic factors (learning in a political context and the rhythm of policy process) that in practice make it difficult to act upon the experience of others.

Overall the use of the OMC is in the surveillance mode rather than the decision mode. The OMC has made an impact on the way in which the Ministry monitors its policy environment in Europe and its access to information. Conceptual use is also prominent. Especially the use of quantified, internationally comparable concepts as an integral part of domestic policy is a major modus of utilization in Norwegian education and higher education policy-making.

Overall data say that the use of the OMC depends on the organizational channels that have been created between the European level and domestic administrative institutions. Organizational factors filter the impact of this type of soft governance. Using the OMC is mainly an activity for mid-level civil servants who are in turn well connected to the domestic policy process. This speaks to the potential for domestic impact within the pockets of domestic policy-making where the OMC has gained a foothold.

The use of EU soft modes of governance in the knowledge policy domain is part of a general picture of going from homespun to European multi-level interwoven policy-making (Jacobsson and Sundström 2006). The Ministry of Education and Research is now among the Norwegian ministries with the strongest international orientation for policy-making in general. The effect of the OMC is then part of the internationalization of policy production at the national level. The national orientation as the policy frame of reference that was dominant only a decade ago has been changed. On this point the evidence is irrefutable. There are several European processes that 'hit' the nation states and these blur and blend the routes of impact. Yet, the evidence presented here shows how the institutionalization of the OMC for the Europe of Knowledge is a central part of this development. Also for these policy areas national policy cannot be understood solely from a national point of view. The influence of European cooperation lies not only at the level of zeitgeist or free flowing ideas, it involves organized links, and regularized procedures and routines, mediated by a non-hierarchical governance mode.

## NOTES

1. A draft version of this chapter was presented at the ECPR 5th General Conference, Potsdam 10–12 September, 2009. Thanks to members of the panel: 'Beyond Bologna:

Determinants and Outcomes of Change in Higher Education Policy' for helpful comments.
2. It has been commonplace in the literature and among practitioners to refer to the OMC as a type of soft law (Abbott and Snidal 2000; De Ruiter 2010; Duina and Raunio 2007; Dunoff and Pollack 2013; Falkner et al. 2005; Trubek and Trubek 2005). However, scholars have made a strong argument that 'soft law' is a misnomer in the case of the OMC because this mode of governance has an 'extra-law' nature and the novel aspects of the OMC set it apart from traditional EU soft law (Borrás and Jacobsson 2004; Borrás and Radaelli 2010).
3. Note that unless otherwise stated the results reported here are filtered so as to exclude respondents whose field of work is not at all affected by the EU, the EEA or Schengen agreements.
4. The interviews were carried out under conditions of anonymity (Chatham House Rule) and the interviewees are only identified by their number within the text.
5. Average score on the OMC use index: 6.7 in ministries; 9.4 in agencies.
6. Council Conclusions of 12 May 2009 on a Strategic Framework for European Cooperation in Education and Training ('ET 2020') (2009/C 119/02), 28 May 2009.
7. These policies were controversial, especially with respect to the underlying logic of measuring and publicizing the performance of school children on national tests of basic skills.
8. Draft joint progress report with annex COM 2005 549 final/2.

# REFERENCES

Abbott, K.W. and D. Snidal (2000), 'Hard and soft law in international governance', *International Organization*, **54**(3), 421–456.

Allison, G.T. (1969), 'Conceptual models and the Cuban missile crisis', *The American Political Science Review*, **63**(3), 689–718.

Borrás, S. (2009), 'The politics of the Lisbon strategy: the changing role of the Commission', *West European Politics*, **32**(1), 97–118.

Borrás, S. and K. Jacobsson (2004), 'The open method of co-ordination and new governance patterns in the EU', *Journal of European Public Policy*, **11**(2), 185–208.

Borrás, S. and C.M. Radaelli (2010), 'Recalibrating the open method of coordination', *Stockholm Siepes*, Report No. 7.

Bulmer, S. and C.M. Radaelli (2005), 'The Europeanisation of national policy', in S. Bulmer and C. Lequesne (eds), *Members States of the European Union*, Oxford: Oxford University Press, pp. 338–359.

Chou, M.-H. and Å. Gornitzka (2014, this volume), 'Building a European knowledge area: an introduction to the dynamics of policy domains on the rise', in M.-H. Chou and Å. Gornitzka (eds), *Building the Knowledge Economy in Europe: New Constellations in European Research and Higher Education Governance*, Cheltenham, UK and Northampton, MA, USA: Edward Elgar, pp. 1–26.

Christensen, T. and P. Lægreid (2008), 'NPM and beyond – structure, culture and demography', *International Review of Administrative Sciences*, **74**(1), 7–23.

De Ruiter, R. (2010), 'EU soft law and the functioning of representative democracy: the use of methods of open co-ordination by Dutch and British parliamentarians', *Journal of European Public Policy*, **17**(6), 874–890.

Dimitrova, A. and B. Steunenberg (2000), 'The search for convergence in national policies in the European Union', *European Union Politics*, **1**(2), 201–226.

Duina, F. and T. Raunio (2007), 'The open method of co-ordination and national parliaments: further marginalization or new opportunities?', *Journal of European Public Policy*, **14**(4), 489–506.

Dunoff, J.L. and M.A. Pollack (2013), 'International law and international relations', in J.L. Dunoff and M.A. Pollack (eds), *Interdisciplinary Perspectives on International Law and International Relations*, Cambridge: Cambridge University Press, pp. 3–32.

Egeberg, M. (2004), 'An organisational approach to European integration: outline of a complementary perspective', *European Journal of Political Research*, **43**(2), 199–219.

Egeberg, M. (ed.) (2006), *Multilevel Union Administration. The Transformation of Executive Politics in Europe*, Houndmills: Palgrave Macmillan.

Egeberg, M. (2012), 'How bureaucratic structure matters: an organizational perspective', in B.G. Peters and J. Pierre (eds), *The SAGE Handbook of Public Administration*, Los Angeles: Sage, pp. 157–168.

Egeberg, M. and J. Trondal (1997), 'Innnenriksforvaltningens og den offentlige politikkens internasjonalisering', in T. Christensen and M. Egeberg (eds), *Forvaltningskunnskap*, Oslo: Tano, pp. 335–363.

Egeberg, M. and J. Trondal (2009), 'National agencies in the European administrative space: government driven, Commission driven or networked?', *Public Administration*, **87**(4), 779–790.

Elkins, Z. and B. Simmons (2005), 'On waves, clusters, and diffusion: a conceptual framework', *Annals of the American Academy of Political and Social Science*, **598**, 33–51.

Eyre, S. and M. Lodge (2000), 'National tunes and a European melody? Competition law reform in the UK and Germany', *Journal of European Public Policy*, **7**(1), 63–79.

Falkner, G., O. Treib, M. Hartlapp and S. Leibner (2005), *Complying with Europe: EU Harmonisation and Soft Law in the Member States*, Cambridge: Cambridge University Press.

Feldman, M.S. and J.G. March (1988), 'Information in organizations as signal and symbol', in J.G. March (ed.), *Decisions and Organizations*, Oxford: Blackwell, pp. 409–428.

Finnemore, M. (1993), 'International organizations as teachers of norms – the United Nations' educational scientific and cultural organization and science policy', *International Organization*, **47**(4), 565–597.

Fossum, J.E. (2009), 'Norway's European conundrum', *Arena Working Paper*, **4**(February).

Gornitzka, Å. (2003), *Science, Clients, and the State: a Study of Scientific Knowledge Production and Use*, Enschede: CHEPS.

Gornitzka, Å. (2006), 'What is the use of Bologna in national reform? The case of the Norwegian quality reform in higher education', in V. Tomusk (ed.), *Creating the European Area of Higher Education: Voices from Peripheries*, Dordrecht: Springer, pp. 19–41.

Gornitzka, Å. (2007), 'The Lisbon Process: a supranational policy perspective', in P. Maassen and J.P. Olsen (eds), *University Dynamics and European Integration*, Dordrecht: Springer, pp. 155–178.

Gornitzka, Å. (2009), 'Styringsreformer i høyere utdanning i Europa – politiske ambisjoner mellom omgivelsespress og sektortradisjoner', *Norsk Statsvitenskapelig Tidsskrift*, **25**(2), 127–156.

186     *Building the knowledge economy in Europe*

Gornitzka, Å. and L. Langfeldt (2008), 'The internationalisation of national knowledge policies', in Å. Gornitzka and L. Landfeldt (eds), *Borderless Knowledge*, Dordrecht: Springer, pp. 141–169.

Gornitzka, Å. and B. Stensaker (2004), 'Norway', in J. Huisman and M. van der Wende (eds), *On Cooperation and Competition. National and European Policies for the Internationalisation of Higher Education*, Bonn: Lemmens, pp. 81–111.

Greenwood, R., C. Oliver, K. Sahlin and R. Suddaby (2008), 'Introduction', in R. Greenwood, C. Oliver, R. Suddaby and K. Sahlin (eds), *Organizational Institutionalism*, Los Angeles: Sage, pp. 1–46.

Hall, P. A. (1993), 'Policy paradigms, social learning, and the state: the case of economic policymaking in Britain', *Comparative Politics*, **25**(3), 275–296.

Holzinger, K. and C. Knill (2005), 'Causes and conditions of cross-national policy convergence', *Journal of European Public Policy*, **12**(5), 775–796.

Ikenberry, G.J. (1990), 'The international spread of privatization policies: inducements, learning, and "policy band wagoning"', in E.N. Suleiman and J. Waterbury (eds), *The Political Economy of Public Sector Reform and Privatization*, Boulder: Westview Press, pp. 88–110.

Jacobsson, B. and G. Sundström (2006), *Från Hemvävd til Invävd. Europeiseringen av svensk statsforvaltning och politik*, Malmö: Liber.

Katzenstein, P.J. (2005), *A World of Regions: Asia and Europe in the American Imperium*, Ithaca, NY: Cornell University Press.

Lægreid, P., R.S. Steinthorsson and B. Thorhallsson (2004), 'Europeanization of central government administration in the Nordic states', *Journal of Common Market Studies*, **42**(2), 347–369.

Laffan, B. and C. Shaw (2005), 'Classifying and Mapping OMC in Different Policy Areas', NEWGOV Reference Number 02/D09.

March, J.G. (1988), 'Ambiguity and accounting: the elusive link between information and decision making', in J.G. March (ed.), *Decisions and Organizations*, Oxford: Blackwell, pp. 384–408.

March, J.G. (1991), 'Exploration and exploitation in organizational learning', *Organization Science*, **2**(1), 71–87.

March, J.G. (1999), 'A learning perspective on the network dynamics of institutional integration', in M. Egeberg and P. Lægreid (eds), *Organizing Political Institutions – Essays for Johan P. Olsen*, Oslo: Scandinavian University Press, pp. 129–155.

Olsen, J.P. and B.G. Peters (1996), 'Learning from experience?', in J.P. Olsen and B.G. Peters (eds), *Lessons from Experience. Experiential Learning in Administrative Reforms in Eight Democracies*, Oslo: Scandinavian University Press, pp. 1–35.

Pierre, J. and B.G. Peters (2009), 'From a club to a bureaucracy: JAA, EASA, and European aviation regulation', *Journal of European Public Policy*, **16**(3), 337–355.

Pollitt, C. (2001), 'Convergence: the useful myth?', *Public Administration*, **79**(4), 933–947.

Pollitt, C. and G. Bouckaert (2004), *Public Management Reform: a Comparative Analysis*, Oxford: Oxford University Press.

Pressman, J.L. and A. Wildavsky (1984), *Implementation: How Great Expectations in Washington are Dashed in Oakland, or, Why it's Amazing that Federal Programs Work at all: This Being a Saga of the Economic Development Administration as*

*Told by Two Sympathetic Observers Who Seek to Build Morals on a Foundation of Ruined Hopes*, Berkeley, CA: California University Press.

Radaelli, C.M. (2008), 'Europeanization, policy learning, and new modes of governance', *Journal of Comparative Policy Analysis: Research and Practice*, **10**(3), 239–254.

Rich, R.F. and C.H. Oh (2000), 'Rationality and use of information in policy decisions – a search for alternatives', *Science Communication*, **22**(2), 173–211.

Risse, T., M.G. Cowles and J. Caporaso (2001), 'Europeanisation and domestic change: introduction', in M.G. Cowles, J. Caporaso and T. Risse (eds), *Transforming Europe: Europeanization and Domestic Change*, Ithaca, NY: Cornell University Press, pp. 1–20.

Simmons, B.A. and Z. Elkins (2004), 'The globalization of liberalization: policy diffusion in the international political economy', *American Political Science Review*, **98**(1), 171–189.

Sverdrup, U. (2004), 'Compliance and conflict management in the European Union: Nordic exceptionalism', *Scandinavian Journal of Management*, **27**(1), 23–43.

Thompson, M. and A. Wildavsky (1986), 'A cultural theory of information bias in organizations', *Journal of Management Studies*, **23**(3), 273–286.

Treib, O. (2008), 'Implementing and complying with EU governance outputs', *Living Reviews in European Governance*, **3**(5), available at: http://www.livingreviews.org/ (accessed June 2013).

Treib, O., H. Bahr and G. Falkner (2007), 'Modes of governance: towards a conceptual clarification', *Journal of European Public Policy*, **14**(1), 1–20.

Trubek, D.M. and L.G. Trubek (2005), 'Hard and soft law in the construction of social europe: the role of the open method of co-ordination', *European Law Journal*, **11**(3), 343–364.

Underdal, A. (2008), 'The organizational infrastructure of international environmental regimes', in U. Sverdrup and J. Trondal (eds), *The Organizational Dimension of Politics*, Oslo: Fagbokforlaget, pp. 186–205.

Vifell, Å. (2006), *Enklaver i staten. Internationalisering, demokrati och den svenska statsförvaltningen*, Stockholm: Department of Political Science, Stockholm University.

# 8. 'Quality agencies': the development of regulating and mediating organizations in Scandinavian higher education

**Hanne Foss Hansen**

## INTRODUCTION

'Cognitive capitalism' has been introduced to characterize societies in which innovation and the accumulation of knowledge constitute the central economic force (Høstaker and Vabø 2005). In the context of cognitive capitalism strategies, Europeanization and globalization, Scandinavian higher education in the last decades has increasingly turned into a commodity and higher educational institutions into companies competing to attract students and staff nationally as well as internationally. At the European level, the Bologna Process aims at increasing student mobility and making higher education comparable across national borders. At national levels higher educational reforms based on new public management are implemented. Focus on leadership is increased and result-based funding systems further developed. An interesting question is how the Scandinavian higher education systems have responded to these multiple ideas and tensions as marketization challenges classical academic values as well as the Scandinavian tradition of regarding education as a free welfare state right.

As in other areas the increasing marketization has brought along requests for quality assurance, transparency and new forms of regulation. And requests are brought forward both in the Bologna Process and at national political agendas. To meet these requests quality agencies, defined as agencies being responsible for quality assurance, have been established. In some cases existing regulatory agencies have been reformed, in others new agencies have been established. Quality agencies have developed international networks which have become places for discussion and development of quality assurance methodologies and policies.

This chapter deals with this development by focusing on how quality agencies in higher education are organized in Denmark, Norway and Sweden. The main research question concerns the role of these agencies in higher education. How are quality agencies regulated? And how do quality agencies practise quality assurance and thus regulation?

Aiming at answering these questions the chapter also relates to the broader discussion in public administration research about regulatory reform, agencification and modernization of government. In recent years comprehensive reform initiatives have been launched internationally. Regulatory reform programmes prescribe high degrees of autonomy for regulatory agencies from political executives as well as from market actors (OECD 2002) and modernizing programmes prescribe strengthening accountability and *ex post* control (OECD 2005). This chapter examines how higher education quality assurance in the Scandinavian countries responded to these seemingly contradictory recommendations.

Radaelli (2005) has studied how regulatory ideas related to regulatory impact assessment procedures have diffused in the European Union among other things due to OECD initiatives. He has also shown, that the diffusion of ideas has not resulted in convergence because national political contexts have shaped the implementation of the regulatory ideas. In this case of quality assurance in higher education, where the European Educational Ministers decide on policies, we should expect a higher degree of convergence compared to the findings of Radaelli. The main findings of the analysis however are, that there is little regulatory convergence across the Scandinavian quality agencies and although European standards have been developed, these are only to a limited extent standardizing the practices of quality agencies.

The chapter is structured into seven sections. The next section presents the theoretical framework and analytical concepts used in the analysis as well as the methodological approach. The following section gives an introduction to the agencies studied and analyses how these agencies are regulated and organized. The fourth section holds an analysis of the international networking and governance of the agencies. The fifth section examines how the agencies practise quality assurance. The sixth section discusses and compares the role of the agencies and the final section concludes the chapter.

## THEORETICAL AND METHODOLOGICAL APPROACH

The analysis of the quality agencies in the field of higher education combines a regulatory approach with an approach anchored in organizational theory. The regulatory approach is concerned with how quality agencies work, the instruments and strategies they use as well as their relationships with the actors regulated, while the organizational approach is concerned with how they organize including how their external networks influence how they develop. Below the two approaches are presented in more detail.

Autonomy and control of state organizations and the process of agencification have been topics for academic discussion in the field of public administration for some years (Christensen and Lægreid 2006; Pollitt et al. 2004). Contemporary agency reform efforts have in many countries split up former integrated agencies into 'single-purpose organizations', one such type being agencies specialized in regulation, inspection and evaluation often named regulatory agencies (Boston et al. 1996; Lægreid et al. 2008).

As the term indicates, regulatory agencies are responsible for regulation. A classic definition refers to regulation as 'sustained and focused control exercised by a public agency over activities that are valued by a community' (Selznick 1985, p. 363). However, as control may be exercised in different ways, much of the literature on regulation is concerned with developing and discussing typologies of different types of regulation. One typology distinguishes between 'hard' regulation (defined as classical rule and control-based regulation) and 'soft' regulation (defined as discursive related to language-use and knowledge-making).

Another typology distinguishes between deterrence, compliance and responsive regulation which models the relationship between the regulatory and regulated (Walshe 2003). In the deterrence model the regulator's view of the regulated organizations is that of the untrustworthy amoral calculator while the regulated organizations' view of the regulatory agency is that of the policeman using many, detailed and explicit written standards. On the contrary, in the compliance model the regulator's view of the regulated organizations is that of the mostly good and well-intentioned, if not always competent, while the regulated organizations' view of the regulatory agency is that of the consultant and supporter accompanying written standards by guidance on implementation. Finally, responsive regulation, sometimes also called smart regulation, is an attempt to escape these dichotomies. In responsive regulation the core concept is contingency. There is no 'one size fits all' approach and no uniform regulatory methodology. Instead, the regulatory regime is highly contingent on the behaviour of the individual regulated organizations. High-performing organizations are deliberately treated differently than low-performing, and amoral calculators are dealt with differently than good-hearted compliers.

The typologies discussed above relate to regulatory agencies regardless of the policy field in which they work. Besides the relevance of the policy generic typologies, the more specific literature on educational evaluation methodologies is relevant when analysing regulatory agencies in the field of higher education. Also educational evaluation methodologies may take different forms. Programme evaluation, evaluation of quality assurance systems (also called auditing) and accreditation have been extensively used but new forms of evaluation are constantly developed. Programme evaluation focuses on the quality of educational programmes and are often organized comparatively, assessing, for example, all national programmes in disciplines such as chemistry, pedagogy or political science. Evaluation of quality assurance systems (also called auditing) normally refers to evaluation of higher educational institutions internal quality assurance systems, a more indirect way to try to influence educational quality. Finally, accreditation refers to evaluation using explicit *ex ante* defined criteria and standards to approve or disapprove either programmes or institutions. It is not unequivocal to sort out the concepts of educational evaluation methodologies because conceptual uncertainty characterizes the concept of quality as well as the concepts of educational evaluation methodologies. Moreover, concepts are used in slightly different ways in different countries and the different educational evaluation methodologies do not clearly match the deterrence/compliance distinction although accreditation approaches most often lean towards deterrence and quality assurance systems approaches towards compliance.

Finally a regulatory approach on quality agencies should be open to the fact that other actors besides national agencies may act as regulators. Expert panels and private institutions may be involved in inspection. The concept of regulatory capitalism has been proposed to reflect the fact that in many areas private regulation institutions in recent years have emerged (Christensen and Lægreid 2006).

In the analysis, especially in the fifth section, the regulatory approach is used as a frame of reference for the analysis of how the practices of the quality agencies have developed in order to shed light on how they respond to the Bologna Process and whether convergence occurs.

The regulatory approach will be combined with an approach anchored in organizational theory, especially theories on public organizations. Regulatory agencies are regarded as open systems (Scott 2003). Regulatory agencies are public organizations not of the type 'public-in-contact' (Blau and Scott 1963) as for example higher educational institutions, but of a type which can be termed 'public-and-public/private-organizations-in-contact'. This means that their target group consists of other organizations and not directly clients or citizens.

As other types of public organizations, regulatory agencies may engage in several networks (Jørgensen et al. 1998). Three main networks are expected to be of special importance. First, regulatory agencies are engaged in a regulation negotiation network including actors who are able to influence the context and the working conditions of the agencies. These actors include authorities superordinate to agencies, for example international organizations, the parent ministry, the Ministry of Finance, the General Audit Office and so on, but may also include Members of Parliament, interest organizations, unions and media. Within this network, law-making, goals, strategies, standards and resources are negotiated.

Second, regulatory agencies are engaged in a regulation practice network including actors in the organizational field regulated, in this case public and private higher educational institutions, their interest organizations and external actors drawn into regulation activities for example experts, peers and student representatives. Within this network evaluation and inspection activities are planned and practised.

Third, regulatory agencies are engaged in a methodological network including sister organizations in other countries as well as experts on higher education regulation. In this network, experiences are shared and methodologies developed.

Within all three networks agencies may achieve organizational legitimacy. Whether this is the case is a point of interest for empirical analysis. Other points of interest for empirical analysis are which actors dominate a network, which is the relative importance of the different networks, how tightly or loosely networks are coupled, how different networks influence or even dominate each other and which roles the regulatory agencies have? Are agencies mainly the auxiliary arms of international organizations and the parent ministries, do they play a mediating role between actors in the negotiation network and actors in the regulation network or are they playing a more autonomous and proactive role setting the agenda and influencing the development of the higher educational field and higher educational regulation?

In the analysis, especially in the sixth section, the organizational approach is used as a frame of reference for the analysis of how the networks of the quality agencies are constituted in order to shed light on the role of the agencies in the development of quality assurance practices.

Methodologically, the analysis is based primarily on publicly accessible documentary data, such as laws, consolidating acts, statutes, year books and other kinds of documentary material. Second, it is based on knowledge developed through participation in the field as a member of the Advisory Council of the Danish Evaluation Institute (EVA) since 2005, the Board of the Norwegian Agency for Quality Assurance in Education (NOKUT) since 2007 and an International Advisory Board of the Swedish National Agency for Higher Education (HSV) 2007–2010. Placing in these contexts has given insight into the dynamics of quality assurance practices which this chapter has benefited from. Before I turn to the more thorough analysis of agency practices, the next section gives an overall introduction to the agencies, their historical development and the international context in which they operate.

## THE ORGANIZATION OF SCANDINAVIAN HIGHER EDUCATIONAL QUALITY AGENCIES

Historically, Denmark, Norway and Sweden have had different higher education quality assurance and development traditions. In Sweden, initiatives to develop a national system for quality assurance were taken already in the late 1960s. In Denmark, similar processes came on the agenda in the late 1980s and in Norway in the late 1990s (Hansen 2009). Today Denmark, Norway and Sweden all have agencies responsible for quality assurance in higher education. However, the organization and regulation of these agencies differ. In the following, the history and the key characteristics of the three systems are described country by country and the development and roles of the international networks in which they participate are discussed.

### Denmark

An agency specializing in evaluation in higher education was established in 1992. In 1999 it was reorganized into the Danish Evaluation Institute (EVA) which was given responsibility for evaluation activities at all educational levels. At the university level the EVA carried through programme evaluations and for a short period of time audits of quality assurance systems at the institutional level. Both activities aimed primarily at further developing quality work and only indirectly at controlling. At the university college level the EVA carried out accreditations of both programmes and institutions aimed at controlling that certain quality criteria were met. While both programme evaluations and audits were manifestations of soft regulatory approaches leaning towards a compliance approach, the accreditations were based on a harder more deterrence leaning regulatory approach.

In 2007 a large reorganization was undertaken and a single-purpose and single-technology agency called ACE Denmark was introduced. The purpose of ACE Denmark was to assure and document quality and relevance of higher education in Denmark through carrying out accreditation of educational programmes. ACE Denmark had the task of preparing and carrying through plans taking all existing Bachelor and

Master's programmes through accreditation within a five-year period. Higher educational institutions also have to apply for accreditation of all new Bachelor and Master's programmes which they plan to offer. The 2007 reorganization meant that except for Ph.D. programmes all parts of Danish higher education are now approached in a hard deterrence leaning regulatory strategy.

ACE Denmark is regulated through one law (called the Accreditation Law) and several consolidating acts. The law lays down the overall framework of the system covering all higher education. According to the law, ACE Denmark is a professional autonomous body established by the Ministry for Science, Technology and Innovation (now the Ministry for Science, Innovation and Higher Education after reorganization in October 2011). Although being a single-purpose and single-technology institution, the organization is very complex. An Accreditation Council is responsible for decisions on accreditation as well as for securing that standards used in the Danish system matches standards decided on at the European level, the so-called 'European Standards and Guidelines for Quality Assurance in the European Higher Education Area' (ESG) drafted by the European Association for Quality Assurance in Higher Education (ENQA) and decided on by the European Ministers of Education in 2005 (ENQA 2005).

The Accreditation Council consists of a chairman and eight members appointed by the Minister for Science, Technology and Innovation. Three members are appointed on the recommendation of the Minister for Education, one on the recommendation of the Minister for Cultural Affairs and one on the recommendation of student representatives. Altogether the members of the Accreditation Council have to have knowledge and experience with quality assurance, higher education, research and the labour market for graduates.

The Accreditation Council is supported by a Council Secretariat preparing the meetings in the Council. The Council uses two different organizations as operators in carrying out accreditation. Accreditation reports regarding higher educational programmes offered by the universities are prepared by a specialist secretariat in ACE Denmark. Accreditation reports regarding higher educational programmes offered by other higher educational institutions above all university colleges are prepared by the EVA.

The consolidating acts lay down the accreditation criteria to be used. Until a reorganization in October 2011, the universities and the university colleges were placed in two different ministries, the universities in the Ministry for Science, Technology and Innovation and the university colleges in the Ministry for Education. In this context slightly different criteria were developed as the ministries so to speak were the 'owners' of the accreditation criteria within their own field.

The criteria regarding the universities were laid down in the political law-making process before ACE Denmark was established, with the Ministry of Science, Technology and Innovation being a very influential actor. In the first years after the accreditation system was introduced ACE Denmark acted mostly as an accreditation machine concentrating on implementing the system. In 2010 a new director was appointed and she chose a more mediating strategy presenting a proposal for a new accreditation system (Akkrediteringsrådet 2010). The proposal was worked out against the background that the existing system had been heavily criticized for being far too bureaucratic.

The criteria regarding the higher educational programmes outside the universities were laid down in a dialogue process involving higher educational institutions, the EVA and the responsible line ministries, especially the Ministry of Education and the Ministry of Cultural Affairs (EVA 2007). Since the accreditation system was introduced, the EVA has played an important role in the regulation negotiation network mediating between the ministries and the higher educational institutions. The EVA is governed by a Director under the responsibility of a Board and in dialogue with an Advisory Council. These bodies however have no formal influence on how the task of accreditation is carried through.

The December 2010 proposal from ACE Denmark to reform the accreditation system initiated a broad discussion on how to proceed in the future. In late spring 2013 a political decision about a new accreditation system was taken. From autumn 2013 the new system based on accreditation of institutions is being phased in. ACE Denmark has changed its name to the Danish Accreditation Institution and staff working in the EVA with accreditation have moved to this institution. The EVA in the future is to be responsible for thematic evaluations of higher education.

### Norway

The Norwegian Agency for Quality Assurance in Education (NOKUT) was established in 2002 and became operative in 2003 (Stensaker 2006). The agency was established as a reform of the precursor in Norwegian named Norgesnettrådet, which had been established in 1997. While Norgesnettrådet had used a very soft regulatory approach by drawing up guidelines for quality work within higher education as well as evaluating a national network structure developed in relation to a reform merging nearly 100 higher educational institutions into 26 university colleges, NOKUT was given a somewhat harder regulation profile.

The purpose of NOKUT was to control the quality of Norwegian higher educational institutions but the law stresses that the control activities of NOKUT have to be developed in such a way that quality work at educational institutions benefits from it. Control and development purposes and hard deterrence leaning and soft compliance leaning regulatory approaches thus go hand in hand. The aim of NOKUT has been expressed as to contribute to societal confidence in the quality of education (NOKUT 2009). In recent years the strategy has been to strengthen quality developing activities.

NOKUT is both a multi-purpose and a multi-technology agency working with audits of quality assurance systems at educational institutions, accreditation of programmes and institutions, reaccreditation, evaluation, approval of foreign education and assessment of applications for centres of excellent teaching. NOKUT also carry through analyses in order to build up knowledge on the higher educational sector.

NOKUT is regulated through sections in the general law about universities and university colleges. According to the law NOKUT is a professional autonomous body. Also according to the law the parent ministry, the Ministry of Education and Research, cannot give NOKUT instructions other than the kind which are laid down in law and regulations. Also, the Ministry cannot reverse accreditation decisions taken by NOKUT.

A consolidating act elaborates on the task of NOKUT and criteria to be used in both audit and accreditation. NOKUT has also formulated regulations further elaborating on these criteria. Recently, the consolidating act and NOKUT's elaboration of this has been revised. This process was organized in a dialogue process with the higher educational sector. In the development processes of the quality assurance system, NOKUT in this way clearly acts as a mediating organization.

NOKUT is as a department organized agency governed by a Director under the responsibility of a Board. The Board has eight members one of these being a student and one a member of staff at NOKUT. The Chairman of the Board is appointed by the Ministry. Alongside being responsible for strategy development the Board also takes decisions in concrete matters related to audits, institutional accreditation and accreditation of Ph.D. programmes. Decisions about programme accreditation below the Ph.D. level are delegated to the director.

**Sweden**

Sweden has had agencies specialized in higher education and working with evaluation since the 1960s (Gröjer 2004). From 1995 until the end of

2012 the Swedish National Agency for Higher Education (Högskoleverket, HSV) was responsible for quality regulation. The HSV was a multi-purpose agency dealing with a broad set of issues affecting universities and higher education institutions in Sweden. The HSV was responsible for quality assurance, evaluated qualifications awarded abroad, supported educational innovation and development, and also provided information on higher education and encouraged student recruitment.

The Swedish government regulated the HSV through law, a yearly budget (reguleringsbrev) and separate decisions (opdrag). The Ministry of Education was responsible for preparing governmental educational policies and the HSV is in dialogue with the Ministry. According to the law (Högskolelag and Högskoleförordning), higher educational institutions were obliged to deliver to the HSV any information requested. The law also gave the HSV authority to withdraw higher educational institutions examination rights and stated that HSV decisions could not be brought before any other authority.

The HSV was headed by the University Chancellor. For some years the HSV was organized with a Board. Later this was changed into an Advisory Council (Indsynsråd). The HSV regularly met with the group of Vice-Chancellors. Whereas the quality assurance technology to be used is legally codified in Denmark and partly also in Norway, there has been no such tradition in Sweden.

In 2012, it was decided to close the HSV from 1 January 2013. The tasks were placed with two new agencies. An agency called the Swedish Higher Education Authority (Universitetskänslerämbetet) is responsible for quality assurance and has to take responsibility also for broader evaluations of how effectively higher education institutions perform. The former multi-purpose Swedish quality agency was thus divided into two more single-purpose organizations. This development is the result of a general administrative policy promoting lean agencies.

## INTERNATIONAL NETWORKING AND GOVERNANCE

Besides being shaped by the domestic political context, the Scandinavian higher education quality agencies are part of and influenced by the development of a multi-level governance system presented below.

A Nordic network of agencies was established in 1992. In 2003, it became formalized into the Nordic Quality Assurance (NOQA). Besides the Danish Accreditation Institution, EVA, NOKUT and the Swedish Higher Education Authority, the Finnish Higher Educational Evaluation

Council (FINHEC) and the Icelandic Ministry of Education, Science and Culture are members of the network.

A European network was established in 2000 and later in 2004 transformed into the ENQA. The ENQA has 40 full members from 20 countries and a large number of network associates.

In 2003, the European Ministers of Education in the Berlin meeting of the Bologna Process, today including 46 countries, called upon the ENQA (Commission for the European Communities 2004, p. 6):

> through its members, in co-operation with EUA,[1] EURASHE[2] and ESIB[3] to develop an agreed set of standards, procedures and guidelines on quality assurance, to explore ways of ensuring an adequate peer review system for quality assurance and/or accreditation agencies or bodies, and to report back through the Follow-up Group to Ministers in 2005.

In 2005, the European Ministers of Education in the Bergen meeting of the Bologna Process approved the set of standards for quality assurance in the European Higher Education Area prepared by the ENQA (ENQA 2005; Vinther-Jørgensen and Hansen 2006). According to these any European agency must at least every five years conduct or submit to a cyclical external review of its processes and activities. ACE Denmark, EVA, HSV and NOKUT have all been approved to meet the ENQA standards. However, in 2012 the ENQA informed the HSV that on the basis of the latest review they could not reconfirm the full HSV membership. The ENQA states that an important principle in the ESG's is that external quality assurance should take into account the effectiveness of higher educational institutions internal quality assurance and that the HSV practice, now practiced by the Swedish Higher Education Authority, initiated by the Swedish government (see fifth section below) does not fulfil that principle (ENQA 2012a and 2012b). Sweden has thus become what is called 'ENQA Full Member under review' for a two-year period and has to go through a new review process.

In 2003, the European Consortium for Accreditation in Higher Education (ECA) was founded. The ECA aims for the mutual recognition of accreditation and quality assurance decisions as the members of the ECA believe that this will contribute to the mobility of students and prevent the necessity of multiple accreditations for joint programmes and institutions operating across borders. The ECA also aims for mutual learning and dissemination of best practices and for providing transparent information on quality. The ECA have 16 members from 11 countries including ACE Denmark and the EVA. Previously NOKUT was also a member, but recently NOKUT decided to withdraw in order to concentrate their international activities. It seems that NOKUT experienced that the cost of participating exceeded the benefits.

In 2007, the European ministers in charge of higher education mandated the E4 Group, consisting of the ENQA, the ESU (former ESIB, see note 3) and the EURASHE, to establish the European Quality Assurance Register (EQAR). The EQAR aims at providing clear and reliable information on the quality assurance agencies operating in Europe. At present 28 quality agencies from 15 countries are members of the register among these the Danish Accreditation Institution and the EVA.

All the Scandinavian quality agencies are members of the ENQA, although Sweden is not a full member at the time of writing, and only the Danish agencies are members of the ECA and EQAR. As will be elaborated below, this to some extent reflects the differences in the quality assurance strategies chosen in the three countries. While Sweden and Norway have developed national distinctive strategies, Denmark has adopted an accreditation model more conventional in central Europe. The key characteristics of the quality assurance systems in the Scandinavian countries are summarized in Table 8.1.

## QUALITY ASSURANCE PRACTICES

Similar to the organizational structures, the quality assurance practices of the quality agencies differ across time as well as across national boundaries. As shown below, Denmark follows a rather 'hard' more deterrence than compliance-based approach, Norway a softer and contingency-based approach and Sweden a learning outcome-based approach.

### Denmark

In Denmark there are eight universities, seven university colleges, nine business colleges and a number of educational institutions within the field of arts and the field of maritime.

Overall, the Danish regulatory approach which as mentioned above now is being phased out can be characterized as rather 'hard', more deterrence than compliance-based and with full coverage. The criteria used are rule-based, only programmes meeting the criteria are approved and all programmes have to go through the accreditation process. Programmes may be conditionally approved and given a time limit of one to two years to document that problems have been satisfactorily addressed. In the political process concerning the accreditation system, it was discussed whether to have a system based on programme accreditation or a more soft system

*Table 8.1   Regulatory agencies in the field of higher education in Scandinavia*

| | Denmark | Norway | Sweden |
|---|---|---|---|
| Agency | The Danish Accreditation Institution and EVA | NOKUT | The Swedish Higher Education Authority former part of Högskoleverket (HSV) |
| Purpose | Single-purpose: to assure and document quality and relevance of higher education (Accreditation Institution). Multi-purpose: to evaluate higher education but also day care centres and schools (EVA). | Multi-purpose: to control and develop the quality of Norwegian higher education and to approve education from non-Norwegian institutions. Control activities have to be developed in such a way that quality work at educational institutions benefits from it. | Multi-purpose: quality assurance, legal supervision, monitoring. |
| Regulatory basis | 'Law about the Accreditation Institution in Higher Education' (Law No. 294 given 27 March 2007) – in 2013 being phased out. | Section in 'Law about Universities and University Colleges' (Law 2005-04-01, No. 15) and section in 'Law about Tertiary Vocational Education' (Law 2003-06-20-56). | Sections in 'Law about Universities and University Colleges' (1992: 1434) and corresponding consolidating act. Statutory instrument with instruction for HSV (Förordning 2007: 1293). |

| | | | |
|---|---|---|---|
| Regulation technology used | 2007–2013: single-technology: accreditation of programmes. From 2013 accreditation of institutions. | Multi-technology: audit of quality assurance systems at educational institutions, accreditation of programmes and institutions, reaccreditation, evaluation, approval of foreign education. | Multi-technology: learning outcome focused assessment of programmes, statistics and information. |
| Does parent ministry have instruction possibilities? | No. | To a limited extent. Only within the law meaning that the Ministry may ask for evaluation of specific educational areas. | Yes. The Ministry often gives the agency assignments (opdrag). |
| Organization | Complex. | Department organized, agency governed by a Director under the responsibility of a board. | Department organized agency, governed by a University Chancellor (Director) advised by several advisory boards. |
| Membership international networks | NOQA, ENQA (full member), ECA, EQAR. | NOQA, ENQA (full member). | NOQA, ENQA (full member under review). |

*Source:* author's compilation.

based on a quality assurance system approach. The political decision-makers went for the hard programme accreditation approach. One interpretation of this is that it reflects that political decision-makers have a low degree of trust in Danish higher educational institutions.

When the accreditation system was introduced, the consolidating act for university programmes laid down four criteria which were further elaborated into ten criteria in an annex. Later this was slightly simplified as a response to critiques from higher educational institutions. Three criteria are important: the relevance of programmes in relation to the labour market, the degree to which programmes are research-based and the internal quality assurance system. In an annex the three criteria are further developed into five criteria.

ACE Denmark has prepared guidelines to the educational institutions as to how to produce documentation in order to meet the criteria. The first guideline to existing programmes preparing for accreditation was a 24-page document including a checklist of around 50 bullet points specifying the information which the programmes were expected to deliver. The current guideline is a 19-page document including a list of around 25 bullet points. The simplification efforts seem to have been rather symbolic.

The system leaves room for expert assessment as accreditation is to be done by an expert panel with international participation. It also opens up for 'regulatory capitalism' as the Accreditation Council may choose to accept an accreditation report made by an international reputable organization, if the criteria mentioned above have been used.

Up to July 2012 the Council had assessed 447 existing university programmes. Of these 82 per cent were approved, 4 per cent were approved but for a shorter period than the normal period of six years and the rest, 14 per cent, were conditionally approved. No existing programmes have been refused. Approval rates are thus rather high indicating either that the system is run in a softer way than one should expect or that the need for this kind of system is not very obvious. Regarding new university programmes assessed 2007–2011, 79 per cent were approved, 10 per cent refused and 11 per cent were withdrawn before reaching a final decision in the Council. Recently, there has been a growth in applications regarding new programmes and the share of refused programmes has gone up. When a new programme receives approval, the Council makes a recommendation to the Ministry concerning, among other things, at which level of finance it is to be placed and which admission requirements to apply. When the Ministry has approved the recommendation the Council gives its final approval.

Higher educational institutions may complain to the Ministry about legal matters but the accreditation approval as such cannot be brought before any other administrative authority. The Accreditation Council has the final say.

The criteria and the processes used by the EVA and approved by the Ministry of Education to assess educational programmes at university and business colleges are slightly different.

As already mentioned the Accreditation Council in 2010 worked out a proposal for a new system (Akkrediteringsrådet 2010). The idea was to combine accreditation of institutions using audits with accreditation of programmes based on random checks. One suggestion was that the result of audits should be a three-graded assessment of the quality assurance systems at the institutions. Institutions being assessed as 'very satisfactory', the best grade, should have the right to establish new educational pro-grammes themselves and only be approached with a few random checks; whereas institutions assessed as 'less satisfactory', the worst grade, would have to send proposals for new programmes to the Accreditation Council and would be approached by more random checks. This proposal thus was clearly based on contingency thinking and represented a responsive type of regulation. The system now being implemented (and already mentioned in the third section) is also based on contingency thinking. The quality systems of higher education institutions may be approved, conditionally approved or rejected. If conditionally approved or rejected, institutions are faced with demands for accreditation of educational programmes.

**Norway**

In Norway 59 higher educational institutions receive budget allocations from the Ministry of Education and Research, among these 23 private institutions. Distinguishing between different types of institutions, there are eight universities, nine specialized universities and 40 university col-leges (Kunnskapsdepartementet 2012, p. 21).

In the Norwegian system all institutions have to have their quality assur-ance systems evaluated at least every six years. In these audits ten criteria are used. These concern the organization of quality work, the linking of quality work to strategic work and institutional management, the active participation of students as well as output from the systems. In the first cycle of audits well above 70 institutions were evaluated. Less than ten institutions did not meet the criteria and had to go through a re-audit which they all passed. Thus also in the Norwegian system the approval rate is rather high. The system is now in its second cycle. This is organized more flexibly to address slightly different themes at different institutions.

In the Norwegian higher educational system there are three different categories of institutional accreditation, giving the institutions different degrees of autonomy in developing educational programmes: university colleges, specialized university institutions and universities. Institutions which have passed audit may apply to move up in the institutional hierarchy. Criteria used in institutional accreditation concerns education and research activities, staff qualifications, organization as well as participation in international networks. To receive university accreditation an institution, for example, has to have at least five accredited programmes at least at five-years duration as well as Ph.D. programmes in four different subject areas.

The system has created a strong drift for Norwegian higher educational institutions to move towards a status as a specialized university or university, a process which from time to time has put strong local and regional pressures on the quality agency.

Norwegian higher educational institutions are authorized to develop educational programmes on their own according to their institutional accreditation. Universities are fully authorized to develop new programmes at all levels, specialized university institutions are authorized to develop programmes at all levels within specific fields, university colleges are authorized to develop study programmes at Bachelor level and programmes at Master's level in fields where they have obtained an accredited Ph.D. programme, whereas non-accredited institutions are not authorized to develop any programme on their own. If an institution wishes to offer a new programme which it is not authorized to, it has to apply to NOKUT for accreditation.

Criteria used for programme accreditation are mostly quality criteria related to the plan for the programme, the academic staff, the infrastructure, the quality assurance procedures and internationalization. Relevance criteria do not play such an important role as compared to the Danish system. Some of the criteria used in the Norwegian system are based on requirements of certain numbers. For example, for Bachelor programmes at least 20 per cent of the staff assigned to the programme are required to have senior lecture or professorial status, whereas for Ph.D. programmes there has to be a research environment consisting of at least eight professors of which at least four are full professors. The numbers-based criteria have been controversial.

The most flexible technology which NOKUT may use is reaccreditation which it can initiate on its own. NOKUT has used this technology on several occasions. The first reaccreditation process concerned all Bachelor and Master's programmes in nursing. Only one out of 31 assessed programmes got a positive outcome. The others received fixed periods to address the shortcomings. Among others programmes in pharmacy, odontology and law have also gone through reaccreditation.

Finally, on initiative from the Ministry NOKUT has carried out broader national evaluations, for example of all general teacher education. These have been organized very much like the programme reaccreditations but they are not directly linked to sanctions or follow-up procedures. Programmes in teacher training, engineering and pre-school teacher training have been evaluated. As the Ministry has not in every case provided the resources necessary for these evaluations, this activity to some extent limits the possibilities for NOKUT to initiate projects on its own. Expert panels are used in all audits, accreditations and evaluations.

NOKUT is also responsible for accreditation of tertiary vocational education offered by special colleges (fagskoler). Tertiary vocational education programmes shall provide competence that may be directly applied in the labour market. Programmes are of a minimum of six months and a maximum of two years of full-time study and cover a broad range of fields from technical vocations to art and health. The field of tertiary vocational education is regulated by a special act and NOKUT has, in collaboration with stakeholders, developed a set of criteria for accreditation in this area.

The Norwegian system is organized with two specialized Complaints Boards with overlapping members: one for higher education and one for tertiary vocational education. The Complaints Boards deal with complaints from institutions on administrative procedures. Institutions cannot complain about decisions based on professional assessments.

Since NOKUT was established the Norwegian system has been contingency-based adapted to the structure and challenges in the higher educational field. The plan for the years to come is to further develop the system in the direction of the responsive regulation type using statistics and analysis as part of the basis for planning evaluation and reaccreditation activities.

**Sweden**

In Sweden there are 47 universities and university colleges. Of these 34 are public institutions. All in all 26 institutions are offering programmes at Bachelor, Master's and Ph.D. levels while the rest are offering programmes at Bachelor and Master's levels. Twelve institutions hold the title 'university'. The Parliament decides which university colleges to establish. The government decides whether a university college may use the title university. University colleges can apply to the HSV to establish Ph.D. programmes.

The HSV has used different approaches to quality assurance at different points in time. From 1995 to 2002 the main task of the HSV was evaluation of quality assurance systems (auditing). To support educational institutions in their development of quality assurance systems, the agency conducted two cycles of audits.

In 2001 the agency launched a plan for programme evaluation under the heading 'From Assessment of Quality Work to Assessment of Quality' (Högskoleverket 2001). Consequently, programme evaluation combining self-evaluation, external assessment by expert panels and follow-up activities became the main task. In the period from 2001 to 2006, the HSV carried through evaluations of all educational programmes (about 1800 in total). Programmes with severe shortcomings (around 10 per cent) were given one year to solve their problems. Due to the authority of the HSV to withdraw higher educational institutions' examination rights there was an element of threat in this regulation approach. Around 40 per cent of the programmes with severe shortcomings were closed down by the institutions themselves. It turned out that it was unnecessary for the HSV to actively use its withdrawal right.

In 2007, a new approach planned for 2007 to 2012 was adopted but never introduced (Högskoleverket 2007). Whereas the coverage of the former systems had been comprehensive, the process reaching out to all institutions and programmes in the same way, the new system was planned to be more selective consisting of the following components. First, quality work at the higher educational institutions should be subject to audit. All levels (even department level) and all higher educational institutions would be covered in this process. Related higher educational institutions would be reviewed in the same year for comparison. Self-evaluation and site visits by expert panels would be the methodology used. The ENQA standards would be the criteria used. On the basis of the reports from the expert panels the University Chancellor would decide on overall assessments of institutions being either 'HSV has confidence in the quality work of . . .', 'HSV has limited confidence in . . .' or 'HSV has no confidence in . . .'.

Second, educational programmes would be subject to evaluation. This process was planned to be organized in three steps: (1) a national picture would be produced on the basis of simple self-evaluations, statistics and so on; (2) on the basis of this national screening picture around a third of the programmes would be selected for a more thorough evaluation based on the normal methodology; (3) programmes selected for in-depth evaluation would be programmes with risks for quality shortcomings but it could also be programmes supposed to be of special interest (for example, because they were innovative).

Third, there would be an accreditation component. As in Norway, Swedish higher educational institutions differ as to whether they are authorized to develop and offer new programmes on their own. Institutions which are not authorized have to apply to the HSV for accreditation.

Fourth, the HSV should continue doing thematic evaluation. Themes could be gender equality, internationalization, student influence and

E-learning quality. Also the HSV should continue a recently started activity related to awarding prizes to especially outstanding institutions.

The approach planned for 2007 to 2012 was however cancelled before it really was rolled out. The background was that the new Swedish government which had come to power in 2006 wished to develop a quality assurance system which could be used also for resource allocation. For a period the situation was unsteady and conflict-ridden. First, the head of the evaluation department stepped back criticizing the University Chancellor. Later the Chancellor stepped down, a new one was appointed and a new system developed according to the government wishes (Wahlen 2012, p. 32).

The Swedish quality agency approach for 2011–2014 is to assess educational programmes focusing in particular on whether learning outcomes meet requirements as outlined in the regulation (Högskoleverket 2010). A very important element in this system is the assessment of the examination work of students. In the system a selection of student reports on the final examinations are assessed. For each programme up to 24 anonymous student reports are reassessed. In addition educational programmes are asked to complete self-evaluations and interviews, and surveys are carried out with former students to assess whether their education helped them entering the labour market. Against this background a panel consisting of professors, students and representatives from the labour market assess each programme and propose a grade from a scale of 'very high quality', 'high quality' to 'lack of quality'. On this basis the University Chancellor decides the grade of each programme. Programmes receiving the grade 'lack of quality' are followed up a year later and the HSV decides whether to withdraw the examination rights at that point in time. Programmes receiving the grade 'very high quality' are rewarded with additional quality money by the government. Grades decided by the University Chancellor cannot be brought before any other authority.

The Swedish approach to educational evaluation is innovative as it attaches so much importance to student learning outcomes and student assessments. However, while Norway (and maybe Denmark) moves in the direction of contingency-based responsive evaluation, this is not the case in Sweden. Here all programmes are evaluated according to a 'one size fits all' model.

The Swedish approach has turned out to be controversial in an international perspective. As already mentioned, the ENQA has decided that the approach does not fulfil the requirements of the ENQA standards. The ENQA is not opposed to the learning outcome approach as such, but to the fact that the new Swedish model is not sufficiently open to give space to various quality assurance approaches (ENQA 2012a). Among other things, the Swedish model almost exclusively focuses on results and thus according to the ENQA does not take into account the effectiveness of the internal quality assurance processes as required by the ENQA standards (ENQA 2012b). The ENQA critique is to be interpreted not as a critique towards the HSV but rather as a critique towards the Swedish government. The ENQA decision has been brought up in the Swedish Parliament, where the Minister of Education has been questioned concerning how he plans to restore confidence in Swedish higher education. The Minister has responded by arguing that the result focus of the quality system will be maintained but adding that the systems as such will be supplemented. The course of events clearly shows how different regulation ideas pushed forward by different actors may clash.

Table 8.2 presents an overview of the practices of the three Scandinavian quality assurance regimes.

## A COMPARATIVE PERSPECTIVE ON THE NETWORKS AND ROLES OF THE REGULATORY AGENCIES

What can be learned from the above description and discussions about the networks and roles of the Scandinavian quality assurance agencies?

First of all, the regulation *negotiation* networks including actors being able to influence the conditions of the quality agencies are quite different across the Scandinavian countries. The regulation negotiation network around ACE Denmark was complex as it was constituted by several ministries acting as criteria owners using several operators. Now the ministerial level has been reorganized and the quality assurance system is being revised. All in all, Danish higher educational institutions are controlled by the government to a higher degree than institutions in Norway and Sweden. This governmental culture is reflected in the accreditation system. Since 2007, even universities do not have authority to develop and offer new programmes on their own. By establishing the accreditation system, decisions have been delegated to a council at arm's length from the ministries. But the Danish regulatory agencies are rather tightly controlled as both methodology and criteria are rule-based. Agency autonomy is limited compared to the Norwegian and the Swedish agencies.

The regulation negotiation network around NOKUT is less complex than the Danish one but constituted by two rather loosely coupled networks related to respectively academic higher education and tertiary vocational education. As NOKUT has a broad portfolio of tasks, some of which may be used more flexibly than others, the autonomy of NOKUT is comparatively stronger than the autonomy of the Danish regulatory agency.

*Table 8.2 Quality assurance practices of quality agencies*

| | Denmark | Norway | Sweden |
|---|---|---|---|
| Agency | The Danish Accreditation Institution and EVA | NOKUT | The Swedish Higher Education Authority former part of Högskoleverket (HSV) |
| Actors regulated | 8 universities, 7 university colleges, 9 business colleges and several academies and schools in the field of arts and the field of maritime. | 8 universities, 6 specialized universities and 23 university colleges, all public institutions. In addition a number of private institutions. | 47 universities and university colleges. |
| Regulatory profile | 'Hard', deterrence leaning and approval-based moving towards responsive regulation. | Combine 'hard' and 'soft', deterrence and compliance elements. Moving towards responsive regulation. | Combining 'hard and 'soft', deterrence and compliance elements, rating, approval and development-based. Rewarding very high quality. |
| Coverage of regulation | All-covering. All programmes both new and existing at Bachelor and Master's level (Ph.D. programmes not included). In the future accreditation of institutions. | All-covering and selective. Quality assurance systems at all institutions. Selective approach in relation to accreditation and evaluation. | All-covering and selective. All existing programmes. Focus on learning outcome. Selective approach in relation to accreditation. |

*Table 8.2* (continued)

|  | Denmark | Norway | Sweden |
|---|---|---|---|
| Formally responsible for regulatory decisions | The Accreditation Council. | The Board/the Director. | The Chancellor. |
| Use of expert panels? | Yes. | Yes. | Yes. |
| Does the agency have information request in relation to the higher educational institutions? | Yes. | No. | Yes. |
| Are there possibilities for higher educational institutions to lodge complaint? | Accreditation decisions of the Council cannot be brought before any other administrative authority. Complaints about legal questions can be brought before the Ministry. | Two specialized complaints boards deal with complaints about administrative procedures. Decisions based on professional assessment cannot be brought before any other authority. | Chancellor decisions cannot be brought before any other authority. |

*Source:* author's compilation.

The regulation negotiation network in Sweden is more homogenous. On the one side the Swedish agencies formally have high autonomy in relation to the Ministry in choosing an approach, on the other side the HSV in its last years was put under strong political pressure. The Swedish agencies seem to have a much more frequent informal dialogue with their parent ministry than is the case in Norway and Denmark. Their close tie has recently ensured that as a result of national political adaptability, the agency was brought into conflict with the ENQA.

Overall Scandinavian administrative traditions and cultures differ. Sweden has a very long tradition for relatively formal autonomous agencies ('verker'). This tradition constitutes the context of the Swedish agencies but is balanced against political adaptability. In Norway and Denmark autonomous regulatory agencies are younger developed along with more contemporary agency reform ideas. The ideas behind the recent Swedish reform aimed at establishing more lean agencies do not have strong support in Denmark and Norway.

Second, the regulation *practice* networks including actors in the organizational field regulated also differ across the agencies. ACE Denmark was constituted by several loosely coupled networks, one for each of the different operators, sets of criteria and groups of higher educational institutions. One network related to the eight universities, one for the eight university colleges and the business colleges, and one for the academies and schools in the field of arts.

The regulation practice network around NOKUT is more homogenous but is partly divided into the different clusters of higher educational institutions with the academic higher educational institutions on the one side and the institutions for tertiary vocational education on the other. The Norwegian agency has more autonomy than the Danish agency, as it may initiate reaccreditation on its own. The most homogenous regulation practice network is that of the Swedish agency.

Third, all the Scandinavian agencies are involved in Nordic and European methodological networks. In addition to being meeting places where methodological experiences are shared and further developed, the international networks also work to create platforms for themselves in the broad European regulation negotiation network related to the Bologna Process. Hitherto primarily the ENQA has succeeded with this strategy. Participating in international networks is important for agencies both in order to develop competence but also in relation to influencing the regulation negotiation network and thus both the content of international governance and national regulation. Table 8.3 summarizes the characteristics of the networks of the agencies.

The frequent reorganizations in Denmark and the conflicts in Sweden

*Table 8.3    The networks of the regulatory agencies*

| | Denmark | Norway | Sweden |
|---|---|---|---|
| Agency | The Danish Accreditation Institution and EVA | NOKUT | The Swedish Higher Education Authority former part of Högskoleverket (HSV) |
| Regulation negotiation network at national level | Complex structure. Different operators. Contact to parent ministry formalized as accreditation plans have to be approved by the ministers. | Two rather loosely coupled networks around academic higher education on the one side and tertiary vocational education on the other. Contact to parent ministry based on recurring formal dialogue and ad hoc informal dialogue. | One network. Contact to parent ministry based on frequently informal dialogue. |
| Regulation practice network | Several rather loosely coupled networks around the different clusters of higher educational institutions. | One network but partly divided into different clusters of higher educational institutions. | One network. |
| Methodological networks | Well-developed network into NOQA, ENQA and ECA. | Well-developed network into NOQA, and ENQA. | Well-developed network into NOQA and previously also to ENQA. |
| Agency autonomy | Limited. | Some autonomy in relation to Ministry in choosing approach. | Formally high autonomy in relation to the Ministry in choosing approaches. At the same time political pressure and adaptability. |

*Source:*  author's compilation.

212

on how to develop the quality assurance system indicate that the organizational legitimacy can be a sparse asset for quality agencies. Quality agencies are placed in a cross pressure between three actors: the Bologna Process, the national ministries in the regulation negotiation network and the higher educational institutions in the regulation practice network.

The control-oriented Danish system can be interpreted as a result of a more general political distrust towards the higher education institutions. If the quality agency is experienced as pleading the higher education institutions cause, its legitimacy is questioned. In Sweden the quality agency historically has had a high legitimacy. But due to a political regime shift the agencies legitimacy became questioned.

Higher educational regulatory agencies try to achieve organizational legitimacy through different strategies. One strategy is a knowledge strategy. Through developing and maintaining a knowledge base to support the development of the educational system, they may be able to be recognized by both international actors, national political actors and the higher education institutions. Another strategy is to act in a mediator role developing quality assurance practices in close dialogue with all actors in the field. Yet another strategy is to use expert panels. In relation to the regulation practice network expert panels are able to adapt criteria in order to make sense of quality assurance practices at institutional and programme levels. In these sense-making processes a conflict may arise between local sense-making and the overall aim related to treating programmes and institutions equally. Such conflicts are most likely to arise in systems where programmes and institutions are assessed individually (for example, applying for new programmes to be accredited). In systems approaching assessments comparatively, clustering programmes and institutions, transparency and equal treatment are more easily achieved.

What do we know about how higher educational institutions experience quality assurance activities? On the one side higher educational institutions often complain about quality assurance requirements creating unnecessary data collection and reporting. Being in the process they claim that resources are withdrawn from educational activities to be used for administrative and bureaucratic procedures. Institutions seem to argue departing from the deterrence model that quality agencies constitute an unnecessary police force.

On the other side *ex post* analysis indicates that there are some positive effects. In Norway an evaluation of NOKUT showed that higher educational institutions report that audits, accreditations and evaluations have had positive impacts on their quality work (Langfeldt et al. 2008). The self-evaluation and application processes provide overviews on the strengths and weaknesses of the institutions and provide input for those institutions to realize improvements. Recently a report on the experiences with the programme evaluations in Norway conclude that the evaluations have had positive effects especially in relations to developing educations and spreading knowledge about good practices (NOKUT 2011). At the systems level having a national quality assurance system helps putting quality issues at the agenda.

In Sweden the HSV made a follow-up analysis of their programme evaluations conducted in the beginning of the new century (Högskoleverket 2008). The analysis showed that the higher educational institutions had been mostly satisfied with the programme evaluation approach. Institutions had used the self-evaluations and the advice from the expert panels to further develop quality. Important programmes with shortcomings had used the evaluations to create pressure to get more resources at the institutional level and rectors had received help to close down programmes with severe shortcomings. At the systems level quality assurance systems seem to contribute to making higher education institutions more visible. Increased visibility promotes comparison and competition. Both control and self-control is reinforced and sometimes counterstrategies are invoked (Segerholm and Åström 2007).

## CONCLUSIONS

The aim of this chapter has been to describe and analyse quality assurance agencies in the field of higher education in Denmark, Norway and Sweden. The chapter has analysed the development and roles of the agencies focusing on whether the practices of the agencies have converged in the context of the Bologna Process.

The analysis has shown that, although having similar purposes related to controlling and developing quality in higher education, the Scandinavian agencies are organized differently. The ways in which they are regulated differ and their quality assurance practices also differ. The special attributes of the Danish system 2007–2013 being the hard single-technology regulatory approach (programme accreditation), the very complex organizational set-up and the emphasis on the relevance criteria. The special attributes of the Norwegian system being the coupling of audit and institutional accreditation and the possibilities/rights for higher educational institutions to apply for moving up into a higher institutional category, a system creating drift towards more universities. The special attributes of the Swedish system being the student learning outcome focus, the formal autonomy of the agency to decide on which technologies to use combined with national political pressures partly conflicting with international standards.

The Bologna quality assurance policy thus has not led to convergence.

The European standards leave considerable room for variations in national solutions. National administrative cultures and national policy agendas matter a lot in order to explain the development of national practices. Also, differences in higher educational systems in structure and traditions translate into differences in the organization and tasks of quality agencies. However, the recent conflict about the Swedish model shows that the ENQA is willing to try to set limits for national policies. What this means in the long run is too early to say. However, one implication could be that the attention towards the European guidelines in national policy development processes increases.

Although differing in organization and quality assurance practices there are also similarities across the Scandinavian quality agencies. The quality agencies all act as mediating organizations. They facilitate dialogue between international and national political levels as well as between political levels and higher educational institutions. In this way they play important roles in regulation negotiation networks at national as well as on the international level. Although formally being autonomous regulatory agencies, the Scandinavian quality agencies are all embedded in consensus-oriented political cultures.

## NOTES

1. The European University Association.
2. The European Association of Institutions in Higher Education.
3. The National Unions of Students in Europe, in 2007 renamed to the European Students' Union (ESU).

## REFERENCES

Akkrediteringsrådet (2010), *Akkrediteringsrådets anbefalinger til et fremtidigt akkrediteringssystem på universitetsområdet*, København, available at: http://acedenmark.dk/fileadmin/user_upload/dokumenter/Aktuelt/Pressemeddelelser/Akkrediteringsraadets_anbefalingspapir.pdf (accessed 13 December 2012).

Blau, P. and W.R. Scott (1963), *Formal Organizations. A Comparative Approach*, London: Routledge and Keagan Paul.

Boston, J. et al. (eds) (1996), *Public Management – The New Zealand Mode*, Auckland: Oxford University Press.

Christensen, T. and P. Lægreid (2006), 'Agencification and regulatory reforms' in T. Christensen and P. Lægreid (eds), *Autonomy and Regulation. Coping with Agencies in the Modern State*, Cheltenham, UK and Northampton, MA, USA: Edward Elgar, pp. 8–49.

Commission for the European Communities (2004), 'Report from the Commission to the European Parliament, The Council, The European Economic and Social Committee and The Committee of the Regions on the implementation of Council Recommendation 98/561/EC of 24 September 1998 on European Cooperation in Quality Assurance in Higher Education, COM (2004)620 final', available at: http://eur-lex.europa.eu/LexUriServ/ LexUriServ.do?uri=COM:2004:0620:FIN:EN:PDF (accessed 10 December 2012).

ENQA (2005), *Standards and Guidelines for Quality Assurance in the European Higher Education Area*, Helsinki: European Association for Quality Assurance in Higher Education, available at: http://www.enqa.eu/files/ESG_3edition%20 (2).pdf (accessed 13 December 2012).

ENQA (2012a), 'Letter to Lars Haikola on "Subject: External review of HSV"', available at: http://www.hsv.se/download/18.485f1ec213870b672a680004340/ Letter_ENQA_HSV_170912.pdf (accessed 10 December 2012).

ENQA (2012b), 'Swedish National Agency for Higher Education: Review of ENQA Membership', available at: http://www.hsv.se/download/18.1c6d4 396136bbbed2bd80002238/HSV_review-ENQA-Criteria-Report-April2012.pdf (accessed 10 December 2012).

EVA (2007), 'Årsberetning 2007', Copenhagen: EVA, available at: http://www. eva.dk/nyheder/om-eva/aarsberetninger/Aarsberetning2007.pdf (accessed 13 December 2012).

Förordning (2007: 1293) 'med instruktion för Högskoleverket', available at: http:// www.riksdagen.se/sv/Dokument-Lagar/Lagar/Svenskforfattningssamling/Foror dning-20071293-med-ins_sfs-2007-1293/ (accessed 3 December 2013).

Gröjer, A. (2004), *Den utvärdera(n)de staten. Utvärderingens institutionalisering på den högre utbildningens område*, Stockholm: Statsvetenskapliga Institutionen, Stockholms Universitet.

Hansen, H.F. (2009), 'Educational evaluation in Scandinavian countries: converging and diverging practices?', *Scandinavian Journal of Educational Research*, **53**(1), 71–87.

Högskoleverket (2001), *Högskoleverkets utvärderingar – från bedömning av kvalitet- sarbete till bedömning av kvalitet*, Stockholm: Högskoleverket.

Högskoleverket (2007), *Nationellt kvalitetssäkringssystem för perioden 2007–2012. Reviderad 2007-12-11*, Stockholm: Högskoleverket Rapport 2007:59R.

Högskoleverket (2008), *Hur har det gått? Högskoleverkets kvalitetsgranskningar år 2007*, Stockholm: Högskoleverket Rapport 2008:17, available at: http://www. hsv.se/download/18.880c3ba1194d1b806c800030041/0817R.pdf (accessed 13 December 2012).

Högskoleverket (2010), *Högskoleverkets system får kvalitetsutvärdering 2011–2014*, Högskoleverket Rapport 2010:22, available at: http://www.hsv.se/download/ 18.4afd653a12cabe7775880003715/1022R-system-kvalitetsutv.pdf (accessed 13 December 2012).

Høstaker, R. and A. Vabø (2005), 'Higher education and the transformation to a cognitive capitalism', in I. Bleklie and M. Henkel (eds), *Governing Knowledge. A Study of Continuity and Change in Higher Education*, Dordrecht: Springer, pp. 227–243.

Jørgensen, T.B., H.F. Hansen, M. Antonsen and P. Melander (1998), 'Public organizations, multiple constituencies and governance', *Public Administration*, **76**(Autumn), 499–518.

Kunnskapsdepartementet (2012), *Tilstandsrapport. Høyere utdanning 2012*, Oslo, available at: http://www.regjeringen.no/upload/KD/Vedlegg/UH/Rapporter_og_planer/Tilstandsrapport_2012_270612.pdf (accessed 11 December 2012).

Lægreid, P., P.G. Roness and K. Rubecksen (2008), 'Controlling regulatory agencies', *Scandinavian Political Studies*, **31**(1), 1–26.

Langfeldt, L., L. Harvey, J. Huisman, D. Westerheijden and B. Stensaker (2008), *Evaluation of NOKUT – The Norwegian Agency for Quality Assurance in Education*, Oslo: Norwegian Ministry for Education and Research.

Law about Universities and University Colleges (1992: 1434), translation available here: http://www.hsv.se/lawsandregulations/theswedishhighereducationact.4.516 1b99123700c42b07ffe3956.html (accessed 13 December 2013).

Ministry for Science, Innovation and Higher Education (2012), 'Skitse til en ny fælles model for akkreditering af de videregående uddannelser', available at: http://esdhweb.ucl.dk/196544.Skitse%20til%20ny%20f%C3%A6lles%20model%20for%20akkreditering%20af%20de%20videreg%C3%A5ende%20uddannelser%20%28dialog%29%20DOK2271464.pdf (accessed 10 December 2012).

NOKUT (2009), 'Strategiplan. Strategi for videreutvikling av NOKUT 2010–14', available at: http://www.nokut.no/Documents/NOKUT/Artikkelbibliotek/Generell/Strategi/2010/NOKUT_Strategiplan.pdf (accessed 10 December 2012).

NOKUT (2011), 'NOKUTs programevalueringer – processer, resultater og kvalitetseffekter', available at: http://www.nokut.no/Documents/NOKUT/Artikkelbibliotek/Kunnskapsbasen/Rapporter/UA%202011/NOKUTs_program evalueringer_prosesser_resultater_og_kvalitetseffekter_2011.pdf (accessed 10 December 2012).

OECD (2002), *Regulatory Policies in OECD Countries. From Interventionism to Regulatory Governance*, Paris: OECD Publishing.

OECD (2005), *Modernising Government. The Way Forward*, Paris: OECD Publishing.

Pollitt, C. et al. (2004), *Agencies: How Governments do Things through Semi-Autonomous Organizations*, London: Palgrave.

Radaelli, C.M. (2005), Diffusion without convergence: how political context shapes the adoption of regulatory impact assessment, *Journal of European Public Policy*, **12**(5), 924–943.

Scott, W.R. (2003), *Organizations. Rational, Natural and Open Systems*, New Jersey: Prentice Hall.

Segerholm, C. and E. Åström (2007), 'Governance through institutionalized evaluation. recentralization and influences at local levels in higher education in Sweden', *Evaluation*, **13**(1), 48–67.

Selznick, P. (1985), 'Focusing organizational research on regulation', in R.G. Noll (ed.), *Regulatory Policy and the Social Sciences*, Berkeley: University of California Press, pp. 363–368.

Stensaker, B. (2006), *Kvalitet som forhandling: NOKUT i norsk høyere utdanning 2003–2006* [Quality as Negotiation: The Norwegian Agency for Quality Assurance in Education in Norwegian Higher Education 2003–2006; in Norwegian], Oslo: Norges Forskningsråd.

Vinther-Jørgensen, T. and S.P. Hansen (eds) (2006), *European Standards and Guidelines in a Nordic Perspective*, Helsinki: ENQA.

Wahlen, S. (2012), 'Från granskning och bedömning av kvalitetsarbete till utvärdering av resultat', in Högskoleverket (ed.), *En högskolevärld i ständig förändring*, Stockholm, pp. 27–36.

Walshe, K. (2003), *Regulating Healthcare. A Prescription for Improvement?*, Maidenhead: Open University Press.

# 9. Economic shocks, federalism and redistribution: exploring the future of Europe through a comparison of the evolution of student financial aid in the United States and the European Union

**Cecile Hoareau**

## INTRODUCTION

The integration mechanisms of the Europe of Knowledge are far reaching and revolutionary, and in this sense of strong research interest, because integration reached a policy area which is traditionally of strong national interest. This chapter explores the potential mechanisms through which the Europe of Knowledge extends the boundaries of European integration by concentrating on the evolution of a policy domain which is not commonly attributed to European competency, namely redistributive mechanisms in the higher education domain.

European integration and redistribution do not match well, the zero sum game nature of redistributive mechanisms making the agreement necessary for further integration difficult. Under which conditions can federal governments increase their redistributive function?

In order to understand the evolution of redistributive mechanisms, the chapter studies more particularly the effect of a negative economic shock on federal integration in redistributive areas, by comparing developments with another major political system recognized as a federal entity, namely the US. This chapter more generally seeks to understand why redistributive schemes are difficult to achieve at the federal level and under which conditions federal governments can increase their redistributive functions.

The term federalism loosely covers the creation of a multi-ordered structure, with all orders of government having some independent as well as shared decision-making responsibilities, and is hence applicable to the US as well as the European Union (EU) (Broadway and Shar 2009).

This chapter explores the case of redistributive transfers in higher education, and concentrates more particularly on publicly subsidized loans. Loans are a form of interpersonal transfer – the transfer element coming from the government using taxpayers' money to subsidize students in the form of interest rate subsidies, and limits on the length of repayments for example. In general, financial aid to students is a redistributive policy, which allows us to observe the evolution of the relative share of responsibility incumbent to different levels of government.

Student loans have been a popular way among governments across the world to support students while – at least in theory – not bearing as much of the costs as with a grant. Student loans have broad social implications for social mobility and encompass significant expenses – in the US, the student loan market represents US$460 billion (Lehman Brothers 2008). Student loans are not federally allocated in the EU. But most EU countries have a substantial financial aid scheme to students including a loan element, as in the UK, Germany, the Netherlands, Spain, Sweden, France and Hungary, and several governments are planning to adopt such lending schemes including the Czech Republic, Portugal, Romania and Lithuania. Recent reforms have modified the dynamics across both continents. For example, the US government decided to reform its student loan scheme in 2010, attributing more competencies to the federal government. In Europe, an effort to establish a federal lending scheme has been proposed by the European Commission in 2011 and is being discussed by the European Council (European Commission 2011; European Council 2012; Hoareau 2010a).

Higher education is an area where the federal level traditionally had limited competencies and which for this reason has typically been undervalued. The EU only has complementary competencies in education according to articles 149 and 150 of the Treaty establishing the European Community (articles 165 and 166 in the Treaty of Lisbon). Yet, European institutions have had a growing role in higher education, extending the scale of its flagship programme Erasmus, as well as gaining increasing political relevance through its support of the Bologna Process, and gaining further relevance through the recognition of the relevance of youth, education and skills in the EU strategy Europe 2020.

Finally, such a case has a strong topical relevance: increasing federal direct redistribution directly addresses the concerns of many national governments on how to finance their public obligations.

Moreover, the case of higher education is particularly enlightening because it benefits from large, albeit variable, public transfers across both continents.

The chapter first provides some background regarding the literature on fiscal federalism. It then maps out current trends in terms of state funding coupled with the increasing costs of higher education. This part aims to illustrate the constraints that state governments are under in terms of further investments in higher education, in order to justify the case for federal intervention.

The following section presents how governments have so far dealt with this increase in costs, namely by splitting the financial burden across the public purse, students and other philanthropists and businesses (a concept known as cost-sharing). This part shows that the cost-sharing does not necessarily presume a proportional shift in the cost-burden from one side to another, and that higher tuition fees still result in a high cost for the state level (using the case of England as an example).

A subsequent section introduces the hypothesis according to which federal governments could have a larger role to play in cost-sharing in order to relieve the financial constraints incumbent on state budgets. This hypothesis is substantiated by a comparison of student loan reforms in the US and the EU, in order to understand under which conditions a symmetric shock increases the likelihood for further federal integration of redistributive competencies. This comparison is timely, occurring in the midst of intense debates regarding the role of European institutions in public finances. The chapter then presents a discussion regarding the theoretical applications of this comparison. The case study analysed points to federal intervention because of limited ability for states to intervene and for markets to provide a similar service at as low cost as the federal government (given the risk structure of student loans). This case study therefore questions the assumption of the part of the fiscal federalist literature which consists in arguing for a limitation of federal competencies in order to preserve the functioning of markets. The last section concludes the chapter.

## A FEDERALIST APPROACH

The intended use of a 'federal' framework stretches the boundaries of European integration. Using the term federalism to qualify the EU has been somewhat of a taboo in the politics of European integration. The EU has traditionally been described as a *sui generis* entity, a political system, or a supranational structure bearing unique features. Fossum and Augustin (2011) show for example that the European Communities were the first constitutional union based on constitutional states which transcend the paradigm of the nation state. Yet, according to international comparativists, the EU has some broad features of federalism. Broadway and Shar (2009) define federalism as a loosely defined and multi-ordered structure with all orders of government having some independent as well as shared decision-making responsibilities. According to them, this definition applies to the US as well as the EU.

Comparisons with the US are understandably prone to methodological limitations, given the different historical developments and underpinnings of both regions. Yet, the EU has, similarly to the US, a multi-ordered structure between EU institutions and national governments, with some exclusive and shared competencies between EU institutions and national governments as defined by the Lisbon Treaty of 2009. The term federal government is used in a generic manner to cover federal institutions in both the US and the EU. Federalism and redistribution are known for not matching well (Oates 2002; Obinger et al. 2005).

A large part of the rational choice literature concentrates on justifying why the federal government should be limited. According to this literature, federalism causes a series of adverse market conditions and a stronger federal intervention leads to revenue extraction. The central government should hence be limited through decentralization (to avoid vertical fiscal imbalances), hard budget constraints (to prevent cases where governments request more funds to the federal system than needed) and competition through a common market to prevent trade barriers.

The US federal government has certain responsibilities in redistributive matters, let alone for the fact that it can raise and redistribute federal taxes. Yet, in terms of education, both the European Commission's Directorate-General for Education and Culture and the US State Department bear some similarities in their limited competencies. The comparison is rarely made as both departments are relatively recent, the US Department of Education was established in 1980; while the Department of Education of the European Commission emerged in 1981 as an integration of employment, social affairs and education – the education and culture portfolio having been a part of the Directorate-General for Research in the 1970s (European Commission 2006, p. 24). Both Department and Directorate-General cannot issue regulations to educational institutions for example, the Directorate-General for Education and Culture being bound to promote cooperation and mobility, while the US Department of Education acquired a remit to provide financial aid to students following the GI Bill of 1965.

The powers of the EU have traditionally been more limited in redistributive areas than in economic and regulatory policies, and, when existent, redistribution has been more likely in the form of intergovernmental rather than interpersonal transfers. A large part of the EU's budget is indeed allocated to regional cohesion policies, a form of intergovernmental transfer. These transfers are market correcting redistributive policies (Héritier 1999). These are areas where the EU has long traditions and established practices in escaping deadlock despite disputes over the power to redistribute funds.

According to Scharpf's (1997) well-known joint decision trap, the super-majority structure means that the federal level depends on individual states to make decisions. The outcome therefore usually relies on the lowest common denominator. However, demand from the lowest common denominator for distribution depends on income distribution. With a full-franchise democracy and a right-skewed income distribution, the poor are more able to obtain transfers from the rich, through interpersonal transfers or other forms of subsidies for goods like education (Boix 2003; Meltzer and Richard 1981; Romer 1975). This mechanism implies intergovernmental or interpersonal transfers negatively correlated with income.

This is unlikely to arise in federations, where such interregional redistribution is hardly likely to happen given that mechanisms such as hard-budget constraints are in place to prevent increases in interpersonal and interregional redistribution, as Rodden (2009) underlined. Indeed, applicability to the EU is more limited than in a national setting given that European institutions have no powers to raise taxes. The EU however has some power to redistribute across member states and directly to citizens (in education for example through the Erasmus programme allocated to mobile students), as well as to generate income through the generation of bonds on the financial market in case of emergency for example.

However, business cycles should affect the likelihood for redistribution in federal contexts. Generally speaking, representatives have stronger incentives to seek resources from federal governments when state governments are under fiscal stress (Rodden 2003). When a negative shock occurs, flows from the federal government to the states should counteract these shocks as well. If the own-source revenues of state governments are pro-cyclical and if they are major public sector employers and the primary providers of public services such as education, unemployment, health and welfare benefits, presumably the assignment of stabilization responsibilities to the federal government requires that the federal government issues guarantees on bonds on behalf of states and bolsters revenues through increased revenue shares, discretionary grants or subsidized loans in the face of a country-wide recession.

Then again, central governments have an incentive to externalize the costs of adjustment to officials at lower levels of government since expenditure cuts are politically painful: externalizations taking the form of 'unfunded mandates' (Wibbels and Rodden 2004). Moreover, in general, revenue-sharing and discretionary transfers are either acyclical or procyclical. While increased budget deficits are common under negative shocks, counter-cyclical expenditure occurred only in two of seven federations they studied, namely Canada and Australia, according to Wibbels and Rodden (2004).

**Method**

Higher education systems in the EU and the US are understandably different, the costs of a degree to students in the EU being on average much lower than in the US. The macro-trends discussed below, for example on the costs of higher education and cost-sharing mechanisms, however apply despite differences in the scale of cost-sharing.

This research was based on 40 semi-structured interviews of an hour, conducted with stakeholders of student loan reforms in the US, both at the state level (relevant university administrations and commissions) as well as the federal level (with law-makers) and experts. The interviews were conducted under the Chatham House rule. In addition, relevant legislative debates were analysed. Interviewees were selected based on their expertise and role in legislative reforms.

## BROAD TRENDS IN THE EVOLUTION OF NATIONAL PUBLIC BUDGETS FOR IIIGHER EDUCATION

National budgets have been constrained for higher education. Scholars of higher education have started to follow the impact of the recession on higher education acknowledging the potentially long-lasting changes which can result from negative shocks.

Douglass (2010) concentrates on the consequences of cuts in state budgets and the extent to which the 2010 federal stimulus package offered a compensation for state cuts in the US. He explained that the Obama administration's first stimulus package helped mitigate large state budget cuts to public services in 2009–2010 and to support expanded enrolments largely at the community college level. But it was not enough to avoid universities and colleges having to adopt drastic budget cutting measures in states such as California.

Eggins and West (2010) provide a global overview of the policy and management trends related to the recession. They explained that developed countries suffered from higher student enrolment inversely linked to the rise in unemployment, and stressed that developing countries' aid programmes were the hardest hit.

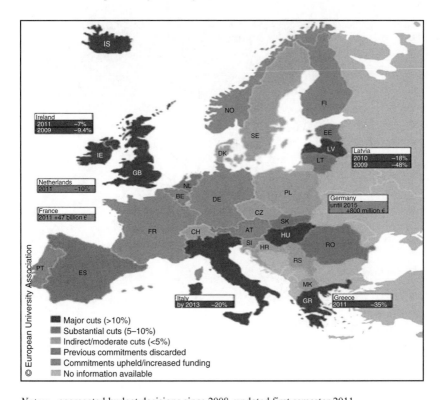

Major cuts (>10%)
Substantial cuts (5–10%)
Indirect/moderate cuts (<5%)
Previous commitments discarded
Commitments upheld/increased funding
No information available

*Notes:* aggregated budget decisions since 2008, updated first semester 2011.

*Source:* EUA (2011a).

*Figure 9.1 Impact of the economic crisis on public funding – EU*

Altbach (2010) underlines international differences in responses to the recession in the field of higher education, and shows that Asian countries were less exposed to budgetary cuts because of political priorities and less exposure to economic upheavals.

In contrast, several EU-27 member state governments have announced cuts in the public budget to higher education institutions (a significant change since public funding constitutes around 75 per cent of European universities' income).

Figures 9.1 and 9.2 represent a rough overview of the reductions in public spending in Europe and the US. According to data from the university representative body European University Association (EUA), 18 member states had announced cuts by 2011 (EUA 2011a). The EUA

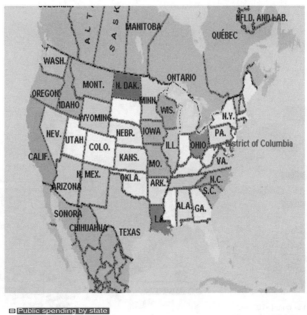

Source: Grapevine (2013).

*Figure 9.2    Trends in state spending – US*

reported cuts in higher education budget of up to 35 per cent from 2010 to 2011 in Greece, 48 per cent in 2009 followed by a further cut of 18 per cent in 2010 in Latvia (with academic salaries cut up to 30 per cent) and a cumulative decrease of 14 per cent in 2010 in Italy (EUA 2011b). Despite uncertainty regarding the comparability of these figures (for example, it is unclear whether the budget includes capital grant or recurrent funding, per full-time equivalent or not), the conclusion according to which a majority of member states are reducing their budget holds.

Yet the governments of eleven European countries have decided to invest in higher education in an effort to boost the knowledge economy. The French and German governments have invested in higher education, in France through a massive public investment plan called the *Grand Emprunt* with €20 billion going to higher education and Germany with around €3.5 billion. The Swedish government is continuing a policy of generous funding to higher education and had minor increases in autonomy in 2009, while maintaining generous financial aid policies. The Danish government also maintains its commitment for higher education, thanks to a long-term strategic governmental commitment for higher education.

At first sight, these budgetary cuts no doubt appear significant, with 66 per cent of state governments reducing their public budgets in the EU. The US higher education sector also had several cuts, 70 per cent of state governments reducing their budgets between 2008 and 2011 according to Grapevine Reports from Illinois State University (2013). These cuts mostly affect public universities in both the US and the EU, direct public funding contributing to anything between one-third of the budget of universities in some US public universities to most of the revenue streams, especially in some European universities (more precisely public funding represents on average 75 per cent of the revenue streams of universities in Europe). But an analysis which goes beyond macro-level data is necessary draw an accurate conclusion of these trends, the 'hidden' public and private financial support, regarding the 'costs' of higher education and the relative public/private contribution are very important to take into account (Schwarzenberger 2008). So far very few comparative studies exist beyond macro-level data analyses, relying for example on indicators from the Organization for Economic Co-operation and Development (OECD) or Eurostat.

The trajectories of costs and available revenues for higher education have in fact been a long-term function of three long-term factors also known as 'cost disease' (Bowen 2012). The idea of the cost disease is simple (Bowen 2012, p. 4):

> [In] labor-intensive industries such as the performing arts and education, there is less opportunity than in other sectors to increase productivity by, for example, substituting capital for labor. Yet, over time, markets dictate that wages for comparably qualified individuals have to increase at roughly the same rate in all industries. As a result, unit labor costs must be expected to rise relatively faster in the performing arts and education than in the economy overall.

The factors contributing to the cost disease include: escalating enrolment, a financial dependence on what in most countries has become increasingly inadequate governmental revenues and rapidly increasing unit, or per student costs (Johnstone and Marcucci 2010, p. 30). Despite the economic recession, Desrochers and Wellman (2011, p. 22) showed that the '2009 spending patterns preserved a ten-year high in average expenditure and revenue spending'.

Figures 9.3 and 9.4 illustrate the macro-level evolution related to the inadequate governmental revenues, and more particularly the decrease in public spending (measured for the US as a negative annual percentage of

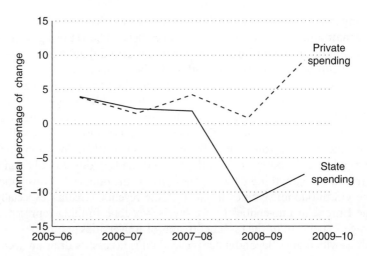

*Source:*   College Board (2010).

*Figure 9.3    Trends in public and private spending – US*

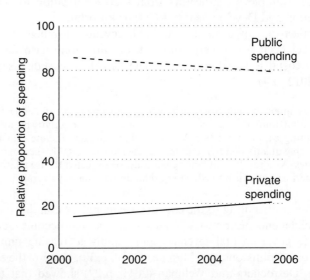

*Note:*   illustrates relative proportion of public and private sources of funds for educational institutions after transfers from public sources.

*Source:*   OECD (2010).

*Figure 9.4    Trends in public and private spending – EU*

change and for the EU in terms of relative proportion of spending for the EU) since 2000.

## A CLOSER LOOK AT REDISTRIBUTIVE MECHANISMS IN HIGHER EDUCATION, THE CONCEPT OF COST-SHARING

Governments deal with constrained national budgets by splitting the cost burden of higher education across several parties, a concept known as cost-sharing. This concept implies a zero-sum game, where the reduction of the burden for one party either results in a shift to one or more parties, or to a loss in revenues (Johnstone and Marcucci 2010, p. 45; also covered by Woodhall 2007). Parties involved in cost-sharing typically include parents, students, donors/philanthropists and governments.

So far, the most politically visible and controversial aspect of cost-sharing in countries with a strong tradition of public funding has been its 'downward' application, namely the increasing contribution that students have to pay upfront (not taking financial aid schemes into consideration). The US is a country well-known for its increasing student fees and related student debt.

The trend of increase in tuition is most visible in public universities, because public revenues have been declining, but is also occurring in private universities. For example, between 2008 and 2009, a Master's degree at a public university has on average a US$225 one-year change in net tuition revenues and US$536 for an equivalent course in a private university (Wellman 2011).

The increase in fees to students (the most politically visible side of cost-sharing) masks governmental transfers. For example, in Europe, England is probably the country which is most known for its increasing student fees, which have occurred in 1998, 2004 and 2010, the most recent reforms having led to much publicized student demonstrations, the National Union of Students leader Wes Streeting qualified it as 'an extraordinary act of self-harm by the Government' (Richardson 2010) and Vernon of UC Berkeley announced that these cuts signified the end of public universities in England (Vernon 2010).

Direct public allocations to institutions are not the only way to measure the relative role of the government (Esping-Andersen 1993; Pierson 1996). For example, in the case of England, the amount available through the universal maintenance grant and publicly subsidized income contingent lending scheme has also increased in parallel to the increase in tuition fees, in a scheme heavily influenced by studies conducted by Barr (2004). According to the calculations of the British government, student loans are predicted to offset the cuts in recurrent grants that institutions had to bear, the change being only over 0.71 per cent. Combined with the cuts to capital funding, the reduction in the budget of higher education institutions amounts to 4.15 per cent, according to the figures of the British government.

Government subsidies for the payment of these fees mean that higher education remains free upfront. Every student remains eligible for a universal maintenance grant. In a loan format not fully dissimilar to a targeted tax, graduates, not students, pay for their fees. This repayment is significantly subsidized by the government. Graduates repay only if they earn a salary above a certain threshold and the interest rates on loans remain largely paid for by the government.

The overall actual cost of this lending scheme to the British government is hard to predict since it depends on various factors, including the number of lenders and their rates of repayment. But the previous loan scheme was very costly, resulting in a student loan debt of GBP30 billion in 2009 (Student Loans Company 2009). The government may even end up subsidising students to a greater extent than it did from its introduction in 2004 for the following reasons. The value of the maintenance grant, for which each student is eligible, has actually increased for the most disadvantaged student from GBP2,905 to GBP5,000. Moreover, the threshold at which students are expected to repay is 40 per cent higher than it used to (from a salary of GBP15,000 per year to GBP21,000 per year). This increase in the income contingent threshold could also lead to adverse selection and moral hazard: students who expect to earn less than the threshold will have more incentive to take a government loan, leading to high defaults, the costs of which will be borne by the government. Graduates may also have an incentive to keep their annual income down, for example by encouraging companies to pay them in kind, to avoid repayments. Increasing tuition fees to students are therefore not necessarily synonymous of a proportional decrease in costs for state governments. The following part of the chapter analyses another option to split the rising cost burden of higher education, for example the involvement of federal governments.

## AN EXTENSION OF COST-SHARING TO FEDERAL GOVERNMENTS

So far cost-sharing in Europe includes national governments, students and other non-governmental donors. But the federal level, including EU institutions, could have a bigger role to play in terms of bearing the costs of higher education in an ideal distribution of tasks.

Exploring the evolution of the US student lending scheme is very enlightening in order to understand how the federal government can contribute to the cost-sharing system. The US federal Department of Education did not traditionally have much power, and was limited to relatively minor education programmes.

Like the current Directorate-General for Education and Culture of the EU, the US Department of Education originally had very little exclusive competency in higher education. Yet, the federal government obtained a role in financial aid when the GI Bill (officially the Servicemen's Readjustment Act of 1944) was adopted to provide veterans with grants and loans in order for them to obtain a postsecondary education. The federal government debated how to allocate taxpayer-funded financial aid, to the institutions for distribution or to individual students. The GI Bill gave loans to students who could use them to enrol at an accredited college or university of their own choice – a precedent that was maintained in later years. The federal financial aid budget consistently increased in the context of the Cold War and scientific competition with the USSR. The 1957 National Defense Act, and then the 1965 Higher Education Act increased both the grant and a growing loan scheme to mostly low income or highly talented students.

These federal loans, which dramatically grew under the Nixon administration of the 1970s, were distributed via private sector banks and the federal government only provided federally guaranteed loans that eliminated default risks for banks (called Federal Family Education Loans, FFEL). This was the dominant approach to providing loans until the 1990s, and led to a variety of programmes, as Table 9.1 indicates.

At that time, the Clinton administration advocated in favour of a 'direct' loan programme, which would include removing the federal guarantee to have the federal government directly allocate the loans, being cheaper to the government[1] as well as faster to allocate by reducing the number of intermediaries (Interview US1, 29 October 2010[2]).

Figure 9.5 illustrates the differences between direct loans and FFEL. Under the FFEL, private lenders, who acted as intermediaries to originate loans, originated these loans against a fee called the Special Allowance Payment (SAP). Various legal complexities increased the profit margin of these lenders. For example, prior to 1 April 2006, lenders could keep any interest paid on the loan which exceeded the SAP. Lenders could also take advantage of 'borrower benefits', which consisted of waving the origination fee that the Department of Education charged for some loans (Lehman Brothers 2008). Bodies at the state level also used to be involved in guaranteeing loans through a guarantee agency such as EdFund in California[3] and generally managing the interaction between loans and other forms of

*Table 9.1    Types of loans*

|       |        | Type of loan | Limit | Interest rate |
|-------|--------|--------------|-------|---------------|
| Public | FFEL | Combined subsidized and unsubsidized | $8,500 | 6.8% |
|        |        | Unsubsidized | $20,500 | 6.8% |
|        |        | Consolidation | ? | Fixed at average underlying loans |
|        |        | PLUS | Cost of attendance minus other financial aid | 8.5% |
|        |        | GradPLUS | Cost of attendance minus other financial aid | 7.9% |
|        | Direct loans | Combined subsidized and unsubsidized | $23,000 | 6.8% |
|        |        | Unsubsidized | $57,500 | 4.5% |
|        |        | Consolidation | ? | Weighted average of consolidated loans |
| Private |       | Private | Variable | Variable |

*Notes:*  means-test determines how much subsidy the government provides on interest rates FFEL and direct loans or not; interest rates post 1 July 2006; limit set in US$ per year for graduate studies.

*Source:*    Finaid (2010).

financial aid in the FFEL programme. The recent move to a direct loan removes state guarantee functions. This move is not unlike the recommendation made by the former President of the University of California, Clark Kerr, in the late 1960s: funding should not be allocated to the states (because that would stifle the process with political interests) but to students directly. This recommendation was made in the context of a political debate stimulated by Carnegie Commission on Higher Education which bore some similarities with the debate which emerged in 2010 (Douglass 2005).

Finally, postsecondary institutions were generally perceived by their administrators as well as students as having a responsibility to find a suitable financial package, which may include loans (Interview US9, 20 November 2010; Interview US10, 20 December 2010). These institutions checked students' eligibility criteria for financial aid. This eligibility calculation, called the Expected Family Contribution, is defined by an Act of

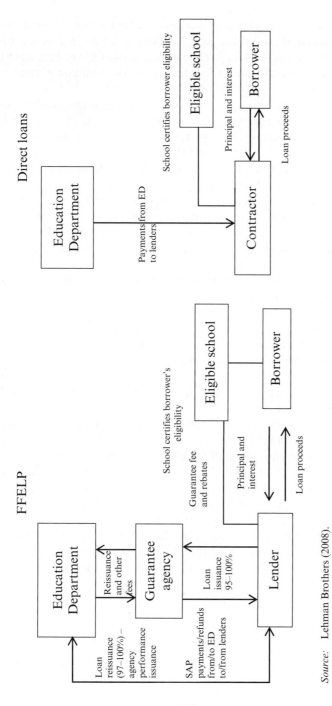

*Source:* Lehman Brothers (2008).

*Figure 9.5    Allocation mechanism for FFEL programme and direct loans*

Congress and is based on the information students provide in their application for financial aid called the Free Application for Federal Student Aid (FAFSA), the data of which are entered in a nationwide system managed by the federal Department of Education called the Common Origination and Disbursement System (COD).[4]

The institutions then notify students of their aid package, which includes an institution-based financial aid such as a departmental scholarship. The data on public loans taken by students are also available nationwide through the National Student Loan Data System for Students.[5] Schools to which the student chooses to release information can access student data nationwide. Unlike the COD, which is only accessible by administrators, the National Student Loan Data System allows students to view their loan and grant information. (Private lenders created their own database system called the National Student Clearing House,[6] a degree and enrolment verification tool, which led institutions in the FFEL programme to enter student data in both databases.[7])

The Clinton administration originally suggested a complete streamlining of loans into direct loans managed by the federal government, which would allow the federal government to manage the loans itself without relying on lenders, originators and guarantee agencies. But streamlining loans into the direct loan programme, as was the original plan from the Clinton administration, meant going against the interest of actors who benefited from the existing loan structure, including large Sallie Mae, which held US$128.1 billion in 2007, NelNet, Pheea and Great Lakes (Lehman Brothers 2008).

Pressures from Congress and lobbies to defend FFEL led the Clinton administration to back off from its original plan and let higher education institutions choose the system of which they wanted to be part (Interview US4, 2 November 2010). The Clinton government had to limit its ambitions to set-up a direct loan in the form of an experiment, which would eventually include not more than 20 per cent of federal loans.

The recession of 2008 allowed the federal government (at the time having a Democrat Congress and President) to push for an extension of direct loans. At that time, more than two-thirds of loans were allocated by private lenders through the FFEL or private loans. But these loans were not designed to absorb major shocks. Private lenders became wary of lending to students through the FFEL programme. These lenders had previously relied on asset-back securities (ABS, which broadly speaking consist in selling a bundled debt to other investors) to finance new guaranteed loans. The collapse of the ABS market led these lenders to face much higher costs.[8] Although 88 per cent of loans were financed by the Department of Education, if one includes direct loans in 2008–2009 (CBO

2010, p. 8), the guarantee provided by the federal government on these loans was insufficient to cover such costs because these guarantees had fixed statutory payments.

Law-makers first responded by passing the Ensuring Continued Access to Student Loans Act in 2008 (ECASLA). The law authorized the Department of Education to provide funding to the FFEL lenders, primarily by purchasing their loans but also by providing them with back-up lines of credit. This law made it possible for students to still receive loans and lowered the costs of allocating student loans, since the federal government did not have to make some of the payments it otherwise would have had to make to lenders (CBO 2010, p. 8). The federal government also provided support to the private lenders to borrow from the Federal Reserve's Term Asset-Backed Securities Loan Facilities (TALF). This increased involvement made it easier for the federal government to justify switching to the direct loan programme in March 2010, where all loans were streamlined to direct loans. (Private lenders were however not entirely dismissed. They were to be contracted by the federal government to service loans and their repayments.)

But the adoption of the student loan reform, an initiative largely conducted by Democrats, was difficult. The law would have been difficult to adopt given state resistance to lose the federal guarantee as well as the Republican support for the alternative Sallie Mae proposal. To overcome a Senate which had a majority of Republicans, the Obama administration and the Congress (led by Congressman Chairman Georges Miller and Department of Education staff such as Robert Shireman), chose to bundle up the education bill and the equally, if not more contentious, healthcare bill as part of a reconciliation procedure for adoption by the Senate on 18 March 2010.

The choice of the reconciliation procedure facilitated the fit of the student loan reforms to overcome institutional constraints, backed by the rhetoric of the economic recession. First, it made it technically easier for the bill to be adopted at the Senate, by lowering the number of Senators and preventing voting on it being slowed down by the Senate by limiting deliberation in the Senate to 20 hours.

Second, as a reconciliation procedure being used to allow consideration of a budget bill, it highlighted the budget savings coming out from the student loan bill, fitting with the rhetoric of the economic recession and the need to limit public budgetary expenditures (which also fitted the Republicans' rhetoric of the time concerned with the shift in the income distribution of their voters).[9] Such legislative bundling was adopted by the Congress and Senate because of growing concerns regarding the capacity of graduates to repay their student debt in times of increasing unemployment and the associated costs related to subsidies of the FFEL programme, which dismisses the fiscal federal argument according to which markets need to be protected from the distortive intervention of federal governments.

The evolution of redistributive schemes in education, and more particularly higher education, at the level of the EU illustrate a similar struggle. Reforms regarding financing for higher education are seldom at the European level and have historically been heavily debated, the flagship European exchange programme Erasmus being a case in point. Erasmus, was adopted by the Council on 15 June 1987 after 18 months. It was the result of lengthy negotiations, even if the budget requested by the European Commission only constituted about four days of agricultural expenditure – the requested amount was 175 million ecus, the EU currency which preceded the euro (European Commission 2006). The Council of Education of Ministers rejected the first proposal for Erasmus on 9 June 1986, and at the following meeting of 28 November 1986 still met with a lot of disagreements from the German, French and British ministers. The programme would provide scholarships for mobile students covering about one-third of the total costs of a year abroad. The Erasmus negotiations illustrate the political conflicts resulting from the sensitivity of integrating education to the remit of European institution competencies (Corbett 2005).

Another example includes the difficulties related to inserting any consideration regarding student financing in the Bologna Process, an originally intergovernmental reform process for higher education. Such difficult negotiations emerged during the ministerial conference in Berlin in 2003, when student representatives lobbied the French Minister for an inclusion of the 'social dimension' of higher education in the interministerial communiqué (see Hoareau 2010b).

Regarding student loans, an EU-wide student loan scheme has been under negotiation since 2010 (Hoareau 2010b). These negotiations illustrate a similar struggle. They started with a European Commission proposal for a European-wide student loan facility in 2011. The European Commission justified the student loan facility in the context of the economic crisis, arguing that the economic downturn would reduce mobility and that further action was necessary to meet the Europe 2020 targets (European Commission 2011, p. 20). The scheme was more limited in nature than its US counterpart, reserved to postgraduate mobile students. The size of the scheme would make it easier to be adopted and is common to the history of spillover effects in the development of EU programmes.

This study led to a loan guarantee scheme financed by the European Investment Bank (EIB), officially announced in 2011, thereby expanding the existing remit of the EIB (which provided guarantees to national lending agencies such as the Hungarian student loans company) to fund individuals.

The EU would act as a guarantor against the possible default on loans, which would be disbursed by financial intermediaries based in the home countries, funded from private sources (essentially banks or student loan agencies) as Figure 9.6 illustrates. The EU lending facility scheme does not have the same resistance from banking interest. The facility fills a market gap in the funding of student mobility, where the losers would be relatively niche providers. Private banks would benefit from the lending scheme, but benefiting from the EU guarantee scheme on a risky loan (European Commission 2012). The lending facility would fund only mobile students, as an addition to the existing Erasmus mobility grant. This lending facility is in this respect is compliant to the principle of subsidiarity, which rules that the EU intervenes only if EU action is more efficient than at the national, regional or local level (Article 5, Treaty of the EU).

As the process of adoption of this student loan scheme is on-going, further analysis of European Council debates (if accessible) would be necessary to claim causality with more confidence. Yet, the timing of the adoption (in less than a year) provides a strong indication that European level redistribution was easier to set-up due to the economic shock of 2008, and would shift the weight of the needs of students to a federal entity. Moreover, the economic shock made a strong rationale for the use of the EIB, with EIB bonds being more stable than national bonds in an uncertain economy.

## DISCUSSION

This analysis of the evolution of state and federal trends in public spending to higher education illustrates diverse trends and has implications for the Europe of Knowledge as well as a broader literature on fiscal federalism.

First, student contributions and redistributive schemes operate in different contexts in the US and the EU, with students in the US paying on average a larger amount towards their studies; but the EU does not escape the cost disease of higher education. The introduction of tuition fees or the discussion to increase fees illustrates a similar trend towards a larger student contribution in Europe (these countries include England and some German states for example).

Europe is actually marked by diverging trends regarding the evolution of national public spending, some governments reducing public budgets while others choose to invest in higher education for long-term growth (Hoareau and Ritzen 2012). The diversity of national spending means

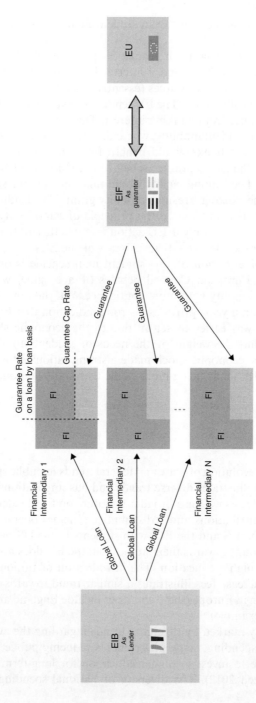

*Source:* European Commission (2012).

*Figure 9.6 Suggested architecture of a European student loan guarantee facility*

that some European member states would have more incentive to request redistribution from European institutions.

A closer look at the case of financial aid to students illustrates the effect of a negative economic shock on federal intervention analysed in terms of competencies rather than net amount spent): in the US, this negative shock facilitated the insertion of the student loan scheme in the reconciliation procedure (meant to decide on budgetary allocation), and hence the avoidance of the lowest common denominator (in the form of Republicans in the Senate). The adoption of the US student loan reform was therefore a mix of various tools, including key actors (in the form of Democrats in the Congress), the use of the economic recession as a powerful argumentation and discourse tool, as well as the legislative trick of the reconciliation procedure. Yet, the objective of this chapter is not to suggest a particular political formula for further integration, in the form of a particular legislative tool, namely the reconciliation procedure. The significance of the economic downturn in the case of the European student loan facility is less explicit, and emerges from the limitations faced by member states in increasing their budgets for higher education (and presumably student support). This chapter's core objective was to issue generalizable conclusions for scholars studying the Europe of Knowledge as well as fiscal federalist literature at large. Regarding the Europe of Knowledge, this chapter shows how economic changes can become an engine for European competency to increase in areas which were politically difficult to tackle (student loans) or considered outside the remit of European institutions (transfer to students). The history of financial aid in the US further illustrates that this engine was synonymous of having the political incentive to bring forward previous issues on the agenda (rather than to initiate new ideas). In Europe, the negative economic shock threatened part of the student aid package for mobile students (under the Erasmus programme). But the European Parliament has prevented cuts to this budget in December 2012 (European Parliament 2012). This finding also applies to the more general debates regarding the future of fiscal Europe.

But this study has a relevance to a broader political science literature. Regarding fiscal federalism, this finding appears to contradict a part of the literature which concentrates on the limits of redistributive schemes at the federal level (Obinger et al. 2005; Wibbels and Rodden 2004). These differences in findings however need to be interpreted with caution. A large part of the literature concentrated on different forms of redistribution including intergovernmental transfers, rather than interpersonal transfers covered in the case of student loans. These differences in findings may also be an artefact of the different levels of analysis used – this study presents isolated policy cases while a large literature concentrates on macro-data comparisons. Such a macro-comparison is made difficult because of the scarcity of accurate comparative data on spending and the costs of higher education. More precise macro-level data, as well as cross-policy comparative study, are necessary to establish further research in order to measure the full costs and spending allocated to education.

A more substantial conclusion can nevertheless be derived from this analysis. A significant condition for the greater intervention of the federal government was the compensation of market failures in the US. This case of market failure is peculiar. It does not include the typical scenario where markets could not provide a particular good (which is the basic justification for the public provision of public goods), but an example where markets wanted to retain the competency at hand in spite of the federal entity being able to provide these goods at lower cost. The US direct loan programme was set-up precisely to prevent lenders and origination agencies from not being able to continue to manage risks and provide loans at affordable costs due to the collapse of the ABS market. It is also worth noting that banks and originators wanted to keep the portfolio of student loans, precisely because the federal guarantee reduced the risks of these products for them.

In the case of the EU, state governments were being constrained in their ability to finance students – one explanation being the lower trust that financial markets provided to their bonds. A European-wide bond to finance student loan schemes would guarantee a higher credibility vis-à-vis the market.

The case presented here appears to present a reverse image to the fiscal federalist argument which aims to limit the intervention of the federal government and see such intervention as mostly distortive. In this case, the federal government should intervene to compensate for a market failure. Further relevant research should therefore investigate the relationships between markets and different levels of governments and the conditions under which federal redistribution is justified by market failure. This research would be particularly relevant in a European context where debates regarding the future of Europe are fiscal and redistributive policies are very timely.

## CONCLUSION

The comparison between student loan reforms in the US and the EU showed how the federal institutions in both regions acquired additional competencies in a period of economic constraint. The chapter suggested that the political idea and need for such student loan reforms existed prior the economic downturn (for example, through increasingly constrained state level spending in higher education). Yet, the economic downturn facilitated the adoption of reforms through the use of particular legislative tools, and the strengthening of the argumentation in favour of reforms. This comparative case study analysis illustrates the significance of federal intervention for market regulation.

## NOTES

1. Douglass (2005, p. 9) explained that government-guaranteed loans cost taxpayers twelve cents for every dollar spent, while direct loans cost less than one cent for every federal dollar.
2. The Chatham House Rule applied for interviews. Around 40 were conducted for the US case.
3. These agencies derived income from insurance premiums, loan process and origination fees, default aversion fees, collection retention fees and reinvestment income loan servicing.
4. See https://cod.ed.gov/cod/LoginPage.
5. See http://www.nslds.ed.gov/nslds_SA/.
6. See http://www.studentclearinghouse.org/.
7. The Oxford Professor Neil Shephard (2010) counts among the European scholars who have advocated a greater role for higher education institutions in the financial aid programme. This prospect is not impossible over the long run as coordinated efforts are made to make higher education institutions progressively gain more autonomy, for example in Europe with the Bologna Process. But such a switch would require considerable investment and institutional adaptation. The US higher education institutions have a large administrative, managerial and financial capacity regarding financial aid. Scholarships, grants and fellowships amounted to US$1.56 billion for the University of California alone in 2004–2005 (loans totalled US$813.7 million). This is comparatively about equal to the entire teaching and research budget for higher education of the Republic of Ireland for 2011.
8. ABS were a relatively 'new' product. They had only been used in the student loan market in the US since the privatization of Sallie Mae in December 2004. Before that date, Sallie Mae was a company owned by public shareholders with the status of a Government-Sponsored Enterprise (GSE), a financial service corporation created by Congress in 1972 to provide liquidity to the student loan market. The GSE status guaranteed Sallie Mae with low funding costs. Upon privatization, Sallie Mae had to release its outstanding GSE debt and issued to do so.
9. Budgetary savings were highlighted because the costs related to the direct loan reform, such as the costs of covering for the defaults of lenders, did not show on the year of the adoption and highlighted the savings from the guarantee. Moreover, the Congressional Budget Office (CBO) reviewed its estimates between the House vote on the 27 of July 2009 and the Senate vote.

## REFERENCES

Altbach, P. (2010), 'The Impact of the Financial Crisis on International Higher Education', interview to *EducationUSA*, available at: http://www.youtube.com/watch?v=9g53AoL8z0s (accessed August 2011).

Barr, N. (2004), 'Higher education funding', *Oxford Review of Economic Policy*, **20**(2), 264–283.

Boix, C. (2003), *Economy and Redistribution*, Cambridge: Cambridge University Press.

Bowen, W.G. (2012), 'Costs and Productivity in Higher Education: is Technology the Answer?', Stanford University, Tanner Lecture 1, 10 October 2012, available at: http://www.ithaka.org/sites/default/files/files/ITHAKA-TheCostDiseaseinHigherEducation.pdf (accessed 13 December 2012).

Broadway, R. and A. Shar (2009), *Fiscal Federalism: Principles and Practice of Multiorder Governance*, Cambridge: Cambridge University Press.

College Board (2010), 'Trends in College Pricing 2010', available at: http://trends.collegeboard.org/sites/default/files/CP_2010.pdf.

Congressional Budget Office (CBO) (2010), 'Costs and Policy Options for Federal Student Loan Programs', CBO Study, available at: http://www.cbo.gov/sites/default/files/cbofiles/ftpdocs/110xx/doc11043/03-25-studentloans.pdf (accessed 13 December 2012).

Corbett, A. (2005), *Universities and the Europe of Knowledge: Ideas, Institutions and Policy Entrepreneurship European Community Higher Education Policy, 1955–2005*, Basingstoke: Palgrave Macmillan.

Desrochers, D. and J. Wellman (2011), 'Trends in College Spending 1999–2009', Washington, DC: The Delta Cost Project on Postsecondary Education Costs, Productivity, and Accountability.

Douglass, J.A. (2005), 'The Carnegie Commission and Council in Higher Education: a Retrospective', UC Berkeley: CSHE Research and Occasional Paper Series.

Douglass, J.A. (2010), *Higher Education Budgets and the Global Recession: Tracking Varied National Responses and Their Consequences*, UC Berkeley: CSHE Research and Occasional Paper Series.

Eggins, H. and P. West (2010), 'The global impact of the financial crisis: trends in developed and developing countries', *Higher Education Policy and Management*, **22**(3), 1–16.

Esping-Andersen, G. (1993), *The Three Worlds of Welfare Capitalism*, Princeton, NJ: Princeton University Press.

EUA (2011a), 'Public Funding Observatory', available at: http://www.eua.be/eua-work-and-policy-area/governance-autonomy-and-funding/public-funding-observatory.aspx (accessed August 2011).

EUA (2011b), 'The Impact of the Economic Crisis on European Universities, Update: First Semester 2011', available at: http://www.eua.be/Libraries/Governance_Autonomy_Funding/Economic_monitoring_June2011.sflb.ashx (accessed August 2011).

European Commission (2006), *The History of European Cooperation in Education and Training, Europe in the Making – an Example*, Luxembourg: Office for Official Publications of the European Communities.

European Commission (2011), 'Commission Staff Working Paper: Impact Assessment on Education and Training Actions, Accompanying the Document Proposal for a Regulation of the European Parliament and of the Council Establishing a Single Education, Training, Youth and Sport Programme for the Period 2014–2020', COM(2011) 788, SEC(2011) 1403, 23 November, available at: http://ec.europa.eu/education/erasmus-for-all/doc/impact1_en.pdf (accessed December 2012).

European Commission (2012), 'Erasmus Master – an EU Student Loan Guarantee Facility, Non-Paper for Education Committee of the Council', COM AC DI 2012.

European Council (2012), '3201st Council Meeting Education, Culture, Youth and Sport', 26 and 27 November 2012, Press release, available at: http://www.consil ium.europa.eu/uedocs/cms_data/docs/pressdata/en/educ/133836.pdf (accessed December 2012).

European Parliament (2012), 'Erasmus: Find out How it Works and How it was Saved', Brussels news, 19 December, available at: http://www.europarl.europa. eu/news/en/headlines/content/20121213STO04619/html/Erasmus-find-out-how-it-works-and-how-it-was-saved (accessed December 2012).

Finaid (2010), 'Student loans', available at: http://www.finaid.org/loans/student loan.phtml (accessed 13 December 2013).

Fossum, J. and M. Augustin (2011), *The Constitution's Gift: a Constitutional Theory for a Democratic European Union*, Lanham: Rowman and Littlefield Publishers.

Grapevine (2013), 'State Fiscal Support for Higher Education, by State, Fiscal Years 2007–08 (FY08), 2010–11 (FY11), 2011–12 (FY12), 2012–13 (FY13) a State Fiscal Support ($)', available at: http://grapevine.illinoisstate.edu/tables/ FY13/Table1_FY13.pdf (accessed 3 December 2013).

Héritier, A. (1999), *Policy-Making and Diversity in Europe: Escape from Deadlock*, Cambridge: Cambridge University Press.

Hoareau, C. (2010a), 'Financing EU Student Mobility: a Proposed Credit Union Scheme for Europe', CSHE Research and Occasional Chapter Series.

Hoareau, C. (2010b), 'Does Deliberation Matter? A Study of the Impact of the Bologna Process on Attitudes and Policies in the European Higher Education Area', Doctoral Thesis, London: London School of Economics and Political Science.

Hoareau, C. and J. Ritzen (2012), 'The State of University Policy for Progress in the European Union', UNU-MERIT Working Chapter, Maastricht: UNU-MERIT, also Policy Paper 51, Bonn: Institute for the Study of Labour (IZA).

House of Parliament (2008), 'Sale of Student Loan Bill 2007–2008', available at: http://services.parliament.England/bills/2007-08/saleofstudentloans.html (accessed August 2010).

Johnstone, B. and P. Marcucci (2010), *Financing Higher Education Worldwide, Who Pays? Who Should Pay?*, Baltimore, MD: John Hopkins University Press.

Lehman Brothers (2008), 'US Securitized Products: an Education in Student Loan ABS', Fixed Income Research, 22 May.

Meltzer, A. and S. Richard (1981) 'A rational theory of the size of government', *Journal of Political Economy*, **89**(5), 914–927.

Oates, W. (2002), 'Fiscal Federalism and European Union: Some Reflections', Pavia: Societa Italiana di economica pubblica.

Obinger, H., S. Leibfried and F. Castles (2005), *Federalism and the Welfare State: New World and European Experiences*, Cambridge: Cambridge University Press.

OECD (2010), *Education at a Glance*, Paris: OECD.

Pierson, P. (1996), 'The new politics of the welfare state', *World Politics*, **48**(2), 143–179.

Richardson, H. (2010) 'University Budget Cuts Revealed', in *BBC News*, 1 February, available at: http://news.bbc.co.uk/2/hi/education/8491729.stm (accessed 13 December 2013).

Rodden, J. (2003), *Hamilton's Paradox: the Promise and Demise of Fiscal Federalism*, Cambridge: Cambridge University Press.

Rodden, J. (2009), 'Federalism and Inter-Regional Redistribution', Barcelona: Institute d'Economia de Barcelona.

Romer, T. (1975), 'Individual welfare, majority voting, and the properties of a linear income tax', *Journal of Public Economics*, **14**(May), 163–185.

Scharpf, F.W. (1997), *Games Real Actors Play. Actor-Centered Institutionalism in Policy Research*, Boulder, CO: Westview Press.

Schwarzenberger, A. (2008) 'Public/Private Funding of Higher Education: a Social Balance', available at: http://www.his.de/abt2/cost-sharing/information (accessed November 2012).

Shephard, N. (2010), 'Submission to the Review on Higher Education Funding and Student Finance', available at: http://www.nuff.ox.ac.uk/economics/papers/2010/w3/submission110510.pdf (accessed December 2012).

Student Loans Company (2009), 'Statistical First Release'.

Vernon, J. (2010), 'The End of Public Universities in England', *Inside Higher ed* blog, 27 October, available at: http://www.insidehighered.com/blogs/global highered/the_end_of_the_public_university_in_england (accessed 13 December 2013).

Wellman, J. (2011), 'Keeping College Within Reach', Statement in the House Subcommittee on Higher Education and Workforce Training Hearing, Delta Project on Postsecondary Education Costs, Productivity and Accountability, 30 November, p. 18.

Wibbels, E. and J. Rodden (2004), 'Business Cycles and the Political Economy of Decentralized Finance: Lessons for Fiscal Federalism in the EU', Chapter Prepared for Fiscal Policy in the 'EMU: New Issues and Challenges' Workshop Organized by the European Commission, Brussels, 12 November.

Woodhall, M. (2007), 'Funding Higher Education: the Contribution of Economic Thinking to Debate and Policy Development', World Bank Education Working Chapter Series, No. 8, December.

# Index